TEAM
SCHUMACHER

TEAM
SCHUMACHER

THE MAN WHO PAINTED F1 RED AGAIN

TIMOTHY COLLINGS

DEDICATION

To Tom-Tom

Published in 2005 by Highdown,
an imprint of Raceform Ltd
Compton, Newbury, Berkshire, RG20 6NL
Raceform Ltd is a wholly-owned subsidiary of Trinity Mirror plc

A CIP catalogue record for this book is available from the British Library.

ISBN 1-905156-03-0

Cover designed by Tracey Scarlett

Interiors designed by Fiona Pike

Printed in Great Britain by William Clowes Ltd, Beccles, Suffolk

ACKNOWLEDGEMENTS

This book, like them all, would not have been possible without the generous help and co-operation of many other people, several giving up precious time to recount their part in the tale of sustained success that made Ferrari and Michael Schumacher such a daunting combination.

First, of course, I am indebted to the talent of Michael himself, without which none of this would have happened. Many others gave assistance, too, in the research and writing, including, in no particular order, the following: everyone associated with the successes of Scuderia Ferrari; Luca Colajanni for his help in arranging interviews and providing valuable background; Jean Todt, for his frankness and honesty; Ross Brawn, for two interviews filled with invaluable anecdotes and fascinating material; Nigel Stepney; Stefano Domenicali; Rory Byrne; Anett Kuehnl; Pat Symonds; Sabine Kehm; Burkhard Nuppeney; Paolo Martinelli; Olaf Bachmann; the staff at the Cavallino; Chris Dyer; Balbir Singh; Willi Weber; Bob Constanduros; Umberto Zapelloni (and his book *Formula Ferrari*); Rainer Schwalb; Regine Rettner; Rachel Ingham; Alan Baldwin; Keith Botsford; Hirohide Hamashima; Kees van der Grindt; Peter Secchi; Luca Badoer; Eddie Irvine; Rubens Barrichello; Martin Brundle; Eddie Jordan; Ian Phillips; Maurice Hamilton; Ray Matts; Jane Nottage; Christophe Schulte; Karin Sturm; *Autosport* magazine; Jurgen Dilk; Udo Irnich; Guido Dilk; Jochen Mass; Roberto Moreno; Harry Hawelka; Derick Allsop (and his book *Formula One Uncovered*); Joe Saward and his website Grandprix.com; Jacques Deschenaux (and his superb reference annual, the *Grand Prix Guide*; Christopher Hilton (and many of his books, notably *Inside the Mind of the Grand Prix Driver*); Russell Hotten (and his book *Formula One*); James Allen (and his book *Michael Schumacher – The Quest for Redemption*); Nick Garton (and his book, *Cavallino Rampante*); Tom Rubython and the magazines *BusinessF1* and *EuroBusiness*); *F1Racing*; *The Sunday Times*; Will Gray, for sterling service when the going became tough and deadlines loomed; Jamie O'Leary; Will Skinner; Amar Azam and Lorraine Varney, for reading and patience; Stuart Sykes, for making things happen when all looked lost; all those others whose help has, I am sure, been overlooked; without forgetting Ruth Collings, who made sure the writer was at his desk on days when it seemed unlikely; finally, thanks to Jonathan Taylor, publisher of Highdown, for supporting the idea and Daniel Balado, who can turn water into wine.

Tim Collings
Hitchin, Hertfordshire
September 2005

CONTENTS

CHAPTER ONE

THE PACKAGE

When I first came into Formula One, I didn't really understand what it was all about. I could drive fast, of course, but I had little idea about the complexity of the whole business, which little wheel you had to set in motion in order to get everything going…
In effect, I just used to drive.

Michael Schumacher, 2003

On a hot July afternoon at the Piazza Libertà in Maranello, it is best to eat your gelato quickly. In the summer of 2005, as barely a dozen people braved the seats and benches in the shade near the tables of the coffee-houses, ice-cream parlours and bars under the trees on the western side of the square, it was imperative. The humidity was high, too; almost intolerable. Visitors to the town, famous all over the world as the home of Ferrari, felt the conditions immediately. It was like walking across an outdoor sauna.

Nearby, at the Galleria Ferrari, and in the car park outside the Planet Hotel, there were clusters of perspiring Americans, drawn like magnets to this relatively small, somewhat ugly and undistinguished place, because on that day a rather special, even fabulous, commercial sale was taking place. It was called 'Sotheby's at Ferrari'. These visitors, ignoring their discomfort in the sweltering conditions as the temperature soared beyond 35°C and the humidity rose above 75 per cent, were there to spend money – hard-earned money, very probably. At the famous restaurant opposite the Ferrari factory's main gates, Il Cavallino, there were English and German voices too amid the hubbub at lunch as Ross Brawn, the Ferrari racing team's technical director, joined the party. Men and women of various nationalities rushed in all directions to ensure the event was part of a perfect day for their guests. It was, after all, one of those 'once-in-a-lifetime' experiences for most people, other than those who were calling in briefly to take delivery, personally, of their new bright yellow Ferraris.

The heat was tiring, and the air-conditioned coolness of the Cavallino's interior was welcome. There, in a room that smelt of Formula One motor racing as much as it did of pasta, ham, olive oil and tomato sauce, there was no mistaking that this was the gastronomic epicentre of the famous Scuderia Ferrari. Its walls were covered in trophies, photographs and memorabilia that left little to the imagination. And many other places in and around the sprawling light-industrial town had been named after people connected with the team or its founder. My car was parked in the Piazza Enzo Ferrari itself, a pretty, tree-sheltered glade not more than five minutes' stroll from the Piazza Libertà; to the north, off the straight speed-testing road known as the Abetone Inferiore, were the side-roads known as the Via Nuvolari and the Via Musso; and to the west was the Via Ferrari itself. Standing there, near the old factory, it was easy to hear the heart-lifting whine and growl of the legendary Formula One engines as they powered a test car around the team's private circuit, the Autodromo di Fiorano. It was possible, also, to close your eyes and imagine Ferrari's team chief Jean Todt peering out of his office at the racing team's headquarters to listen to the sound, and to visualise Brawn doing much the same. They work, after all, within earshot of the track, or nearer. A stone's throw, really.

But of course Brawn, whose reflections on life in Italy with Ferrari make constant references to what he calls 'the group' and what others have dubbed 'the dream team', was not there in his office that lunchtime. He was at the Cavallino with the Sotheby's crowd while the air outside burned with the intensity of an early summer heat-wave and the travelling tourists bought their souvenirs in the shops that decorate a town seemingly dedicated to one famous brand above all others. After five successive championships, Brawn deserved to be fêted. From the turn of the millennium in 2000 to the end of 2004, Michael Schumacher had dominated Ferrari, Formula One and world motor racing. He had won seven world drivers' championships in all, beating the fabulous record of five wins by Juan Manuel Fangio along the way.

This extraordinary run of success, which was unprecedented in the history of the world championship, reflected itself in the range of goods for sale in the shop across the road from the Cavallino known as the Ferrari Store. There, where the shopping bags are bright red and cavernous, there was also an extensive range of merchandise dedicated to the image of Schumacher himself. His face grinned from nearly every wall. Schumacher's supremacy, on the track and in the battle of the images, was starkly represented in the Ferrari Store, where copies of the catalogue for 'Sotheby's at Ferrari' were available for a price of 50 euros. Trade for these seemed slow that hot afternoon, while demand for Ferrari and Schumacher souvenirs was brisk. This suggested that the success of the modern Ferrari team, the one headed by Schumacher and supported by his Brazilian partner Rubens Barrichello, had captured the imagination in a way – at least, commercially – that previous Ferrari teams had not. Clever marketing, global sales, widespread media manipulation and other skills had come into play to make Ferrari not just an evocative name with a grand tradition, but a winning machine that had brand association and an image to sell. People wanted Ferrari shirts, jackets, ties and caps, not to mention leather luggage and cars, and they wanted a choice of colours, sizes and styles. They also wanted all that, and more, with a Michael Schumacher logo or endorsement. And the tills were ringing and ringing.

If the Ferrari Store confirmed the manner in which the team had decided to mould its future, the Cavallino represented the team's history on its walls. Inside there were yellow tablecloths, red-jacketed waiters, rampant stallions on the walls and black-and-white photographs everywhere. Some of them depicted the 'Old Man' in his sunglasses with Niki Lauda and Luca di Montezemolo, both looking startlingly young. They were a reminder of years past, for Enzo Ferrari died in 1988, at a time when Schumacher had not yet even entered Formula One. The big, old silver trophies gleamed and winked.

Il Cavallino is the tourists' delight, but it prompts questions. Is it what it seems? Is it a traditional (and very good) *ristorante*, or is it merely a tacky kind of vaudeville? And what would Michele Alboreto, Nigel Mansell, Gerhard Berger, Alain Prost et al think of their place on these walls now alongside Schumacher? The modern Ferrari seen at Maranello on such days is the face of a union of many qualities. It has been made by the mystique and the traditions of Ferrari, but also by Schumacher's raw speed, his ruthless racing instincts, his rock-chiselled character and professionalism; the organisation and leadership of Jean Todt; the technical mastery and management of Ross Brawn, and others; and the vision of di Montezemolo, who brought them all together. Not for the last time, another question arose: is this really a team built around the myth and legend of Ferrari, or is it a team built around the practical strength and speed of Michael Schumacher?

As the noise grew louder, as the song of the *ora di pranzo* rose and fell, as the Lambrusco di Sorbana oiled the human works and eased smiles across happy faces, it was easy to roll back the years and remember the days before the Ferrari Store, before the Planet Hotel, before Schumacher. That was an era when things were different, when the fruit of the heritage created and left behind by the Old Man was singularly individual, private, and stubbornly defended from the march of commercialism, globalisation and such other forces as threatened in any way to dilute the sound and majesty of twelve cylinders roaring or horses prancing high. Things were very different then. Yes, as L.P. Hartley noted, the past is another country. Where once the place was drab and devoted to nothing more than cars and racing, the sound and fury and speed, now there is a restaurant, a hotel, a shop and a gallery, and more shops around the town. There are windows resplendent with crimson glitter, yellow, black and blue eye-catchers, all the hues of a clever marketing rainbow that glistens and shimmers in the wet heat as black-clad widows shuffle by. They are a dark signal of the contrasts.

Girls in pink hot pants sit in the shade in the square late in the day, not far from posters celebrating Schumacher's and Ferrari's unending successes of the previous years. They share cigarettes and sip ice-cold drinks, and they giggle. The noise from the Fiorano test circuit goes on booming into the evening, reminding those who understand these things that it is not all about glamour in this seductive sport, but about money, technology, power and long hours. Ferrari is selling this day. This is Ferrari For Sale. This is Luca's World, where cash flow, public relations and partnerships with Shell and Marlboro and the rest make money and carry Schumacher to triumph after triumph. This is the team built for Schumacher carrying all before it. But is it the team that Michael made, or is it the team that Ferrari forged? And afterwards, when the wins and the seasons and the glory have turned to statistics in old record books, will people say, 'Wasn't Michael Schumacher lucky to be at Ferrari with that fantastic group, that wonderful team?' Or will they ask it in reverse: 'Weren't those guys at Ferrari lucky to be there at the time when Team Schumacher landed at Maranello and took control?'

Have you ever competed hard and won? Have you ever finished triumphant in a race, a game or a match? Or even a tournament? It is tough to win in team sports. It is very tough in individual sports, and especially difficult in motor racing.

The driver, the man or woman who risks his reputation and his life, is dependent on a hidden group of other people – those who design and make, tune and set up the car, and those others who provide the money required to create the 'package' without which all drivers are lost. For any racing driver, the first win, even in karting, is memorable. The second is elusive, more difficult and more important. Every other win, every success that follows, at another race, in another series and at another championship level, is progressively more difficult. Remember all of this. And then think of your own best achievements in competition.

Again, think and reflect, this time on what it takes to win enough races in motor sport to be spotted, and then to have a chance to succeed again and to reach Formula One, the pinnacle. Once there, after having clawed, climbed and struggled with a ferocious will to win to reach the top level, imagine what it takes not just to survive, but to flourish. With every competitive instinct bristling, think of the challenge to avoid failure, to survive and to compete, and then to succeed by winning again.

Not many reach Formula One. Not many win a Grand Prix race. Not many experience the champagne atop a Formula One podium more than a handful of times. But some find a way to get there, to hold on to that feeling, to discover the elixir that is somewhere within them and brings them victory after victory after victory. And that is important too, because you need it to win a championship. If you are to do that you must win, and then win again and again and again.

And once you are a champion, can you defend your prize? There are one-time champions, and then beyond them, out of their orbit and reach, there are multiple champions, the magical breed of men who can control their own destiny, influence and lead others, transform some from uninspired journeymen to key decision-making team players. Men such as Juan Manuel Fangio, Jackie Stewart, Alain Prost and Ayrton Senna, competitive sportsmen whose feats turned them into icons for a generation of awe-struck fans. And among them, now standing head and shoulders clear with his seven drivers' titles, is Michael Schumacher. A competitor through to his bone marrow, he has amassed more successes than any man before him in Formula One, from his earliest childhood days in karting at Kerpen in northern Germany to the succession of drivers' titles he reeled off in the opening years of the new millennium. Like them all, it must be remembered, he started and finished by competing to win.

So, this is a story of a man of speed, and how he became so fast, so successful and so rich that his feats grew into a legend that, most summer Sunday afternoons, left sports editors all over the world torn between awe-struck rapture and an angry boredom, stimulated by the constant repetition of one car and one contestant's success. It was, for them, as if this gifted racing driver from Germany had been instructed to deliver a demonstration of the greatest Teutonic virtues, to exude ever-increasing confidence and power, to overwhelm all his rivals (sometimes with help from his team, who issued orders to command his team-mate to slow down) and to rewrite history with barely a revelation of emotional weakness along the way. He was, said many of his jealous detractors and critics, an arrogant person, a committed and cold man who was so focused on his own career goals that he showed an unusual lack of interest in other diversions. His supporters praised his single-minded sense of sacrifice and his ability to concentrate on his objectives at times when other people would have allowed outside distractions or emotional issues to undermine their performances.

For decades, sportswriters and fans had talked of the great Juan Manuel Fangio and his unbeatable record of five drivers' titles. His personality and his achievements were regarded with a respect that diminished the feats of many more fine, if not great, drivers who collected victories and titles. Men such as Jackie Stewart, who won three championships, bowed to the memory of Fangio and his legendary status. To them, and to sports editors in offices from London to Singapore, from Sydney to São Paulo, it had seemed that the muscular Argentine's position was unchallengeable. Yet from a land that had never before produced a convincing winner in Grand Prix motor racing came a boy of precocious poise, talent and instinct for pure pace who was to reduce all that lay before him, including the near-sacred image of a grinning and brawny Latin American hero wiping oil and dust from his face, to a pile of statistical rubble. Where Fangio had been and set records, others had followed. Stewart reeled off 27 wins, a record beaten by Prost. No other man, said the Frenchman's fans, could do better. And then, in a career that has seen triumph and tragedy, along came Michael Schumacher.

As the cooling fans whirred on hot afternoons, or nights, in sweaty newsrooms, there were some who almost willed anyone else to win, to loosen the grip the man from Kerpen, near Mannheim, seemed to hold, almost permanently at times, on the leader's place on the time-sheets, or the monitor screens, and, ultimately, the top step of the victors' podium. But the driver took no notice. He was a winning machine, dedicated to his ambition. He drove fast, he was sure, he made few errors – though some in his earlier career were as spectacular as they were controversial – and he had behind him, beneath him and around him a red package that carried him to glory, fame and fortune. His career blossomed like no other, thanks in so many parts to the team around him, a team that had come together, moulded itself to his needs and extraordinary talents, and then delivered with almost monotonous regularity a series of victories that made them arguably the greatest group of motor racing men to work together in the sport's history. This 'group', as Brawn called them, were admired and envied. The ferocity of their competitors' efforts to overhaul this elite and, for a time, apparently invincible combination of men, machines and driving talent only confirmed their place in history. They swaggered and celebrated, as well they might, at each season's end, and there were few by the end of 2004 who argued that they did not deserve it.

Schumacher's record as it stood at the end of 2004, before the start of the 2005 season, reflected his and Ferrari's supremacy. He and his close colleagues became rich men. Schumacher himself became one of the richest sportsmen of all time. But he built his fortune on solid foundations: the best career statistics recorded by a Formula One driver in the history of the world championship. Before he embarked on his pursuit of an eighth drivers' world title, Reuters published a résumé of his career. It contained the following:

MILESTONES
First race – Belgium, 1991
First podium – Mexico, 1992
First win – Belgium, 1992
First pole position – Monaco, 1994
First championship – 1994 (with Benetton)

RECORDS
Titles – seven (1994, 1995, 2000, 2001, 2002, 2003, 2004)
Longest unbroken run as champion (since October 2000)
Wins – 83

Wins in a season – 13 (2004)
Successive wins in a season – seven (2004)
Second places – 36
Fastest laps – 66
Points – 1,186 (including 78 in 1997 when he was excluded from the final standings after colliding with Canadian Jacques Villeneuve at Jerez)
Points in a season – 148 (2004)
Podiums – 137
Wins at the same race – seven (Canada, France)
Wins from pole – 37
Hat-tricks (pole, win, fastest lap) – 20
Successive races in the points – 24 (2001–2003)
Successive podiums – 19 (2001–2002)
Winning points margin – 67 (2002)
Fastest title – 2002 (won in July with six races to spare)
Schumacher is the only driver to have finished an entire season on the podium (in 2002)
Schumacher and his Brazilian team-mate Rubens Barrichello also have the most one-two finishes of any pairing in Formula One history – 23

Schumacher, a bricklayer's son from the northern flatlands west of Cologne in Germany, was, quite simply, a driving force, a catalyst and a record-breaker. When he came to Formula One, as a near-unknown, he was hailed as a *wunderkind* because of his audacity in showing the experienced Andrea de Cesaris a clean pair of heels in practice on his first weekend on arguably the most daunting racing circuit in the world – and without ever having completed a lap of the place before (except on a bicycle). On a track where even the most seasoned racing men gulped and held their breath as they swooped and swung around high-speed corners and through forests of pine trees, the boy quickly earned the respect of his rivals. It was the start of something special, as so many noted. It was, in short, the arrival of a champion. The most successful multiple champion of all.

The success of Michael Schumacher since his debut at Spa-Francorchamps in 1991 has been phenomenal. He is one of the best-known, most successful and richest men in the world, yet he has retained a degree of privacy most public figures would envy. He has remained unchanged as a person in many ways from the man-boy who walked into the paddock at the Belgian Grand Prix in 1991 and gave Eddie Jordan cause for a wide, ear-to-ear grin that was to last for barely a week (he signed for Benetton almost immediately and raced for them at the next event in Italy). He has introduced new standards in all areas of his sport: his level of fitness, his sense of competition, his utter commitment, his pragmatism and ruthlessness on and off the circuit, and his commercial life.

But he has not done it alone. Not by dint of speed itself. No, he has achieved his success through hard work and, above all, an understanding of the kind of teamwork he required. Schumacher, perhaps more than anyone else at any time in motor sport, realised the value of creating a package for success and then making sure it worked. To do this, he ignored issues he felt were not relevant to him and he delegated responsibilities. He accepted management of his career, his businesses, his image and his brand, but took the deepest possible interest in his own performance. He allowed his team to build him, nurture him and replant him, as and when necessary, to sit in the warmest sunshine, the most stimulating light and the best climate for sustained personal growth. While he retained ultimate control over each of his decisions, most obviously in the cockpit of his racing cars, he revelled in the freedom he gained through delegation of other responsibilities so that he could concentrate, unfettered by distractions, on the honing of his body, his mind, his competitive ambition, his racing instincts and his speed. And as this system of development and growth proceeded, he added more and more components until, as some have suggested in the land of Planet Ferrari, it was difficult to see the difference between Team Schumacher and the Scuderia itself. Remember, Ross Brawn was with Schumacher at Benetton in 1994 and 1995 before moving to Ferrari where, later, they repeated their championships and gained even greater success together. Remember, too, the same could be said of the man who designed the cars, Rory Byrne.

Jean Todt, the man whose arrival at Ferrari signalled a change of mentality in the management of the Italian team, also became an integral part of the era of success. He was, if not its architect, most certainly the alchemist who made it work at a time when, to some, it seemed that Ferrari and Schumacher were destined to suffer failure and disappointment together. Todt, seen by many as the Napoleon of the pit-lane because he is a diminutive Frenchman with a flair for authority and management, would disagree heartily with any suggestion that Schumacher, or the notion of a Team Schumacher, could even exist as a successful force, let alone be bigger or more influential than Ferrari itself. He would argue against it, declaring that everyone employed by Ferrari worked only for the Italian team. But, if the two are seen as synonymous in this great period of success, then it cannot be ignored that he was at the heart and head of the entire operation. Indeed, some might say it was the team that Todt built, rather than either Ferrari or Schumacher. Who cares? In reality, it was the sustained success of five years of Schumacher victories that moulded the brand. When people recall the 2000 to 2004 period in Formula One history, they will remember it as the Schumacher era. Yet it was the era of Schumacher and Ferrari. The two are entwined, but it is the core of the team built around the spoon-jawed German that produced the results that made him appear to be so supreme and invincible.

And no one understood the value of a team approach to motor racing more than Schumacher. From the start, he knew he needed others: his father, his sponsors, his patrons, his engineers and mechanics, his friends and his family. When he joined Ferrari, as he has admitted, it was a career decision, a move made for technical, financial and political reasons. He was not aware that he was joining an Italian family club that would influence his entire life. But he knew the value of creating a team to work around him. It had always been a feature of his approach to the job, a confirmation that he saw sport essentially as a team effort. He loved football too, because he understood how important it was for any great individual to ensure his talent was exercised for the benefit of the team. In the midst of his five championships, he said, 'I was once criticised for saying, after visiting the factory [at Maranello] for the first time, that Ferrari's engine workshop looked like my mate's at the go-kart track. However, Ferrari is now a team that is up-to-date in every respect. But I have never claimed that was due to me. Without my team, I would be nothing. As I have always understood it, Formula One is a team sport. Starting with the people in the factory at Maranello, everyone contributes to my being able to sit in a car like this …' In 2004, Ross Brawn stated, 'I'm not sure any other driver has become as closely integrated with a team as

[Schumacher] has with Ferrari. I can't imagine him really wanting to drive anywhere else.' He added, 'It's almost a unique position in Formula One.'

So, who are the people who made Michael Schumacher the greatest success story in the history of Formula One? How did it happen? Inevitably, it is impossible, or virtually impossible, simply to list a series of names and to say, 'Hey, here, these are the guys who did it.' There are too many of them. And many have played walk-on roles in his career, from early karting days to multiple championship success. To embrace them all, to make this explanation of Schumacher's stunningly successful career make sense and to remain accurate and fair, it is necessary first to accept, at least in principle, that perhaps the cleverest thing Schumacher did was to protect himself within each team he raced for by assembling his own 'team' within the team around him.

Other drivers before him had generated great loyalty within a team during their own tilts at glory, forged close relationships with team owners and senior engineers, and even distanced themselves from their team-mates. The classic duel at McLaren between Alain Prost and Ayrton Senna in the late 1980s is a good example. Indeed, Senna helped develop the cult of the driver as something more than a mere servant to the team by operating with press and media assistants, managers and advisers, who helped protect his position and his interests long before such arrangements became almost *de rigueur* in the sport. Others followed suit. When the Williams team were dominant in the 1990s, it was common for the drivers to develop loyal bonds with the men on their side of the garage and in their half of the team. Indeed, when Jacques Villeneuve left Williams to join British

American Racing, he took his race engineer Jock Clear with him. But Schumacher, it appeared to some, took this development of loyalty and devotion to another level. When he was at Benetton, for example, with Johnny Herbert as his team-mate in 1994 and 1995, the popular English driver complained bitterly that he had little chance to compete successfully against Schumacher within the team because his computer readings were taken from him and given to the German. 'I could never do a comparison of his laps and mine,' he said. 'It was not fair for me. He had all the information I didn't have …'

In Schumacher's career, too, perhaps due to the intense sense of loyalty he generated, he collected close confidants as he progressed. Perhaps, this was due to the circumstances created by his craving success and his father's inability, as a man of modest means, to fund him automatically to do as he, or his talent, pleased in motor racing when he was young. In other words, as he grew up, he learnt quickly to fend for himself and make sure he had the best equipment he could find. He learnt to seek out and take advantages. Indeed, such was the obvious star quality of Michael Schumacher as a youngster that as he grew up, and as his father's financial support evaporated, there were always, it seemed, a stream of other people ready to help finance him, somehow or other, to take the next step up the career ladder towards eventual success in Formula One. The best known of these was Willi Weber, but it would be unfair to suggest that Weber alone helped take Michael from his formative days in karting all the way to the top. Indeed, it would be inaccurate.

First among those who worked to help the young Schumacher, in his teenage years, was his father Rolf, supported by his mother Elisabeth. He started him, did his best to develop him, helped him repair and improve his kart, often with parts discarded by richer rivals, and only faced his personal limit when required to buy an expensive new engine to keep his son on the road. When Schumacher senior turned down that request, luckily for his oldest son there were others willing to provide assistance – men such as Gerhard Noack, who had been successful in the carpet business; Willi Bergmeister, in whose garage Michael went to work as a mechanic after school hours; and Jurgen Dilk, a one-time slot-machine businessman who sponsored the young Schumacher during his European karting career and again, notably, in Formula Ford. Without Dilk, Schumacher has often remarked, he might not have made it to Formula One at all. These men and their families were truly vital to the early days of Michael Schumacher – before Weber took over, before Mercedes-Benz became involved, and before he found his way into the paddock at Spa-Francorchamps for his debut Formula One drive.

Weber, who helped to guide Schumacher all the way from Formula Koenig to Formula One, has been a controversial figure at times, but no one can deny that he has done his job as manager of the most successful driver in the history of Grand Prix motor racing well. He guided him sensibly, found deals and openings when they were required, and – even if allegations have been made about some of the methods used in various quarters at various times – succeeded in not only landing him his chance at Jordan, but also in moving him to Benetton, where he won two drivers' championship titles, and to Ferrari, where history was made. That Weber may have dabbled in other businesses that brought him trouble, that he also managed Michael's brother Ralf and others, that he became high-profile for his alleged misdemeanours as much as for his successes, should not hide the fact that where Michael Schumacher is concerned he did his job well and, famously, made himself a very rich man into the bargain. In the line-up of Team Schumacher, Weber is the Money Man. The reasons are self-explanatory.

Later, in his years in Formula One, as he established himself, his methods, his style and his speed, Michael made his own judgements and found his own successes with engineers, technical directors and designers. In their own way, and in their own time, therefore, Ross Brawn, Rory Byrne and Jean Todt became irreplaceable stalwarts of the structured organisation around him, notably at Ferrari, while many others in that team played important if lower-profile roles – men such as Paolo Martinelli, Stefano Domenicalli, Chris Dyer, Balbir Singh, Nigel Stepney, and others too numerous to mention, men who not only played a part in producing a fast car but, more importantly for Schumacher, a reliable one.

In other places, reliable emotional rocks such as his brother Ralf Schumacher, his wife Corinna, his children, his friends from Switzerland and his friends in Italy all contributed to the complex story that made up Schumacher's roller-coaster years of sustained success. They were all different, each working in different departments of this organised man's very organised life. Private and public affairs were kept separate; media and technical obligations were in different compartments; family and Formula One were at arms' length. But they all played a part in his package of success as Team Schumacher evolved into a formidable tale of triumphs.

Above all, Michael Schumacher is, and has always been, a family man. His wife and two children give him a home life and a base that has always been at the core of his professional racing life. Before Corinna, Mick and Gina-Maria in Switzerland, it was Rolf, Elisabeth and Ralf in Kerpen, in Germany. Of course, there were places in between, but it is difficult not to sense the homeliness in Schumacher. It was there when he started out, and it is there as he contemplates his finale, seven drivers' world championships later. In January 2005 he said, 'My family is a very underestimated support for me. You need an environment where you get your strength from; when you have tough moments, you have someone to lean on, like Corinna and my kids. When they feel like the need to slow me down, they pull on the handbrake. They are always there. We deal with any problems together. I take strength from that.'

It was presumed, therefore, at the time that the whole family had agreed without rancour when he made his decision to donate ten million euros to the victims of the tsunami in south-east Asia soon after the disaster on Boxing Day 2004. 'I have always done something when I felt it was appropriate,' he explained. 'I am lucky that I earn a lot of money in my job. In F3, when I was able to win in Macau, I earned for the first time substantial money. When I knew I was going to win and how much prize money I was going to get, my initial thought, during the race, was that I was going to help some people with this. More inside my family, but I have always tried to balance out the unevenness we have around the world … Seeing what we have seen, we have all been affected. It is my way of contributing. It is a little bit personal in a way. It is tough to deal with and it is tough to explain to your children. The donation was a way of trying to help.'

There is no doubting that in the complexity of life within Team Schumacher, Michael's family is a paramount consideration and a source of inspiration and energy. He cares for them so much. This was clear, too, when he travelled to Dublin to carry out supporting promotional work on road safety for the European Union, the Irish government, the World

Health Organisation and the International Motoring Federation (FIA). It was a typical non-racing, non-testing but working day for the world champion on 6 April 2004 as he learnt that 1.2 million people are killed on the roads worldwide every year and that something needed to be done to improve things. That figure averaged out at a daily 3,200 – 'a 9/11 each day' as Max Mosley, the president of the FIA, put it succinctly. Schumacher was shocked. He lives in an isolated and privileged world most of the time, but he cares about his family, and he cares about the wider family of the whole world. 'Look, I'm a father of two,' he told a reporter, who was prodding him with questions. 'So, yes, I tend to relate things to my own life and my own family. That video we saw was very affecting – all those stories about kids being killed on the roads in developing countries. I was shocked, yes. I hadn't heard all those statistics before. I wasn't aware that there were quite so many road deaths in the world. And, as people like Ari shared their own personal experiences, yes, of course, I was deeply affected. Whether I am a racing driver or not, I'm also a father. And just like with the charity work I do, I think that gives me greater motivation to do things that, you know, make a difference. And I know I'm fortunate, and that my kids are fortunate. As so, you compare yourself with others who are less fortunate. And it makes you want to change things, to make a difference.'

In his own book, *Schumacher – The Official Inside Story of the Formula One Icon*, his wife Corinna provides another insight into the man, his high activity levels and his sense of team and family, as well as his honesty. 'Michael is such a family man,' she said. 'One of the reasons why I love him is the way he is with our children. He always has time for them and it is wonderful to see how much he enjoys it. He is never happier than when he is playing around with Gina and Mick. He is always thinking of things to do with them: climbing, trampolining, playing around – those sort of things rather than singing or reading with them. That's where I come in. Michael is the more active one. He can hardly ever sit still. We never spend the day on the sofa together, or simply hanging around. Never. He is incapable of it. Obviously, we sometimes watch a film together, but afterwards we get on with things again. He is unstoppable. He always has to do things, and always he finds something. He has a go at everything. And, above all, he can do everything.'

Yet, despite all of this, Schumacher's success story is not one that has warmed the hearts of every Italian fan who loves Ferrari. Nor has it spread love and affection across Europe. He is a man who has earned respect, and earned it completely and utterly after such long-held domination over his peers, but not one who has been given unquestioned admiration. He is a family man, and he is admired for this, but to the public he is a racer, a winner and a champion – and for that, within the context of his team, his family are just a part. However, as we shall see in *Team Schumacher*, the role of family and home – of his father, his brother, his wife and his children – is as important as any other, if not more so. In the package of people and qualities that make up the essence of the team, it is the family that is at its heart.

CHAPTER TWO

HOME FRONT I

My family is everything to me.
They are always there.

Michael Schumacher, 2005

Michael Schumacher is not a man without a weakness. He may be capable of speed, a determined intensity of focus, a single-mindedness in racing that cuts out all non-essential matters, but when it comes to ordinary everyday life he is like everyone else. He enjoys most things, and he likes to keep his life simple. At end-of-season parties, when he lets his hair down, he dances, sings and drinks. He smokes cigars, mixes Cubalibres for his friends, and has even been known to indulge in karaoke. But his most consistent weakness is probably his sweet tooth, which sometimes forces him to take an indirect, shadowy route through the Formula One paddock's motor homes to find the kitchen of Karl-Heinz Zimmerman. There, where he is usually greeted like a prodigal son by the Austrian chef who is one of Grand Prix motor racing's greatest characters, he likes nothing better than to be given a large slice of apple strudel. He also adores ice cream (he once had a special liking for a cup of spaghetti ice cream) and chocolate. Hardly, you might think, the preferred diet of a slim-line, super-fit Formula One world champion.

In fact, such revelations suggest that the man is normal after all – just a normal family man. And that is what he is. Indeed, without the solid base provided by his family, from his youngest days all the way to his seventh title triumph, he might not have sustained any of it. For Michael Schumacher, home has always been vital to his stability and success, from Kerpen to the northern shoreline of Lac Leman in Switzerland.

He was born in Hurth-Hermuhlheim on 3 January 1969. His father Rolf and mother Elisabeth lived a modest, happy and ordinary family life into which they added another racing-mad son, Ralf, in 1975. Their home town, Kerpen, was in an agricultural and light-industrial region west of Cologne where fields of cereal crops and sugar beet were broken up by small factories and a network of roads that connected dozens of villages. Simplicity, order, discipline and community values ruled. The Schumacher brothers grew up without fear of hard work and no expectations of wealth or fame. Everything had to be earned. Cars were nearly always second-hand or older, driven to their end and then replaced. Meals were eaten together, quickly, without pomp; his mother's cooking was never left long on the table. Old-fashioned values were respected.

Rolf supported his family through hard toil, but found time to help Michael's racing when he showed a talent for karting. He would assist with organisation, repairs and maintenance at the local kart track, the Europe Moto Drom, where Elisabeth would run a fast-food stall. Money was in short supply. There were no luxuries. If Michael needed a new tyre for his kart, it had to be recovered from other people's discarded goods on a rubbish heap and used again. 'My karts were not so much made from second- or third-hand parts, but from tenth-hand or twelfth-hand parts,' he once joked. Everything was made to last, not least the values Michael learnt from this childhood, values that have served him well.

From the start, Michael learnt that nothing was achieved without hard work. It was apparent in his family. It was clear all around him as he grew up. Modesty, too, was taken for granted. Even after his son had become a champion and a millionaire, neither of his parents launched themselves into lives in the limelight. Indeed, Elisabeth may have suffered in the glare of Michael's success as she struggled in her own life after separation from his father. Her premature death, in Cologne after a fall at the family home, on the Saturday night of the San Marino Grand Prix in 2003 was a sad indication of this likely state of affairs. Both her sons flew to her bedside that evening, after qualifying for the race. The following day Michael won. His integrity and dignity were palpable through that entire weekend as he fought to keep his emotions under control.

Like most great racing drivers, Schumacher understood how important it was to keep each part of his life in a box separate from the rest. The racing man was never the same person as the husband, the son or the father. He had to shut out the non-essential material from his mind if he was to be as effective in his car, on the track, as his potential promised. His upbringing and his willingness to work and to obey simple commands for good reason were great allies to him in ensuring this happened.

His escape from school and family routine was in his karting. He started as little more than an infant. He crashed for the first time, into a lamppost, when he was only four. 'I was so enthusiastic about karting when I was young,' Michael said. 'I would be there all the time. I spent hours there practising. If I had the chance, I would have gone professional. I never really thought of anything else.' His first kart, supplied by Rolf, was a pedal kart. It was later improved when his father added a small engine taken from an old motorcycle. 'That's the way it started,' said Schumacher. 'First, we went to the green. Then on the pavement until – and you know this story – I had a meeting with a lamppost. Then we changed to a race circuit. The first proper one was quite close to home, just ten or fifteen kilometres away at Kerpen-Horrem. I joined the club and became a member. I was the youngest driver, and straight away I was in the newspaper. From there, everything started! I was four at that time, and when I was five I got the cheapest go-kart ever built.' This kart was made of pieces of equipment thrown away by other people. It was put together by his father. 'But it did run and we even won races with it,' said

Schumacher. 'That was the most important thing. It had a 100cc engine. My father had to cut a piece out of the chassis and then stick it together again because it was too big for me to reach the pedals. In the end, it worked.'

The world of kart racing might have been everything to Michael Schumacher at this time, but it had no extensions for him to Grand Prix motor racing. 'I lived in Kerpen and the go-kart track was my world. Formula One was beyond my wildest dreams,' he said. 'I never bothered with it. Any old crate on wheels suited me! Formula One was completely remote and out of my reach, which is partly why I had no posters of the great drivers on my bedroom walls. I just wasn't the kind of child who had idols.' Nor did the family have any pretensions to grandeur. Cars, usually second-hand or older, were treated as nothing more than a mode of transport. As a boy, Schumacher had no desire for prestige cars. 'For us, at home,' he explained in *Schumacher – The Official Inside Story of the Formula One Icon*, 'cars were the means to an end. No more than that. They were usually old, and when they were finished, we bought another old banger. It wasn't until later that I learnt that a car could also be a luxury article, that aesthetics and style could be involved. I have never been a dreamer. Even at the stage where I was working my way through the formula classifications, I always tended to be pessimistic. I was satisfied with what I had. Because Formula One was considerably more than I could ever have envisaged, I always thought, "Good, if the next step happens, wonderful. I'll have to grab the chance." But at the same time my attitude was always realistic. I never wanted to hope for things which might never become reality. I have always been a rather pessimistic person.'

Rolf Schumacher gave all he could to help his sons. To increase his income, he took a second job, working at the old Graf Berghe von Trips circuit at Kerpen-Horrem, repairing karts and renting them out. Together, he and Elisabeth kept a close eye on their eldest as he grew up and spent most of his life out of the classroom, at the kart track. By the time he was six, Michael Schumacher had won a club championship for the first time. It was clear that the boy had talent. It was equally clear to his father that it was going to cost him a lot of money to nurture that talent. Rolf did his best, but in the end overtime and unmatched dedication to the task were not enough. He simply did not have the money required.

The breaking point came when Michael wanted a new engine, which was going to cost 800 Deutschmarks. Rolf said he could not afford to buy it. Other means of financing its purchase had to be considered, and in that instant one of the greatest careers in the history of motor racing was decided.

The Schumacher family chose not to give up or give in; instead, swallowing their pride, they would support any scheme that enabled Michael to capitalise on his extraordinary ability. It was a decision taken on the premise that the end would justify the means. In itself, it was no bad thing, but there have been times in Schumacher's extraordinary career when even he has questioned the outcome of various incidents when his desire to fulfil his talent, or even his destiny, has been decided by a similar philosophy. In tandem with this decision, Schumacher became a commercialised sportsman, someone who through accepting patronage and sponsorship owed a debt to his backers. This, of course, empowered his backers, and meant that they would have an opportunity to use this association to their own advantage, whether it was to be through endorsements, media activity or other kinds of promotional or marketing work. 'I was never raised to spend more money than I had,' Michael often remarked later in his life, when money was plentiful. He also, as frequently, explained his feelings of obligation towards his personal sponsors, the companies whose funds helped to steer his career. 'If they have helped me, then the least I can do to repay them is to always try my best to succeed. I cannot slacken off and relax, can I?'

This sense of loyalty, his consistency and his honesty in these matters, stayed with him. His father Rolf has also remained a supporting figure in his career, always close as Schumacher became more and more successful. The simple early rules of life were the ones the family stuck with, and they were not to change. At the same time, some critics suggested, this simplicity was a convenient way for Michael to ignore any issues or features that were deemed wrong or unwanted when they were drawn to his attention by other people. Some called this tunnel vision, or single-mindedness; others regarded it as an extraordinary ability to focus on the things that mattered most. But the purity that was evident in the support and love he received from his parents, even as he grew into the dedicated kart-racing champion of his youth, was no longer dominant once he took to the roads with his sponsors. Then, in a wider world, there were other forces at work. Still, as we shall see, family values and 'home front' security provided a thread of consistency through his life and career.

His academic background certainly did not play a great role in his formative years. He went to the Otto-Hahn Realschule, where he showed promise in many subjects including English and mathematics, but shone in sports, particularly judo. His teaching staff, however, took second place to those he created for himself in his alternative school of life at the kart circuit. It was no real surprise when he left school that he chose to eschew the road to university and instead took up an opportunity to become an apprentice mechanic at a local

Volkswagen and BMW garage. It was a different kind of education.

Schumacher owed this obsession with racing to the guidance of his father. In this respect, Rolf Schumacher was the founding member of Team Schumacher. The love of racing and karting in particular has never left him. In 2001, after winning his fourth drivers' titles, he was back at the track at Kerpen-Mannheim in October for the final round of the Super-A World Championship. It was an event he could not resist, a call from his childhood, a return to his roots. He explained how much he loved working on go-karts. 'In Formula One, you can't do anything yourself. All the mechanics are there to do the things that here you can do yourself. When Ralf was go-karting, I was his mechanic, and I really loved it. This is my world. It is part of my natural rhythm, part of my childhood. Some of my happiest memories relate to this place and karting. I'm convinced that if I weren't a Formula One driver, I would be driving or hiring out go-karts. I certainly wouldn't have got rich doing it, but I would have been just as happy.'

His own experience as a mechanic, his enjoyment of karting, his inheritance of the satisfaction his father found in repairing karts and improving their performance – all of these features help explain why Schumacher relates so well with his own mechanics in his race team at Ferrari, and also why he has been able to weld together a formidable shield of loyalty around himself and his team. All of Ferrari has adopted the same team spirit and family feeling. This is the side of Michael Schumacher that connects with ordinary people, everyday values and honest working lives. This is the part of a complex man that is easy to understand. It is the part of Schumacher that comes from the original home front back in Kerpen, where Rolf and Elisabeth brought up their sons in a sensible, hard-working home and kept their feet on the ground. Money was valued, not wasted, and opportunities for advancement had to be taken without hesitation.

In the creation of a multiple Formula One drivers' world champion whose career rewrote the record books and established new standards, however, it was not the only factor involved.

CHAPTER THREE

THE WIZARD OF ROSS

You're great, Ross. You are great, Ross.
All of you guys. Oh my God! Yahooo! Oh!
We did it! We did it! Ohhh! … I can't believe it …
We did it … Give Corinna a big kiss from me …
Ross, you are simply the master of our team.

Michael Schumacher, after winning
the Japanese Grand Prix on 8 October 2000

There are times in sport when great achievements and thrilling events dwarf all else around them. It may be a winning goal scored in football, a diving catch in cricket, a spectacular, breathtaking running try in rugby union, a supreme passing shot in tennis, or an audacious overtaking move on a race circuit. They trigger noise, emotions and excitement that can lead people to lose their self-control. Vast crowds of spectators join the triumphant sportsman, or sportswoman, or team, in unbridled celebrations. Legends are made. History is rewritten. Eras end. They are the moments to cherish, unforgettable and spine-tingling. The nights when lives are changed, ambitions fired and landmarks set. For the victors' supporters they are more than memorable, they are life-enhancing. For the rest, they are stunning and inspiring.

It is not just about the statistics and the victory. It is the meaning and the substance of them. Everyone knows about Pele's three World Cup wins with Brazil, in Sweden in 1958, in Chile in 1962 and in Mexico in 1970; Martina Navratilova's sustained, spirited run of glory at Wimbledon; the heart of Muhammad Ali, notably in his victory against George Foreman at Kinshasa, Zaire, in October 1974; Emil Zatopek winning the 5,000 metres, the 10,000 metres and the marathon at the Helsinki Olympic Games in 1952. They, and many more, have stayed alive in the minds of those who were there – or believed they were, after reading reports, watching footage and reliving the moments. In recent times there have been the nights when Manchester United (in 1999) and Liverpool (in 2005) lifted the European Cup after stunning and unexpected recoveries; the day in November 2003 when Jonny Wilkinson kicked England's rugby team to World Cup glory, against Australia in Sydney; the elegant supremacy, and the tears, of Roger Federer as he won his first Wimbledon tennis title; and, in Formula One, the long-awaited revival of Ferrari, confirmed when Michael Schumacher clinched their first drivers' world championship in 21 years with his victory at Suzuka in October 2000.

For the Italian team and their loyal *tifosi*, it was not just the end of a long quest after so long without any championship glory, it was a seminal moment too. No one knew it then, but it was to be the first of five back-to-back Schumacher titles and the second of six constructors' championships for Ferrari. It was the start of a new era, a period dominated by the scarlet *scuderi*; and it was the end of years of duality when the title nearly always seemed to be wrapped in the blue ribbons of Williams or the red-and-white, later black-and-grey, of McLaren. But it was also a great victory, won after a great race that concluded a stirring season. No wonder, as he crossed the line and began his slowing-down lap, that Schumacher was lost for words when Ross Brawn, the Ferrari team's technical director, pit-wall boffin and tactical guru, invited him to explain how he felt on an open radio link that was being recorded for use by the world's media and was later published in full audio format on the AtlasF1 website. Schumacher's reply was as passionate and unrestrained as it was lacking in formal language and preparation. His weeping, screaming response, including profanities, was all he had left, but it summed up the feelings of a man who had waited five years for his third title, and as long to make his mark for a team that was paying him a king's ransom to end their decades in the doldrums.

He and the team had endured bitter disappointments in 1997, 1998 and 1999 after mounting serious challenges. The way in which the 1997 championship ended, at Jerez, where Schumacher collided with the eventual champion Jacques Villeneuve, resulted in uproar, controversy and, ultimately, the

Ferrari driver's exclusion from the championship itself. This was why, when the triumph did come at the 2000 Japanese Grand Prix, it tasted so sweet. As a group they had shared the bad times, and as a group they were ready to drink deep from the trough of good times. It is also why, when the moment came, Michael's first thoughts were not for himself, but for the team. It was a team he had built, with his speed and his talent, and he knew he was a winner thanks to them. He has never for one moment shirked from warm tributes to the men around him – Ross Brawn, Jean Todt and the rest – who supported him through thick and thin.

Indeed, when it comes to Brawn, it has to be said that the bespectacled boffin from Manchester has been through nearly all of the down times Michael Schumacher has experienced from the earliest days at Benetton in 1991 and 1992. Only in 1996, when Schumacher experienced a lonely and sometimes dispiriting first year at Ferrari – a period during which he learnt of the team's great strengths, traditions and history while at the same time seeing for himself its weaknesses, bad habits and lack of discipline and organisation – did Brawn work apart from him. Schumacher had departed Benetton after winning his second drivers' title, wanting, it was said, to distance himself from the damaging innuendo that had surrounded his first title-winning year, and to prove his huge talent again by working as part of the massive rebuilding programme that Ferrari, under the guidance of Luca di Montezemolo and Jean Todt, represented. Brawn, having been joined at Benetton by the two ex-Ferrari drivers Jean Alesi and Gerhard Berger, who replaced Schumacher and Johnny Herbert at the Enstone-based team, also passed a year of gentle disillusionment, wondering what he had done to deserve such a reward after his hard work had produced so much success with another driver. The demands of the two wealthy veterans of the F1 circus were entirely different to those of the young tyro who had departed for his new Italian challenge, and it left the technical director pondering his future.

When Ferrari sent out their first feelers, it was clear in which direction Brawn's future would be set. He did not know it then, but it was to be the greatest roller-coaster ride, from frustration and disappointment to the highest thrills. Indeed, Brawn's journey with Ferrari was like a ride on the famous big wheel in Suzuka's own extraordinary playground-cum-parkland. But there was one difference this time round: once Brawn had found his way to the top, he was able to make sure he and the rest of Team Schumacher stayed there for as long as possible.

One man who understood the contribution that Brawn made to the Ferrari–Schumacher success story, when it began in October 2000, was Johnny Herbert, the English driver who had partnered the German to his second title at Benetton in 1995. By then, Herbert's career had taken him to Jaguar, where he partnered Eddie Irvine, newly departed from Ferrari after three years as number two to Schumacher. Herbert was a veteran of the circuit. He knew the people, and he knew how they, and their teams, operated. 'Ross has done a great job,' he said on the eve of the decisive race. 'He should get more praise than Michael if Ferrari win the championship. He has been a very, very important guy. He is the one who has brought the team together. He was there with Michael at Benetton, and he has used that experience at Ferrari. He has also proved he is a great tactician when it comes to winning races.'

That Schumacher won the race, a thrillingly memorable Japanese Grand Prix, to become the first Ferrari driver to win the world championship in 21 years was both a ringing endorsement of Herbert's opinion and a vindication of the massive cost, to Ferrari, of assembling their dream team. Team Schumacher came of age in those months, and they celebrated long into that early October night. They had won four races in succession to seize the drivers' title, entering that last Grand Prix with an eight-point advantage over McLaren's Mika Hakkinen, the defending champion from Finland who was seeking, against the odds, to complete a hat-trick of title triumphs. When nerves, mistakes and destiny might have interfered, they stayed strong and calm. The team delivered. In particular, Brawn delivered. Indeed, in many respects the 'dream team' was created more in the character of this owlish, calm, thoughtful and methodical man than it was from the inspired example of Schumacher's speed and robust competitive racing.

The driver knew it, too. 'All my life, I shall never forget that radio signal from Ross Brawn,' he recalled. 'I was driving down the pit-lane after my second stop, desperate to know if I would make it out ahead of Mika, and Ross said over the radio, "It's looking good, it's looking good." I was very tense and fully expecting him to say it was looking good, but, suddenly, he said, "It's looking bloody good!" Honestly, my heart leapt in the air. It was as if it had skipped a beat.' In that instant, Schumacher and Brawn knew that the drivers' world championship was within their grasp. The driver's pure talent for speed had always enabled him to deliver stunning laps almost on demand, and Brawn's trust in this special ability had enabled him, in turn, to calculate race tactics that could leave rivals sighing or banging their heads on the pit-wall in frustration. In his own account of the race, Michael reported that he had not believed his two laps prior to that second pit-stop were fast enough to give him a good chance to re-emerge in the lead. He said he had been delayed in traffic, including a Benetton that had spun off the circuit. 'And then came Ross's radio message … unbelievable,' he said.

The man from Kerpen's exploits had commanded that a vast army of Germans rose early that Sunday morning to follow the race on television, knowing that if he made no mistakes in the drizzle on the dark parts of a circuit with many newly resurfaced patches, he would become champion again. He duly achieved it. The outburst of relief and glee spread from inside his car, across the circuit, through the pit-lane and into the huge crowd. On his final lap after winning, he wept. He drove on and on. Brawn was feeling the emotions too, but it was more difficult to tell.

When Schumacher finally made it back to the Parc Fermé, the whole of the Ferrari team were there to cheer him in. 'It was just fantastic,' he recalled. 'Those faces, those shining eyes. Everyone cheering. I could have thrown my arms around them all and kissed them all. I did try to – and, thank God, Corinna was there.' Corinna, the girl who had married Michael in August 1995 at Petersburg, near Bonn, at a place normally used by the German government to entertain special guests, joined the celebrations with enthusiasm. She was a major part of the team, bringing a stable family connection to the day, as she always did. In her way, she kept Michael's feet on the ground, even if she did her best that evening to make sure they both danced and partied late into the night. But it was Brawn and Todt who were at the heart of it all as the early celebrations began in makeshift surroundings at the back of the garage in the sloping Suzuka paddock, in the rain. As always, the partying brought out the Rheinlander in Schumacher as the team began eating, drinking and singing. Champagne was flowing everywhere. Wet through, in the midst of it all, his spectacles steamed up, stood Ross Brawn. It was, for him, a fabulous confirmation of his own special role in the great crimson team. Schumacher acknowledged this. 'Today, the pit-stops were perfect,' he said. 'Everything was perfect. Simply, it was great. Ross is the man to thank for this. He, in the final moment, is the person who takes the right decision. He made us the world champion. On the other side, he needs all the support the great engineers and mechanics in the team can give him.'

Two weeks later, Ferrari completed the Formula One 'double' of drivers' and constructors' championships when Schumacher won the Malaysian Grand Prix at Sepang, near Kuala Lumpur International Airport. Sportingly, McLaren Mercedes-Benz, beaten after a thrilling contest, congratulated their rivals as the paddock filled with champagne-soaked people dancing and celebrating in scarlet wigs. The hairpieces were an ironic reference to past seasons, most notably 1997, when Jacques Villeneuve and his supporters had donned blond wigs for the day. At the post-race news conference with the top three finishers, Schumacher and his team-mate Rubens Barrichello, who finished third, wore red wigs. More surprisingly, so too did the second-placed finisher David Coulthard, of McLaren. 'Now,' said McLaren chief Ron Dennis, 'is the appropriate time to congratulate both Michael and the rest of the Ferrari team for their drivers' and constructors' championships. I hope they party for at least three months in order to give us a head start for next year.'

Jean Todt, then working in the role of sporting director for Ferrari, held a plastic beaker of champagne in his hand, smiled, and said it was a moment of great personal and professional satisfaction for him. 'I came here to build up the team, to put the pieces into place and to achieve this success, and for me it is a very satisfying and very special feeling to have done it. The season could not have finished better than this – with two drivers on the podium. The statistics are fantastic this season – ten wins, nine for Michael, one for Rubens, a record year. This time we only needed three points, but we did it properly.' Ferrari president Luca di Montezemolo, one of the most superstitious of the team's supporters, had flown into Malaysia on the Sunday morning of the race, but instead of watching the race at the circuit he had chosen to stay away and follow it on television from his hotel room. 'But he wants to join the big party tonight back at the hotel, and we will all enjoy ourselves with him,' said Todt. 'That is why he came. For us all, it has been a long time coming to achieve this, and we will have a real celebration.'

As Todt smiled, his lieutenants nearby were already working for the future. Brawn, who had been the architect of so many of the team's wins, was already reflecting on their achievements and assessing the challenges ahead. At Suzuka, his decision to keep Schumacher out for three laps after his rival Mika Hakkinen had gone in for a second pit-stop virtually decided the outcome – as Schumacher conceded. Brawn, however, was first to pay tribute to the amazing driving skills of Schumacher when he looked back, and then ahead. 'It will be a little bit different next year,' he said. 'Now that we have achieved this, I think the intense pressure will disappear and the team will be a little more relaxed. It will feel different. I think we might see another notch on Michael, too. To me, he's the best driver out there. I think we had a very good car this year, and he used it. He is such a loyal and genuine guy. He has been here with Ferrari five years, and maybe with another team he could have won the championship before, but he stuck with us, with Ferrari, and he never let up in the time he has been here. He has been so involved. He is much more involved than many other drivers. He encourages everyone. He spends a lot of time with the mechanics. He is the man who has been deeply involved in making Ferrari really work as a team. No one can doubt Michael's ability as a racing driver, but as a person he's a great human being, and not a lot of people see that.

'When I came to Ferrari, it was my ambition to win the world championship. We won the constructors' title last year [1999], so, now, to win the drivers' championship is the ultimate step. It takes a while for these things to sink in, and to be honest, I suppose I'm still waiting for it all to sink in now! We have been so close to this before.' He need not have worried. After all the near-misses, the frustration and the pressure, he was to go on and repeat the trick again and again and again.

Ross Brawn was born on 23 November 1954 in Manchester, England. His family lived in a street of terraced houses and he grew up in a close-knit community in which everyone was friendly with their neighbours and everyone felt secure. He has described it as his *Coronation Street* background – a reference to a famous and long-running soap opera on television in England where most of the characters have become more famous than most modern celebrities. He also grew up as a Manchester United supporter.

His father worked for a company involved in the motor industry, and he followed motor racing. When Ross was eleven, a job offer meant that the family moved south to Reading, close to London. It was an upheaval for the young Brawn, but he settled down in the 'dormitory town' and went on to study engineering. He was taken on as a trainee at the British Atomic Energy Research Establishment at Harwell, near Didcot in Oxfordshire, where he studied instrumentation, and later joined March Engineering at Bicester to work as a milling machine operator. He also worked for the Formula Three racing team as a mechanic. In 1978 he joined the newly formed Williams Grand Prix Engineering racing team, then based in a former carpet warehouse at Didcot, working his way up through the ranks to the research and development department under Frank Dernie. Following the team's move to Basil Hill Road in Didcot, Brawn worked as an aerodynamicist. After eight years under the eye of Patrick Head, the long-serving technical director of the Williams team and partner of Sir Frank Williams, Brawn moved on to be an aerodynamicist with American Carl Haas's FORCE-Beat team. Neil Oatley, who was with him at Williams, also left to join the cigar-chomping Haas.

When that team folded at the end of 1986, Brawn was offered the job of chief designer at Arrows, where Jackie Oliver was in charge. Luckily for Brawn, this was at a time when the Milton Keynes-based outfit was enjoying a good budget, supported by the American investment company USF&G. The team was using Megatron (ex-BMW turbo) engines and, with cars created by Brawn, had some modest successes. The A10 car and its successor, the 1988 A10B, delivered consistently, and the team finished fourth in the constructors' world championship in 1988 with the popular Derek Warwick in the drivers' line-up, enjoying several impressive results but not a victory. Both Arrows cars, notably, came home to score points at the famous 1988 Italian Grand Prix at which Ferrari scored a triumphant one-two just weeks after the death of the team's founder Enzo Ferrari. Even on that hot, sunlit afternoon in the old park at Monza, Brawn was creating an association with Italy that foretold future events.

His ability with a drawing pencil, as the saying goes, then attracted the attention of Tom Walkinshaw, who was looking for someone to design a Jaguar sportscar for him at Kidlington, near Oxford. As a result, and following an attractive offer to leave

Arrows, in 1989 Brawn joined Tom Walkinshaw Racing (TWR) and, after establishing a design centre, produced the XJR-14, the first sportscar to have state-of-the-art F1 technology. It was invaluable experience for the challenges he was to face later in his career. Brawn-designed XJR-14 Jaguars won the 1991 World Sportscar Championship, defeating a Mercedes-Benz team which included a young Michael Schumacher in its ranks, and after Walkinshaw invested in the Benetton team in July of that year, Brawn was duly appointed technical director of the Formula One outfit's operation. He took control of all technical aspects of the team while Rory Byrne, a South African engineer about whom much more was to be heard, took charge of the design of the cars.

The following month the noticeably talented Schumacher followed them both into Formula One having been plucked from the FIA World Sportscar Championship by the Jordan team. Schumacher was 22 and supremely talented when he made his debut at Spa-Francorchamps in August 1991. So impressive was the young German's first race that Benetton boss Flavio Briatore and Walkinshaw snapped him up for the Italian Grand Prix at the beginning of September. Thus began the first real forging of the 'dream team' that was to carry Michael Schumacher to success, both at Benetton and Ferrari. Together, Brawn and Schumacher worked towards their first Formula One victory, which came almost exactly a year later at the 1992 Belgian Grand Prix. Two and a bit years after that they won their first title, when Schumacher controversially took out rival Damon Hill to secure the championship at the season-ending Australian Grand Prix.

After another championship the following year, and a constructors' championship to go with it, Schumacher left Brawn and Benetton for the dream Ferrari drive. But it soon became clear that the sum of the pair was greater than the individual talents of the two parts. By the end of the 1996 season, Williams, associated with neither Brawn nor Schumacher, had moved into the ascendancy. Schumacher finished third in the championship with 59 points for his new Italian team, 38 points behind title winner Hill. Brawn's Benetton team, meanwhile, finished third in their championship, and with 68 points were 107 points behind Williams.

It wasn't long before the pair were reunited, for at the end of 1996 Brawn followed the same path as Schumacher, taking his wife Jean and daughters Helen and Amy with him, though they, in fact, still spent most of their time in education in England. He, too, had to learn Italian. It was not easy at first, but the Italians soon recognised that he could communicate with ease when it came to racing cars. His sense of order, discipline and structure, and his organisation of the team and the workforce around the car, added to his great skills and knowledge as an engineer and his excellence in the selection of race tactics when sitting on the pit-wall, would help turn Ferrari from also-rans into champions. From Ross Brawn's office, with the windows open or closed, you can hear the sounds of speed as someone – Michael Schumacher, Rubens Barrichello, or Luca Badoer perhaps – laps the Fiorano test circuit at the end of the road. It is a sound as typical of Maranello as the smells from the ceramic factories and the restaurants. It is a spacious office, and it has a relaxed atmosphere. Brawn, big, open-natured and warm with his visitors, has a businesslike approach to being interviewed, but it is pleasant and not at all defensive. He smiles frequently. He seems to enjoy talking about himself, his life, his career and his colleagues. He talks, too, as if he understands the needs of his interviewer, weaving in detail and anecdotes that enliven what could, from another person, be much more anodyne fare.

'I was born in Manchester in a little terraced house,' he volunteers to a leading question about his background and childhood. 'I was fortunate because someone sent me photographs of the place where I used to live. It turned out to be from the archives of Manchester Council. Someone made the link somehow and sent me photographs. There was actually a photo of my mum walking down a street, full of these terraced houses in Manchester! It was a wonderful community, a very close community, very friendly. Our front door was open all the time. It was one of those communities that were relatively poor, but you didn't know that because it was such a nice community.

'My father was always interested in motor racing and worked for the Firestone tyre and rubber company, and they offered him a job looking after the racing division factory in Langley so we had to move, to the south of England, when I was eleven. That's where I finished my schooling, in Reading. I used to go to the racing with my dad and in some ways it wasn't anything special to go to a race meeting. It was interesting, and I used to enjoy it, but it was kind of part of my life. I used to tag along with my dad, and my brother Roger used to come as well. He used to mess around in the paddock with Damon Hill. I used to go to races quite often. I remember Dad used to be away a lot because he did races in Europe, and in America he did the Daytona and Sebring races, so he used to travel a lot. He'd often bring back these silly movies of stuff he'd taken while he'd been away. We'd sit and watch that, and it sort of had some relevance because we were a motor racing family in a sense, and that's where it started.

'I was always interested in engineering. I played around with go-karts myself, but soon realised I was no good as a driver so I decided to concentrate on the engineering. I did a mechanical engineering apprenticeship, and while I was at college in Reading I saw a local advert placed by Frank Williams. I went along to see him. Frank didn't know that I was my dad's son, but I made him aware of it later. Patrick [Head] interviewed me. He didn't offer me a job, so I went back to college. A few months later they rang me up and said there was a job there if I wanted it. I thought I was putting my college studies on hold for a year to go off and play with motor racing, and I thought I was going to go back, but I never did. I was studying for an HNC in mechanical engineering and I never finished it, so I'm not actually a qualified mechanic. I got an honorary degree from Ancona University though, which was nice.

'The other interesting thing about my life at that time is the reason why he [Patrick Head] took a couple of months to offer me a job: the guy who was offered the job turned it down at the last minute! So I was the second candidate. Whoever that guy was I really do owe a favour to him, because if he had taken that job I wouldn't be here today. Or at least I doubt it.' It is a thought to consider. If Brawn had not gone into motor racing then, thanks to the Williams team and an unexpected second opportunity to work for Patrick Head, not only his career but those of many other people, Michael Schumacher included, might not have unfolded as they did. Indeed, the interview in Brawn's sprawling office at Maranello might never have taken place, and this book might not have been written.

Moreover, no one would have considered asking him if he missed Manchester, for no one would really have cared. As it is, it is interesting to know what the hugely successful technical director of Ferrari feels about his background as a boy, for it was an upbringing not entirely without similarities to that experienced by Michael Schumacher. 'I miss the community,' Brawn says. 'There was a community spirit which we didn't have in Reading. My parents moved to a bigger house in Reading, and it was in many ways a nicer area, but they didn't have a community spirit there. I know my mum missed that enormously because my dad used to travel. He was away and Mum missed her friends, so, yeah, she missed Manchester. Being younger, I hadn't got into the social scene of Manchester, which was pretty lively, so I didn't miss that, but I did miss a lot of my friends. But when you are young, you adapt pretty quickly. They all used to tease me for my strange accent. My mum sadly passed away last year, but she always retained her Mancunian accent until she died. My accent became a little bit of a mixture …' Typically, he laughs.

His affability has helped him settle in Italy where the value system is built around the family, and life has a rhythm. For Brawn, working at Ferrari is as much a pleasure as it is a job. He has loved living in Italy, and the experience has changed him, developed him. 'I like the Italian way of life. I never regretted for a moment joining Ferrari. Even if we hadn't achieved the results we have had, it would be a wonderful experience because of the people, the country and the culture. At my stage of life it was the right time to try, successful or not. And I've been lucky because it was successful. I love the people, I love the culture, and even when I stop working for Ferrari I would like to keep a link with Italy.' Does he see similarities between the community at Maranello and the one he left behind in Manchester as a boy? 'Possibly, yes. It took me a little while to adjust to Italy. With the friendliness, you are a little bit defensive. If you're a southerner, you build up a few barriers. It's very common and natural for an Italian to come up and put his arm around you, and for an Englishman that's a little bit alien at first. Once you adjust to it, then it's pleasant, it's nice, it's friendly. There is a genuine friendliness, genuine warmth. It did relate to my early life in Manchester and the family spirit. Just the fact that in Italy you can take your kids to a restaurant. You can take your dog to the restaurant. It's a more relaxed lifestyle in many ways. They are more family-orientated.'

The move south from Manchester to Reading had perhaps been more of a culture shock than the move from England to Italy. 'Reading Grammar School was a little bit of a shock for me because I was a simple northern lad who got dumped into a grammar school in the south of England,' Brawn recalls. 'That was a bit of a different environment. I had a reasonable time at school, but I left early. I left after taking my O Levels. In fact, I did far better in my O Levels than my headmaster predicted, so he was a bit shocked. Then he said he wanted me to stay on, but at that stage I had decided I wanted to get involved in mechanical engineering and I took an apprenticeship at the Atomic Energy Research Establishment at Harwell. I did my engineering training there. I did four years of an apprenticeship and then two years at college afterwards. I did the engineering ONC and I started an HNC course, and then, towards the end of it, I got the call from Williams.

'Because of the way Williams grew, I kind of continued my education on the hoof. I had done a little bit of fluid dynamics at college, but not enough. At Williams, I realised I had to get all the textbooks out again and start to understand what aerodynamics were all about. It was a great time at Williams because there were so few of us that you had to do everything. I remember when I started I was sometimes drawing something that I would then go on the machine and make, and I would then go to the car and fit it! Then I would go to a race track and look after it as a mechanic, and maybe even drive the truck to the race track as well. It was a wonderful education. It all evolved from there.'

It is startling to think that this man, the brains behind Schumacher's successes, did not complete the work that would have enabled him to qualify as a mechanic. As is the case with many of the men now in his position, his thirst for knowledge was superseded by his thirst for motorsport, for hands-on, on-the-job training and experience. His academic education was a means to an end. If it were possible to reach that end before ending the course, well, why wait? The similarities with the 'hands-on' experiences of Michael Schumacher's early career in motor racing remain strong. The driver supreme learnt how to bring the best out of his karts, how to repair them and tune them, doing it all by himself or with a few friends, and then had to find his own sponsors, transport and help; the technical director supreme found his own way too. Both took a practical approach. Both ended up missing out on formal higher education.

His approach, Brawn admits, made him 'a bit unpopular' with his tutors. It all worked out for the best, but would he do it again? 'Well, at the time motor racing seemed like a big adventure and I figured I could always go back again if I wanted to. But it's not a course of action I would recommend to anyone. A lot of people write to me asking how they can get started and I try to encourage them to follow a more conventional line because the sort of opportunity I had, quite frankly, doesn't really exist now. To be given that opportunity is very, very rare in motor racing now. People really have to get good degrees or show good skills in what they do to achieve positions within motor racing. But for me, fortunately, it worked out.'

It is worth remembering that Schumacher also became an apprentice mechanic in his early career, but did not complete the full period of time normally required. Like Brawn, he found a short-cut in his career that took him into motor racing. Both men seem to have been completely unruffled by the notion that they might 'not be popular' with their tutors. Still, an academic background is usually regarded as a prerequisite for Brawn's kind of job, so what did he actually learn from his coursework? 'The HNC was largely theoretical,' he replies. 'But it was a very good apprenticeship at Harwell because I used to spend two weeks in the workshops there and one week at college, so it was a sort of split course. For four years, every third week I would spend at college, and then the HNC was a day-release course: one day a week I would go to Reading Technical College and study my HNC. There was a lot of in-house training. A mechanical engineering apprenticeship and a mechanical engineering training covers all the basics – materials, structures, calculations. You have to have a reasonable head for mathematics. In fact, my particular apprenticeship was as an instrument maker working on very high-quality, low-tolerance components, and these things were being used for experiments relating to atomic energy and so on. So they had to be pretty good.

'At that time I didn't really have a plan about what to do next. Actually, I have been very fortunate in life because most of the things that have happened to me I haven't really planned. I have had ambitions, but I didn't really set out with a career path. There have been some funny stages in my life because my parents thought it was just a passing phase, but luckily my dad had been involved so it wasn't so unusual for them. They were very broad-minded in the sense that as long I was doing something I enjoyed, then it was OK. My father was the type who would say, "Get an apprenticeship behind you, lad, and you'll be OK," so he was reasonably happy, but none of us knew how long it would last. I've been married more than 25 years and I particularly remember when I met Jean's father to ask if I could marry her. I always remember him saying, "Well, it's OK, but when are you going to get a proper job?" We often joke about that.'

To many observers, it might seem that his father-in-law was

right. There is no such thing as a proper job in motor racing. Some say too that there is nothing in motor racing that can be called work. Or is there? What, for example, did Brawn do in the early days under Patrick Head and Frank Williams? 'Well, I was taken on as a machinist. The first job I had with Frank was operating a lathe and a mill, because I had confidently gone along there and told them that I could do everything. So they wanted me to prove it. That was at the end of 1976. I worked for Frank for a year, and then Frank sold the company to Walter Wolf and went off and regrouped. So for a year I worked for a Formula Three team, and that meant doing everything again – and by that I mean I was a mechanic, I was engineering the car, I was driving the truck, and I was fitting the tyres, because that's what you did. A Formula Three team was a driver and a mechanic; it wasn't quite the works March team. They ran a satellite team out of Reading, from March Engines. Peter Hass ran the team.

'I did a year with March, and then Frank re-formed in Didcot. Frank had finally got some money to build his own car – he had been running a March Formula One car for Patrick Neve as a customer – and I had an invitation to come back as I had kept in touch with Frank and Patrick all the time, and they were keeping me abreast with what was happening. The job was doing everything. Neil Oatley and Patrick Head were drawing the car, but they couldn't handle everything so a lot of the bits were made on the hoof. Patrick would come down and say, "I need someone to do this, or do that," and you would try to use your skills to create it. There were eleven people at Williams [in 1978], but six or seven years later, when I left, we had 200 people. So there was enormous expansion.

'It became clear that aerodynamics was the key performance area of a Formula One car, and I was very interested in that. I had been mucking about with model aircraft so I had studied aerodynamics for all sorts of reasons. No one else in the company seemed to know very much about it, so we read the textbooks and got stuck in, and it developed from there. In the end, I was running the research and development department. We built a wind tunnel while I was there, which was an interesting project. It was a great formative period in my career. I bought all the textbooks I could. I'd been lucky because we started to do our testing at Imperial College and I built up a friendship there with Dr John Harvey and he was always very enthusiastic. He spent a lot of time helping me understand the principles and the basics. John was a great influence on my early understanding of aerodynamics.'

How much of that hard-earned knowledge has he been able to use at Ferrari? 'Just an understanding,' he says. 'For example, I read the report today of some work we did at Fiorano yesterday. It was an aerodynamic programme, and of course I can understand what the guy is talking about. But it's far more sophisticated now. When you get into the area of computational fluid dynamics, using a computer to simulate aerodynamics, I get a bit lost on that because it's very complex now, but in terms of the fundamentals, and in terms of the basics of aerodynamics, I think I have a good understanding. The principles are still the same. As long as I don't forget them, they are still very useful. Up until recently, I was still doing a lot of structural calculations. When I worked at Arrows, at Jaguar and during the early days at Benetton, I was far more involved in the design of the car. I had to do a lot of structural calculations. At Arrows, I designed the chassis. Nobody else did it. There was no one else there to do it. I designed the chassis, and had to do all the calculations on it. They were relatively unsophisticated compared to what we have now, but you had to do the basics to make sure they were strong enough and safe enough. These days, I don't do so much. I have an understanding, which is important because when I want to talk to the engineers I need to understand what they are doing, what they are talking about. But the use of computer simulations has taken us into a different area. We use computer modelling for everything now – structures, vehicle performance, aerodynamics – and there's a new generation of engineers coming through with that knowledge and that experience. The only thing I draw now is my salary – every few months! Well, sometimes I will sit down with a set of drawings with Rory [Byrne], or some of the engineers, and we will discuss a problem. I will sketch some ideas I have, but I don't design components any more. That really stopped for me during my Benetton period. That's the last time I probably designed a component.'

So, the notion of Ross Brawn sitting at his desk with a pencil and a blank sheet of paper, a cappuccino within easy reach, belongs in the past. Not since Arrows has he truly been a designer. Instead, with his wide range of experiences, he has become a manager and an organiser, as well as a strategist, in the broadest sense. 'I have a range of responsibilities at Ferrari,' he explains. 'As technical director I'm ultimately responsible for all the work on the chassis. Rory and his people do a great job, so it's really a matter of sitting in on the meetings and briefings and sitting in on, let's say, the concept discussions to decide the direction the car's going in. I get involved with specific issues if we have a particular problem. The early part of one year we had difficulties with the transmission, and I stayed close to that to try and solve those problems. I'm also responsible for all the manufacturing at Ferrari, including the manufacturing of the engine. We have a manufacturing director and he reports to me, so I have the responsibility for, let's say, the engineering at Ferrari. It's a very good structure. It's something that only takes

interesting for a young engineer to get involved in. We are involved with four or five Italian universities and one English university as well. We agree projects each year that those students can work on. And periodically we do take students on because they have shown particular ability in those areas. Once or twice a year we take on students and bring them through our organisation. It's how we like to do things. Ferrari is now getting to be a fairly stable organisation where we don't have any massive expansion plans so we can introduce people gradually into our system. We don't need them to be producing designs or components from day one. We've got the time to assimilate them into our system gradually and hopefully turn them into useful engineers and craftsmen. A few years ago, unfortunately, we had to build an organisation very quickly, and it's not so easy to do that, but now the past five or six years of stability has enabled us to be working in those areas.

'I'm talking now about the chassis side, but I often get students writing to me and they ask what they should be doing to get into motor racing. From the mechanical engineering point of view, it's coming down to two or three areas where racing teams will continue to make demands – demands which aren't always fulfilled – and one of the areas, for sure, is aerodynamics. We are always looking for the strongest people we can find in aerodynamics because aerodynamics is a performance area. We do get recommendations from universities. They come to us and say, "Look, this is an exceptional graduate and we think you ought to take a look at him." We always find room when we see somebody who is exceptional.

'The other area is vehicle simulation. More and more we are using computers to understand the behaviour of the car in the design of the car – before we arrive at the circuit, while we are at the circuit, and after the race – to understand what the car was doing. So vehicle dynamics is another key growth area in Formula One. We are always interested in good mechanical designers. We don't always take those guys on straight from university. We look at people who have done a good degree course and they've had a couple of years of experience in industry in an interesting environment, not necessarily motor racing. So those are the areas we are interested in, certainly for the moment, and I imagine in the future.

'Then again, Formula One has reached a stage where all areas are absolutely critical. I don't want to give more credit to one area than another, but aerodynamicists have to be fairly creative people in terms of understanding what's going on. If you can improve the car by one or two per cent aerodynamically you will go faster, there is no question about it. All other things being equal, you will find lap time in improved aerodynamic performance. In fact, it's much more complex because it's rare to find a one or two per cent improvement without changing some other aspect of the performance – and you have to make the comparisons to see what the ultimate performance is going to be. But it's like engine power: if you get another ten horsepower you will go faster. It's a very clear-cut area.'

For anyone obsessed with the idea of finding a job in Brawn's special group, then, in the team that makes and runs Michael Schumacher's car, it is clear that the highest standards are required as well as a clear understanding of the role to be pursued. 'I do feel,' Brawn continues, 'that a student should try and focus on a particular area – vehicle dynamics or aerodynamics – because just to have a mechanical engineering degree doesn't stand out. If we get a résumé from a student, just to have a mechanical engineering degree, even if it's an exceptional degree, doesn't stand out, whereas if a guy's been to Cranfield or Southampton, or one of those universities that specialises in topics specifically related to motor racing, it's always more interesting.'

In other words, the young Ross Brawn would have had next to no chance of landing a job in his own team. It is an irony that amuses him. Like Schumacher, he has not emerged easily from a privileged background and walked through life finding every door opening for him. For both men, it has been necessary to make and take opportunities, to 'duck and dive' a little, as others might say. Their paths to Team Schumacher and the Scuderia may have been different, but there are enough similar characteristics to help understand the bond that holds them, and others involved, together.

Deep-rooted within both is an early introduction to karting – not abnormal in a racing driver, but a more unusual factor in forming what Brawn has become. As previously mentioned, his father's association with karting allowed Brawn to learn the business, learn the people, learn the motor racing way. And with Damon Hill, a future world champion and the son of legendary racer Graham, playing in the paddock with his brother, he was with the right people to steer himself a course to the top. 'We used to go to a lot of the British races Firestone were involved in,' he recalls, 'and it was genuinely the old days I'm talking about, those times when you could walk around the paddock, talk to the drivers, touch the cars and all that sort of stuff. It was that sort of era. Later on, when I was doing my apprenticeship, I bought a kart. It was a Villiers-engined kart and I did two or three seasons of kart racing, but never very successfully. I concluded that my efforts were best spent trying to design the things rather than trying to drive them. I always felt I had a bit of a weight penalty! That was my excuse …'

It mattered little. From the karting arena, both Brawn and Schumacher progressed through the school of hard knocks, learning how to move forward in life, how to take chances and how to succeed. It was no wonder, as their quite different careers burgeoned, that they later found themselves competing against each other, working for different teams in the World Sportscar Championship, before eventually working together so successfully.

May 1996. Jean Todt is in his room at the Hotel de Paris, a sumptuously appointed and internationally renowned palace in the equally famous Place du Casino in Monte Carlo. It is just a short stroll from the world's most famous gambling tables. He is, as always, thinking hard, working on problems and challenges and making plans. He is not one for undue risks, so the short walk across the square to the portals of the casino is not an attractive diversion. Besides, as the sporting director of the Scuderia Ferrari, he has no shortage of appointments.

He has been a Ferrari man since July 1993. That means expectations are now high. The previous August, he and his boss, the company chairman Luca di Montezemolo, recruited the world champion driver Michael Schumacher to lead the team into the new season. After five races of the 1996 campaign, the former Benetton driver has produced the following results: third in Brazil, at Interlagos, and two second places, at the Nurburgring and, on 5 May, at Imola, where he started from pole position. Two weeks later, in front of a huge audience of spectators hanging from every vantage point around the picturesque Mediterranean harbour, and in front of a worldwide television audience of millions, Schumacher is in Monaco bidding to deliver his first win for his new team and reward the sponsors who have poured money into the dream Montezemolo has held since returning to Ferrari, as president and managing director, on 15 November 1991. And it would be a dream result if he could win the 1996 Monaco Grand Prix. In 1993, Ferrari failed to win a race. In 1994 they won once, in Germany. In 1995, again just once, in Canada. That meant one win apiece for Gerhard Berger and Jean Alesi. Now, in an exchange he hoped would reward him, Todt had Schumacher and the two seasoned veterans of Formula One were at Benetton. But, as yet, he had not tasted the victor's champagne.

Todt has talked to his new driver in depth many times. He has evaluated the team around him, many of them staff he inherited from the old days – the time before the death of Enzo Ferrari himself. He has been given his instructions, and his goals, by the chairman. Success is not an ambition, it is the destiny of the team. But, so far, it has proved elusive. There has been progress, but not enough. Todt has continued with the programme he inherited for the production of cars. That means they are designed in England by an organisation run by John Barnard, a highly respected engineer and designer who is in his second association with Ferrari. But Todt is not happy about this. He knows there is something amiss. He wants something else. After long contemplative thought, he knows he needs another man – a man who knows how to get the best out of Schumacher, a man Schumacher trusts, a man Schumacher has recommended – to run the entire technical operation. He has talked and consulted, the first approaches have been made through intermediaries, and a meeting has been arranged.

When he hears a knock on the door, he makes sure it's Ross Brawn. Then he steps aside, effectively hiding behind the door as he opens it. Todt does not want anyone to know he is meeting the Benetton team's technical director. He does not want to be seen. But from Brawn's perspective, it is odd. The door opens. There is nobody there. He pushes it open and walks in. Todt is standing in his room wearing only his underwear. The following winter, Brawn reports to Maranello as the newly appointed technical director of the world's most famous and historic Formula One racing team.

Of course, when in the summer of 2005 he is tracked down to his big, airy, comfortable office at the Ferrari headquarters – it is not as sumptuous as the room at the Hotel de Paris, but very nice all the same – Todt denies that the meeting took place in the circumstances described above. In typical fashion, he says he cannot recall it. He checks his diaries – big A4 *cahiers* in which he has kept his appointments and agendas for years. He has a collection of them close to his enormous desk in a room that is steeped in the history of Ferrari. The walls carry photographs, the cabinets bulge with trophies. He spends much time searching through his files, but still says he cannot believe the story is true. But Brawn, one of the most successful and important recruits ever to be made by a Ferrari team chief, is insistent. He has a clear memory of the meeting. When Todt is told this, he half-smiles. His eyes show some amusement, but since it is a mere trifle, best forgotten, he protests again.

Brawn's version of events is straightforward. When asked to explain how it came about that he left the 1995 champions to join Ferrari, he begins, 'It's an interesting story. I had some commitments from Benetton that they would change the way they ran the team, but that didn't happen. I became a little bit disappointed that the things they promised me over the winter of 1995/96 didn't actually happen, so when I received a phone call from Willi Weber saying, "Any time you're free, I'd like to have a chat with you about the future," I agreed, and this led to my meeting with Jean in Monaco. I went to the Hotel de Paris, went up to his room, and knocked on the door. It seemed no one was there – because Jean was behind the door. He was a bit anxious that someone would see us together. So the door opened, and Jean was in his underpants and vest, getting changed. We sat on his bed and we had this conversation, and I think he didn't put any more clothes on when we had our discussion. He doesn't actually remember that! I came back to him on this once and he said, "Are you sure that was the case?" Well, I can tell you, I wouldn't forget that! That will stay with me for ever.'

Ross Brawn joined Ferrari with an open mind and no idea of what might lie ahead. He felt it was a no-lose situation for him. Ferrari had been in the doldrums for so long that effectively it meant he was starting from scratch. 'I had no expectations,' he recalls. 'I didn't know what the problems in Ferrari were or what needed to be done. I knew some of the people in Ferrari. I was lucky that during the period I agreed to join, so too did Rory, so I knew I had a colleague and comrade joining, so at least we could cry on each other's shoulders. I really didn't know what to expect, but I took the view that it would be a great experience and nobody outside the team would crucify me if it didn't get any better. I could see the challenge that was Ferrari, and I knew that if we could achieve success it would be fantastic.'

And he was right. He soon found levels of work satisfaction he had not experienced before. 'Let's say that the personal rewards for success at Ferrari have been far more than I could ever have expected,' Brawn states. 'And the warmth and gratitude of the Italian people have been exceptional. It's something you will never experience in England. No matter how successful you are in England, you will never experience the rewards you get in Italy for the success we had at Ferrari. When we'd won the championship in 1994 with Benetton and we came back to the factory, there was a protest group outside complaining because Michael had knocked Damon Hill off – and that was our reward for winning. What we did when we won it with Ferrari was a bit different. You came back to an airport and you couldn't move. There were crowds of people. It's a different culture, so to have experienced that, even if it all stopped now, has been just fantastic. And honestly, I don't think it will stop when I'm no longer here, or Jean's no longer here, or Rory's no longer here. We've developed a culture in Ferrari that gives people the confidence to continue in our way. You can't win every year, and things will come, things will pass, but we do enjoy our racing. We enjoy working with each other and there are a lot of rewards here doing our job.'

Given his and the team's success, it would not be surprising if Brawn and his group have been approached by rivals with offers to leave Ferrari. He concedes that this has happened. 'One or two, yes, but nothing serious and nothing I've treated as serious because I'm quite happy here. Sometimes your mind strays to what you're going to do after Ferrari, but I don't honestly know, because for me Ferrari is a pinnacle and I don't know if I could do this job – as technical director – anywhere else any more because of what I've experienced here, what I've achieved, and the respect people have shown me at Ferrari. I don't think I could get that anywhere else. So it's never been a consideration.'

To most observers of the sport of Formula One motor racing, Brawn established himself through the years of success at Benetton and Ferrari as the outstanding pit-wall tactician of his time. But, he says, that is not the full story. It does not do justice to the team around him. 'People always seem to have a perception of what you do and where you fit in, and very few people know exactly what you do,' he says. 'I mean, the pit-wall is a tiny bit of what I do, yet it's the bit people always refer to. If

I'm introduced anywhere, it's as Ferrari's chief strategist, but it's a tiny bit of what I do, although I enjoy it a lot. I have a very good rapport with the drivers, especially Michael, so it's an easy part in that respect. It's not an easy job, but it is an easy rapport, so that's been a very rewarding side and a fun side of the business.

'But this perception of what you are and what you do is very rarely a true measure of what's going on. Most of my working activities at Ferrari are in organising and making sure that people can do their jobs. My objectives at Ferrari are to create the right environment, create the means by which people can get their jobs done. My task is to make sure that the engineers and technicians and all the people have clear directions, the right facilities, and the right environment to achieve their objectives. They have a clear message of what is expected. That is really my main task at Ferrari, and it's helped because I have an established relationship with Michael and a partnership with Rory. I have many "marriages", in fact! With Rory, it's probably more successful than a lot of marriages because I can never remember having a strong disagreement with him. Inevitably we have different views on things, but it's never been such that we couldn't sit down and talk it through and decide which way we are going to go. I'm very fortunate in that respect, in having that relationship with Rory and being able to rely on him to take care of a large part of the business – the designer side. And he's relied on me to take care of the racing side. It's been a great partnership for us both.'

The 'dream team' was born out of these professional 'marriages' to Schumacher, Byrne and the rest of the men he refers to as 'the group'. Brawn, however, does not see himself as the lynchpin in a grand plan. He always says there is far more to Ferrari than the men who front the team. And, in line with the Scuderia's philosophy, he always makes sure that he knows it. It is a trait laid down by Enzo Ferrari and maintained by Luca di Montezemolo, the belief that 'we win together, so we lose together too'. This shared sense of responsibility and worth helped Ferrari survive the frustrating years of 1997, 1998 and 1999, when they took their championship challenge to the final race but lost. In the bitter disappointment of those defeats, they all shared their feelings and the team was strengthened. The whole Scuderia grew together, and within it, so too did the team that was assembled around Michael Schumacher.

'It is something we tell them all the time – that they are an intrinsic and vital part of the success of Ferrari,' explains Brawn. 'A lot of the guys have been here 20 or 25 years. They have been through some very tough times and they are now getting the rewards for the hard work they have done. They are a vital part of our success, and every individual that works for Ferrari plays a very important role. You have several hundred people working behind the scenes to achieve that success, and every person's role is vital. If one individual, for instance a chap working in the inspections department, doesn't see a problem with a component and that component goes on the car and the car fails, then that is a race lost. So everybody is vital. Obviously there are some people in Ferrari who have a higher profile than others, but that is not to take anything away from the whole team. People think I spend all my time on a pit-wall, but in reality, around 90 per cent of my time is spent away from the race track. When I go to a circuit I perform the role you often see, but then I go back, have a series of meetings and discussions, and get the cars designed. It is a team working together overall. Michael makes a big effort within this. I have often said that Michael, as well as being a fantastic driver, has been a very good catalyst for Ferrari. He has often made the effort to come to the factory and meet the people. When we have won championships, Michael has spent a lot of time making sure he personally thanks them all for their efforts. He recognises very much that it is a team effort.'

Teamwork, in all of its guises and hues, has always been an integral feature of the Ferrari tradition. The drivers, subject to contract, are expected to follow whatever orders are issued on behalf of the Scuderia. Until the Austrian Grand Prix of 2002, that sometimes meant one man having to sacrifice his own efforts to win by pulling over to allow his team-mate through to claim victory. On that May afternoon at the so-called A1-Ring, a new circuit built out of the remaining majesty of the old Zeltweg, Rubens Barrichello was asked to slow down and allow Schumacher to win in the interests of the team. The manner in which this act of 'team orders' was carried out created uproar and, for public consumption at least, resulted in a ban being introduced to prevent such contrivances happening again. Even the *tifosi* were upset. Barrichello was, after all, a Ferrari driver in a red car, and he would have deserved his victory; it would still have been a majestic Ferrari one-two. The Italians who had travelled across the border for the race were disgusted that the team chose to put the interests of Michael Schumacher and the drivers' championship ahead of those of his Brazilian team-mate and the Scuderia. It was a significant afternoon, and a revealing one too.

Brawn, the man who master-planned the racing, was at the heart of events that day alongside Jean Todt, the man who made the decisions. Understandably, he was at pains many times during the interviews that followed the race to explain his views on how 'team orders' should be exercised. 'We were surprised at the crowd's reaction,' he revealed. 'If we had expected it, maybe we would have modified our approach to a certain degree ... We need to consider our fans, because we do care a great deal about them. We are human, and we have learnt from the experience.' The incident provided a clear demonstration that there was a team within the Scuderia.

'We have no pre-determined team orders apart from the fact that we don't want the drivers to end up knocking each other off,' Brawn later told Will Gray for the AtlasF1 website, 'Of course, that situation can change before the end of the season in certain circumstances [i.e. if Ferrari have won both championships]. But, at this moment [with the championships open and unresolved], and with an advantage, we don't want to waste it, and we would look very silly if two cars were in the gravel trap having been first and second, and in the last five laps they both ended up off the track. That would be very frustrating, and at this stage of the season it is something we do not want to do.'

It would indeed look silly, especially as what the team most prizes in their cars is reliability. Without it there are no finishes, no wins, no points. That is why, as soon as Brawn arrived at Maranello in 1996, he looked very closely at ways of improving the cars' quality. 'Ferrari had a very good quality control system when I arrived, but we strengthened and improved that,' he says. 'There are strategies, approaches that you can take with the car. You don't always finish the race with a car that is working at 100 per cent. Often you have little problems, and you have to have systems to take care of that. We have a lot of recovery systems built into the cars, and if something goes wrong we can keep racing, we can keep running. Sometimes they are working and people don't realise. There have been one or two times during our best seasons when the car has had a little problem and we have managed it from the pit-wall, or with some settings which have coped. The important thing is to finish.

'I think a lot of this comes from our culture and philosophy that, any little problem we have, we hit it 200 per cent. You cannot afford to have the slightest problem. All our people understand that the slightest problem has to be dealt with at maximum effort. For example, we once had a little problem with the gearbox, and SKF – a very big company, but not necessarily, let's say, built for rapid response – managed within a week to manufacture new bearings to fix this problem. That takes a tremendous effort from a company like them. To create a completely new design in one week – that is the sort of effort Ferrari and its partners make to try to ensure reliability. The stress on reliability meant also, in turn, that the two Ferrari drivers were not free to race against each other in a passionate, no-holds-barred style. They were constrained to ensure that both cars finished and the team's instructions were obeyed. These instructions, many times, have pointed to a favouring of the interests of Schumacher above all else.

This is how Lorenzo Gotti of Ferrari 1, an unofficial Ferrari fan club website, reported Ross Brawn's prickly meeting with the Italian media after the race in Austria on 13 May 2002:

At the end of the Austrian Grand Prix which produced a one-two finish for the Prancing Horse, Ferrari Technical Director Ross Brawn met the press and, naturally, the first question related to team orders handing the win to Michael Schumacher. 'For three years in a row we lost the title at the final race,' said Brawn. 'We simply did not want to run the risk of finding ourselves in the same situation again. I can understand the public's reaction up to a certain point, but the race result did not take away anything from Rubens' performance, as he ran a fantastic race. People have to understand that Ferrari's main aim is to win both championships. I can see that some people might find that hard to grasp, but that is the reasoning behind what happened. We feel this decision puts us in a better position in the fight for the title. The FIA knows that Formula One is a team sport and accepts that, as can be seen from the fact that team orders have always been part of motorsport. The situation would have been different if Rubens was ahead in the points table, but the reality is that, prior to this race, Michael had 38 points more, and that is why we have focused on him to take the title. Rubens understands this, and if he finds himself in a similar situation in a future season then he will be able to fight for the title.' Brawn does not feel the sport has been damaged by this decision. 'This is just part of Formula One,' he maintained. 'We could have called Rubens in for a pit-stop which was not strictly necessary, but we chose to act honestly, so that everyone could see this was Rubens' race and that he handed victory to Michael, simply for the points involved. Michael rates Rubens, and even for him it was difficult to see his team-mate having to accept this sort of decision. He definitely did not ask him for it. But he doesn't run the team.

The 'team orders' furore continued to flare, notably at the United States Grand Prix in Indianapolis later in 2002, when the dominant Schumacher eased off as he approached the finishing line and allowed Barrichello to draw up alongside him. It required a photo-finish to separate the two Ferraris and give the Brazilian a victory that, he said, he presumed was a gift in recognition of his own sacrifice in Austria. The synchronised conclusion to the race was a red rag to an American public raised on much more homespun racing.

For Brawn, it was just another controversial episode in a series of events relating to team orders, and other issues, that seemed, as they did with Michael Schumacher, to punctuate his career. At Benetton, he was involved in a team that was accused several times of stretching the regulations to and even beyond the limits. These incidents included the removal of a filter from a refuelling rig in 1994, a misdemeanour for which the team was widely castigated and made to appear at a hearing in Paris; the infamous 'black flag' fiasco during the 1994 British Grand Prix at Silverstone; and Schumacher's title-clinching collision with Englishman Damon Hill's Williams car in the Australian Grand Prix at Adelaide. Further allegations about irregular software, rumours about traction control, and other rumblings of discontent continued to dog the team in 1995. Nothing was ever done to prove that Brawn was directly involved or responsible for any wrongdoing, but as with any such period when envy and disappointment permeate rival teams, and often the media, it is difficult to wash the stains away after the mud, thrown with or without reason, has become unstuck. According to the conspiracy theorists, Brawn had learnt how to win motor races by means other than the straightforward creation of a more powerful engine and faster car. He worked to understand and to interpret the sporting and technical regulations to his and his team's advantage, they said. It was a half-stated piece of innuendo that followed him from Enstone to Maranello and resulted in further controversies during the seasons when Ferrari were improving and leaving their opponents clutching at straws.

One such occurred in 1998, when constant paddock rumours about the legality of the Ferrari led to checks by the FIA stewards at several races, including the Austrian and Monaco Grands Prix. In an interview, he dismissed all the allegations and explained how hard he and his team worked to keep their car fast within the rules. 'Every time we have a modification or a new package on the car it is checked at the factory to make sure that it is completely legal,' he said. 'The engineers are responsible for making a scrutineering check every day at the circuit, so they go on to the equipment the FIA supplies and check the car out in the same way that the FIA check it. It's quite a complex set of measurements. The FIA kindly make their facility available so that we can, for example, check that our car complies dimensionally to all of the limits that are in the rule book.' This thorough approach, typical of Brawn's attention to detail and made necessary by working for a team as famous as Ferrari, ensured that there were fewer problems than there might otherwise have been.

At times, though, he had to become more aggressive in defence of his and his team's reputation. In 2003, for example, during a feisty news conference at Monza on the eve of the Italian Grand Prix, Brawn carried the fight to his rivals, in verbal terms, by defending his decision during the previous month of August to question the legality of the tyres used by other teams, including Williams. Alongside him on the platform as the questions and answers flew and became increasingly barbed was his one-time employer Patrick Head. Still, as Reuters reported, Brawn did not hesitate when the atmosphere became heated amid accusations that he and Ferrari were spreading false rumours to enhance Schumacher's challenge for the drivers' title. He 'stepped into the hot seat to defend his team's sporting reputation and accuse angry Formula One rivals of paranoia', the agency reported. 'As we know, paranoia runs rife in Formula One,' Brawn declared. 'All the suggestions of Machiavellian plots are just the normal paranoia that runs in Formula One. I think it is a fantastic championship. I don't think this is going to make a huge difference.' Head, a senior figure not only at Williams but in the Formula One paddock as a whole, angrily interrupted Brawn to ask him why Ferrari had waited for 38 races before questioning a design Williams had used since 2001. 'If you had this view all this time, it seems an odd time to raise it, Ross,' said Head. He added that Williams had never had any doubts about the tyres, which had been approved by the FIA. 'Do you really think a company like Michelin would deliberately create a tyre that was outside a regulation and run it ... without checking very, very thoroughly? What we have got here is a change of interpretation,' he added, referring to a regulations clarification issued by the ruling body following a meeting with the Ferrari hierarchy at Maranello. Head said Williams had suffered disruption in the run-up to Monza because of the tyres controversy, but conceded that such furores were all part and parcel of the closing stages of any closely fought championship season in Formula One.

Brawn, having won four consecutive constructors' titles for Ferrari, had made his point – effectively. Sometimes, as he knew well, attack is the best form of defence. It was a lesson learnt the hard way. Like Schumacher, Brawn had experienced some moments in life that had taught him how to make quick decisions, and right decisions. His work on the pit-wall proved that. He had also gained confidence and strength from the way in which Team Schumacher stuck together in a crisis and fought to the final breath.

There is no better example of this than the 1999 season, and in particular its finale. This was the year in which Eddie Irvine won races; Michael Schumacher broke his right leg at Silverstone at the start of the British Grand Prix on 11 July, and then recovered to support the Ulsterman's bid to win the drivers' title for the Scuderia. The German's return to competitive action at the inaugural Malaysian Grand Prix at Sepang was stunning. He had not raced for months (the Finn Mika Salo had deputised very ably), yet he took pole position and dominated the race, twice moving over to give Irvine the lead. He 'rode shotgun' to ease Irvine to victory and secured a glorious one-two for Ferrari that breathed new life into the final embers of the championship. It left Ferrari and Irvine leading McLaren Mercedes-Benz and Mika Hakkinen by four points respectively with one race remaining, the Japanese Grand Prix at Suzuka – Irvine's favourite circuit.

Irvine was already on a plane bound for Hong Kong after the Malaysian race had finished when the drama that overshadowed that season erupted. Both Ferrari cars and their drivers were disqualified by the stewards because their 'barge boards', otherwise known as side deflectors, were claimed to be one centimetre outside the regulated size. The announcement caused uproar and pandemonium, but resulted in Brawn and his team facing a crisis immaculately. A series of phone calls followed, including one to Italy where the car's designer Rory Byrne was on hand to go into the Maranello factory and perform measurement checks on the other barge boards at the factory. It was the start of a convincing fightback by the team. Brawn, his frame drenched with sweat like everyone else's under the arc lights at an impromptu media news briefing, demonstrated that the Ferrari deflectors were not illegal at all. The team, they said, were prepared to appeal against the decision. And they did.

Todt defended his team vigorously. If their Malaysian one-two was taken away, the titles were almost certainly bound for McLaren and Hakkinen. 'This disqualification is unjust and we shall do all we can to fight it,' said Todt. The appeal was heard in Paris where Ferrari were represented by the impressive pairing of Henry Peter and Jean Pierre Martel. The Scuderia argued that the instruments used to carry out the measurements in Sepang were not good enough for the job and had proved nothing. They offered alternative measurements and argued that the deflectors were legal. The appeal judges accepted their argument and Ferrari's drivers were reinstated. Brawn, Todt and the team, pushed into a corner, had fought back and won. The championship, finally, went to Hakkinen, but Ferrari took home the constructors' title for the first time since 1983.

Ross Brawn often muses over how Schumacher could ever want to drive for another team during the many moments when he is asked about their relationship and the emergence of the 'dream team' success story at Maranello. It is hard to imagine him being wrong. The 'group', the 'team', have enjoyed so much success. At the start of 2005, after a series of five successive drivers' triumphs, Team Schumacher was so dominant it was difficult to imagine it ever ending. But, of course, it had to. They were all growing older together. Their motivation was declining, inevitably. Or was it?

In March at the Malaysian Grand Prix at Sepang, where Michael Schumacher had often demonstrated his supremacy, Brawn agreed to explain why he believed the 'dream team' could stay on top. 'If you consider in Formula One that we all have different drivers, different tyres, different engines, different cars, different designers, and we are all a few tenths of seconds off each other, it's abnormal. At least, in a way … because if you took those ten teams and we all designed a Formula One car in isolation we'd all be tens of seconds apart. Why? The reason is that we all drive each other on, so whoever is the reference point then becomes the objective, and all the other teams try to beat them. If we fall behind, we have a new reference point we have to try to match. Periodically you need to be beaten because it just rejuvenates the whole thing. In 2003, we were almost beaten and it was as good as being beaten. There were lots of periods during the year when we didn't know we'd win the championship, and I think that rejuvenated the team.

'There is a cyclical effect where you do the best job you can, but then you see someone else is doing a better job and you have to decide whether you step up and try to beat them or whether you have had enough. So far, everybody in Ferrari has said we want to step up and beat them. Maybe we were a reference point in some years, but we don't feel like that. We always look on the opposition and see what they are doing best, and we are trying to do a better job. I think that as long as everyone feels that way then this will continue, and I don't know when it will stop. Presumably it will stop one day, but I don't know how and when. As long as we wake up in the morning wanting to do a better job than the opposition, then it will continue. And when the day comes that we don't want to step up any more, I guess that will be it. There is a lot of responsibility to support your friends and colleagues in the team, and if you are a part of this team, you have to pull your weight and do your job. You can't be half in and half out. We have this responsibility, but it's a nice responsibility because you are part of the team, part of the group of people.'

So, the 'dream team' can go on and on? Can Team Schumacher, the great group within the successful Scuderia, grow in strength with age? 'Yes, I think so,' says Brawn. 'I really don't know how it's going to end, whether it's with a bang or just a change around. We've got little bits of a change around going on already, but they involve people who have worked together for seven or eight years now, so they know each other very well and it's a kind of natural transition. It's seamless. You can't see the joins, and that will probably happen in other areas as well. I don't think there will be a dramatic change at all.'

Brawn's comments are always underlined by the prospect of change that permanently lies below the surface at the Scuderia, an energy that may ensure that long after the Team Schumacher 'dream team' has laid down its racing gloves and helmets, given up the pit-wall and the track, there will be a vibrant group to continue the modern Ferrari approach. He may be limited in his team's mother tongue – 'I can order a glass of wine and find my table in a restaurant, but I don't speak as well as I would like, and I'm spoilt here because everybody in Ferrari speaks such good English' – but Brawn is an articulate speaker and a positive thinker who is married not only to his job but to the company. In Formula One, a driver's time at the top is limited by his athleticism and his commitment to attack, but an engineer's is simply limited to his desire to succeed. There is no doubt that Brawn, with Team Schumacher, has succeeded beyond his wildest dreams, but he, like Ferrari, cannot stop and enjoy their achievements; they are always wanting more, as he has demonstrated year on year at each birth of a new creation, each dawning of a new step in the Ferrari era, each time they unveil their latest Formula One machine.

In January 2004, after a hard-fought title battle the preceding year, Brawn explained, 'One of the reasons we are able to progress each year is stability. It is a stability that bonds the team during difficult periods, such as in 2003, but it also allows us to grow from within. For the past few years our objective has been to develop key members of our staff so that they will become the Rory Byrnes and Ross Brawns at Ferrari in the future. As part of this plan we have made a number of changes for 2004.' Those changes saw Luca Baldisserri become the team's chief race engineer, with responsibility for race engineering activities, including race strategy. Design office manager Aldo Costa took on more overall responsibility, with the promise of even more responsibility on the horizon in the next few years. And John Iley joined as head of aerodynamics – one of the key positions in the team yet to have a seriously well-known name assigned to it.

'Many of our key staff are expanding their fields of responsibility and we can look forward to the future with optimism,' Brawn said. 'One of the key elements to our eventual success in 2003 was our Technical Partnerships. We had a tremendous response and support from all of our partners, without exception. Perhaps the most crucial partnership is with Bridgestone. What must be understood is that during a tyre war of the intensity and level we have experienced in the last few seasons, no tyre company can be totally dominant. We will succeed or fail on the strength of our tyres. This does not mean that we expect Bridgestone to shoulder that responsibility alone. We are not going to step back and say, "It's up to you, Bridgestone." No, we have built a strong technical and human partnership, and both partners must share the responsibility of producing the most competitive tyres. We will succeed together and we will fail together. And if we fail, then we will need to work harder and work smarter. 2003 was an extremely challenging year and many difficult questions were asked of Ferrari. We faced those challenges and answered those questions with the spirit of which we are all proud. We cannot guarantee to win, but we can guarantee to always try our best. Forza Ferrari!'

One year on, those steps forward had turned Ferrari from near-fallen champions to dominant destroyers of the opposition once again. In an unprecedented season of success, Schumacher won thirteen of the eighteen races and the 2004 title was dead and buried long before the end of the season. And still there remained the underlying interest in challenging for more success, consolidating their position at the front, and looking to the future. As the wraps came off the 2005 challenger in January, Brawn reiterated, 'I mentioned last year that we had begun the process of succession at Ferrari, and this continues. Aldo Costa has the main responsibility for the design and development of this car. He is ably supported by Marco Fainello, Vehicle Dynamics, and John Iley, Aerodynamics. Tiziano Battistini has taken Aldo's previous role of design office manager. Rory has been a "fatherly" figure in this transition and he remains as committed as always, but now in a different role. This transition has been extremely smooth and seamless because Rory and Aldo and the rest of the technical team, chassis and engine, share the same philosophies, the Ferrari philosophies, the philosophies they have created together and the philosophies of our team.

'There are no radical features on this car, but logical progressions in all the areas that we feel make a good racing car. I am not afraid to again say that I think it is the best car we have produced … so far. I mentioned the requirements for the tyres for 2005, and again, our partnership with Bridgestone will be crucial. The new technologies required means that at the present time there is an extremely steep learning curve. Undoubtedly our opposition have the benefit of numbers at this stage. Our calculations show that Bridgestone and Ferrari have only been able to complete less than 20 per cent of the mileage in testing than the Michelin teams at this stage. But we believe in quality as well as quantity, and with the support of Bridgestone we believe our partnership will succeed.

'Other critical technical partnerships for 2005 include Shell, particularly for the extra demands placed on engine mileage;

Brembo, with whom we have developed an innovative braking system; Magneti Marelli; Sachs; SKF; and BBS. All of these companies have made a huge commitment to the Ferrari Formula One programme, and they share in our successes and failures. We have brought in [driver] Marc Gene, who has brought an extra depth to our team, and we are delighted he has joined us. His technical feedback and contribution has been excellent, and he will be heavily involved with the tyre test programme. In my opinion, we are facing one of the most interesting and challenging seasons for some years. The change of regulations will definitely split the field, particularly at the beginning of the season, and the one-tyre rule will bring a fascinating element to the races. As always, we cannot guarantee success, we can only guarantee that we will try our best. Forza Ferrari!'

As always, Brawn made little mention of the race drivers. He does not heap praise on Michael Schumacher. He knows that in the end his car is the most important component of all. It carries the drivers, to success or to frustration. But the 2005 campaign proved a disappointing one for Ferrari. If Brawn and his men can regroup to score further successes, it would be amazing. Nobody can say they have not given their all.

CHAPTER FOUR

HOME FRONT II

I just could not continue if I did not have a sponsor. At that time he was in a good business, and he said, 'OK, I will do it, and the only thing I want to have is your trophies.' So I said, 'That's fine for me – I can drive and you get the trophies ...'

Michael Schumacher talking about Jurgen Dilk, 1994

Buchinger as Schumacher's personal media manager, concluded that his great sense of self-confidence came in part from knowing, as his successful career unfolded, that he had been able to pay his dues. 'He grew up feeling that he owed many people,' she wrote. 'There has always been someone who helped him, who supported him in this expensive sport, and to whom he felt particularly indebted – a patron, a benefactor, a financial backer. People, for example, like Gerhard Noack, who out of enthusiasm for Michael's abilities put a go-kart and his tuning expertise at his disposal. Or Jurgen Dilk, the father of a boy his own age who first lent him his son's kart and then later, year upon year, would take the young Michael with him to the races. Without him, says Michael, he would never have made it to Formula One, because Dilk stood as security for him at a decisive time of his upbringing. Or Adolf Neubert, who allowed the teenager to practise his tuning skills. Or Willi Bergmeister, who gave him days off during his apprenticeship as a mechanic, because he could see how important racing was to him. And then Eugen Pfisterer and Helmut Daab, who enabled the young Schumacher to get his first Formula Koenig drive.' To those names can be added others such as Gustav Hoecker, a Lamborghini dealer, of all things, who helped to provide the car in Formula Koenig; and, of course, Willi Weber, who supplied the support for his first Formula Three drive and laid the pathway to Formula One. Some remained close to the team that was being built longer than others, as is natural, and some departed from the association acrimoniously, but they all deserve a place in the story, the squad, even if they were unable to finish up in the close-knit group that makes the final selection.

Noack, who was a friend of Michael's father Rolf, was a businessman who had done well in the carpet trade. His support provided the first platform, and is not forgotten. Dilk and

Bergmeister gave more sustained, if different, levels of backing to Schumacher. Dilk, having done well with slot machines, supplied financial support, but also a sense of security, as well as much-needed assistance with transport around Europe. Bergmeister, in whose garage Michael used to work after school, gave him advice, a chance to learn about cars and racing, and a chance to become an apprentice mechanic. He also allowed him the days off he needed to pursue his racing career. The combination of Dilk's and Bergmeister's efforts, and those of his family and others, meant that Michael did not have to borrow money to go racing.

'I think I was about seventeen and a half when I left school,' Schumacher recalls of his time with Bergmeister. 'I had nothing planned. I was not top-class at anything, because the only thing I really concentrated on was go-karting. I loved it. I became good at it because I did it constantly and I had the talent for it. I just did not have the same talent for judo or football, which I also did. Well, not as much talent as you need to become as good as I had to for Formula One. That is how I left school. I went to the garage and I did my normal exams in the garage. It lasted two and a half years. At the same time I was following a course that suggested I might become a professional go-kart driver or something like that. I was so keen. I was also asked to test a Formula Ford 1600 car, but I went on and passed my exams. I thought it was necessary to have some qualifications. If nothing happened, I knew that I would need something, so I was planning and preparing for that.' He readily concedes that his apprenticeship at the local Volkswagen and BMW garage under Bergmeister was time well spent. 'In car racing, that can only be an advantage for a driver. If you have a good knowledge of technology, you can describe what a car does much more easily. You may also have ideas about what can be changed or improved. But it was something I did not particularly enjoy then! Quite a lot of the work was really boring.' During this period, Schumacher spent a year or so away working in the same capacity in Darmstadt. 'It was an important time for me as I was away from home for the first time and I had to learn to handle my own life … I went home at weekends to work with my father and to earn some more money. It was a growing-up time.' When he returned to Kerpen, he completed his apprenticeship with Bergmeister in eighteen months – a year less than was usual. 'He was incredibly helpful to me,' says Michael.

Among his loyal friends of that time was Udo Irnich. They had grown up together at the Kerpen kart track. There, says Irnich, it was clear that Schumacher, even as a baby-faced boy, had a gift for speed in a kart. 'He was so small then, just a little boy. He weighed less than 50 kilos – but he drove the karts so fast! He was interested only in them. He would go to school, he had some friends, some girlfriends too, and he would go to the cinema or play football, or sometimes go to a party, but most of his time he was at the kart track or he was training. That was his life. You have to remember that, as he was growing up then, he entered the German, the European and then the world kart championships. So he was away all weekends, and when he was not away he was training and getting ready, preparing himself and his kart for the next race. He liked cycling too, but he was very professional about everything he did, even as a little child. All the way, he has been the same.'

It was Dilk who began to fashion the young racing driver by introducing training for his physical and mental fitness. It was Dilk who made sure he was prepared, ready and punctual. And it was Dilk who stepped in with the money when it was required. No wonder the experienced German motorsport writer Christoph Schulte remarked, 'He was like a second father to Michael. He looked after him from when he was a schoolboy and he always supported him in his racing. He really loves Michael. He helped him so much. When the family did not have enough money to go on with the karting – when Michael was, I think, about ten – his father told him he could not pay for everything any more. Mr Dilk had two sons and one of them was a kart driver, but he did not work too well. Mr Dilk said, "Well, I will do something," and he went and bought a new kart. About the same time, I think he realised that Michael was a true hot-shot so he decided to give Michael all the equipment he needed. This was amazing for Michael. He later, I think, helped him to get into Formula Ford and then into Formula Koenig as well. I don't think Willi Weber became involved until Formula Three.'

Given all of this, it is no surprise that Michael has felt a debt to Jurgen Dilk and has never stopped paying him back. His own recollection of those days supports Schulte's remarks. He remembers the two Dilk boys clearly. 'By 1983, when I was fourteen, we knew each other quite well and we had become friends. I was helping his sons and he saw the problems that I had [financially]. I just could not continue if I did not have a sponsor. At that time he was in his business, and we agreed how it would work ...' This was the arrangement through which Dilk provided the funds and necessary support and Michael handed over the trophies. 'We became closer, as friends, and it was just a very good time altogether for me. Then I went to Darmstadt, but when I came back we continued. I had been driving a kart for nothing for a dealer in the European championship. When I went to Formula Ford 1600, Mr Dilk and I were together again. Again, I needed a sponsor, and he agreed to do it. He just signed the contract for me, which was for very little money. It was for about £10,000 for ten races, but I could not have signed because I did not have that money. I did not even have £100 then. So he did it for me. And the rest of it, everybody knows from then on.'

As a mark of his affection and regard for Dilk, Michael has hosted him at Grands Prix all over the world over the last fifteen years. Dilk was also installed as the inaugural president of the official Michael Schumacher Fan Club, which he helped to launch. Modest, honest and direct, he was a man upon whom Michael knew he could depend in all circumstances – a true supporter. Bearded, open-faced, bespectacled and, in recent years, a little portly, he cuts an intriguing figure in a Grand Prix paddock. He is more at home in the campsites of the fan club where he and his family, and many others from Kerpen, have congregated in support of their local hero.

His son Guido was born two years earlier than Michael. At the age of fourteen, he was the boy who was 'blown away' by the twelve-year-old prodigy when he first began to show his speed in karts. 'We used to race and play together and it became a friendship,' he says. 'My father saw he was a very good driver so he invited him to go with us, and we went racing all over Germany together. We went to every kart race we could at that time, always together, and we slept in the van. It was good. We had some very good times. At thirteen or fourteen he was a very, very good driver. By that time, after a couple of years of this, I had started my job in a coalmine and I stopped racing. Michael carried on, of course, and my father carried on taking him to the races, but not me. My family was able to help him … But he did not only do that – he also went out and found sponsors for Michael too.' These early sponsors introduced by Dilk included a Mercedes-Benz dealership, and local butchers, bakers and candlestick-makers. 'Michael was always a very popular guy, very nice and easy to get on with,' adds Guido, whose grasp of English remains superior to that of his father. 'He taught me about karting later and he started to train hard too. He took himself seriously, and when we went away, or he was away with my father, he would always go to bed at ten o'clock. He had no time to play around then. Not with us or with the girls. Racing was his life. It was all his life.'

Jurgen Dilk took Michael Schumacher on many trips around Europe. They went to kart events in England, Italy, Spain, France and Belgium. It was an embryonic Team Schumacher: the racer and his manager-driver-sponsor, one concentrating on the track, the kart and the race, and the other on everything else. On one occasion, in Germany, in a German championship for juniors, Michael demonstrated the value of this developing teamwork and also the special value to him of his work as an apprentice mechanic. 'Michael was leading,' recalls Dilk. 'Then, on the second lap, he knew he had a problem. He put his hand on the engine, where he felt he had a carburettor problem. He left his hand there for eighteen laps, driving with one hand on the wheel. He won the race. Afterwards he told me what was wrong: apparently there were two small screws loose on the fixing of the carburettor. That victory helped him win the German championship, when he was about fifteen or sixteen, I think.' It also illustrated the exceptional mechanical sympathy the young Schumacher possessed, a trait that was to be of benefit later in his career too.

Michael, in those days, also used to rely on Dilk to make protests and deal with them at race meetings, as Michael was under-age. This was an arrangement agreed upon by the Schumacher family. Michael said that Dilk, at this time, was like 'my father, teacher and my pastor rolled into one'. It was a close and special relationship, but it almost came to an end after talented German Formula One driver Stefan Bellof was killed at Spa-Francorchamps in September 1985. Aware of the dangers, Dilk did not want to be around if anything similar happened to his protégé. He told Michael he did not feel he could stay with him in Formula One, if they succeeded in going that far together. But, according to Guido, Schumacher called him back and persuaded him to stay with him. 'Please come with me,' he told him. 'I want you to be with me in Formula Koenig.' Dilk changed his mind.

Now, twenty years later, Dilk flies around the world whenever he can to follow Schumacher. He is always received with open arms. 'It was not my money which I gave to him then, it was my time and my heart,' says Dilk. 'I did what I could and I helped him to find sponsors. It was always so nice to work with Michael. He had an open mind. He listened to all that was said. There was always a good feeling in working together because he is a wonderful person. Everything I have given him, through those years, from my heart, he has given me back.'

One of the qualities Dilk deserves some credit for in the Team Schumacher story is the driver's phenomenal level of fitness and preparation. Dilk knew that Michael had the restlessness of a serious athlete within him, and that with good advice and direction he could become a better racing driver if he was fitter than all of his opponents. When Schumacher was only fourteen, Dilk hired a former professional football player, Peter Stollenwerk, to help him with his training and to build up his strength and stamina. 'I remember at the beginning that it was obvious that running in the woods was not Michael's thing, and I couldn't help smiling as Michael struggled behind Stollenwerk up the hill behind the kart track [at Kerpen],' recalls Dilk. 'Later the trainer rang me up and asked if I could come over to the track. I got there just as they were starting their run, and very soon Michael was well ahead of Stollenwerk.' Such a competitive spirit needed only the harness supplied by loyal friends to bring out the best in Schumacher.

CHAPTER FIVE

THE MONEY MAN

There was a little story that Willi was asked
if I knew the Spa track, and he said that I had already
driven it, which wasn't true. Luckily, they only asked
Willi! I just kept quiet and said nothing.

Michael Schumacher on how he landed his debut
at the 1991 Belgian Grand Prix

The headline by itself was damaging enough. 'Millionaire manager to face charges of bribery' it read, as printed in the sports pages of *The Times* on 2 April 2005. In the article, written by the newspaper's experienced motor racing correspondent Kevin Eason, the full story was explained:

> The manager of Michael Schumacher was reported last night to be facing corruption charges in a German court. Willi Weber, one of the richest managers in sport with earnings from Schumacher alone thought to top £100 million, is alleged to have bribed a witness in a civil trial. The charges centre on a feud between Weber and a former collaborator with Schumacher, who claims that he is entitled to a substantial slice of the commission from the Ferrari driver's earnings. Weber became involved with Schumacher when the German emerged as a teenage star in karting. Schumacher's salary from Ferrari is estimated at £23 million, but endorsements and merchandising more than double that figure.

Weber, who sports a tidily trimmed grey beard, was hardly likely to have been caught by surprise, because the events and the unproven allegations leading to this story's publication had been known to him for some time. Even so, he may have sighed wearily when he first learnt of the details. The story had also been published, in much longer form with wider claims and implications, in a specialist Formula One motor racing business publication. He had every excuse to pause and reflect, if he did so, during his early-morning shave, or as he sipped his coffee at breakfast-time. Then again, this was not a new experience for

Wilhelm Weber, a man of much experience whose career has been punctuated by allegations of brushes with various institutions and authorities. Like many businessmen who have learnt how to make and take their opportunities in life, he had at times done things that left others raising their eyebrows, and along the way a few people had also found it financially remunerative to take up positions as critics of the hugely successful Michael Schumacher and his management.

It should be said in fairness that Weber was not the first man connected to Formula One to have faced allegations of involvement in various activities that may have been outside the law. Rumours, always refuted with a mischievous grin, had persisted for years that the sport's main impresario, Bernie Ecclestone, was the brains behind the so-called Great Train Robbery. Others, sometimes even team owners, had been in trouble for financial misconduct, fraud, and even involvement with drugs smuggling. By one of those rich ironies that surface every now and then in big-time sport, Weber had been able to land Schumacher his chance to make his Formula One debut at Spa-Francorchamps in 1991 not only by taking advantage of the opportunity created when Jordan's established driver Bertrand Gachot was imprisoned in England following an altercation with a London taxi driver, but also by suggesting that his driver knew the circuit when he did not.

As Weber contemplated the inconvenience of being required to go to court in Stuttgart to defend himself while his most famous client was attempting to defend his status as a seven-time world championship winner on the Formula One circuits of the world, there were claims and counter-claims on both sides. It was a maze of allegations. In the end, by the time most of the Formula One circus had fled for their August holidays, and after a handful of court appearances, Weber agreed to pay a sum of 50,000 euros to a public institution before the end of the month, at the invitation of the Stuttgart county court. The case was thereby brought to an early conclusion, even though it was reported that the court had elaborated on its decision to reach this provisional ending, and the dropping of the charges, by stating that the evidence had proved insufficient and difficult and that there was no prospect of that situation improving. In short, the charges against Weber were unproven; but he was still invited to pay 50,000 euros. It was an ambiguous way for such a case to end, but it no doubt brought relief to Weber. He paid the money, the case was dropped, and, finally, the story ended. The threat of a serious punishment, even a possible prison sentence, had gone, so he would have had good reason to smile whenever he shaved from then on.

His association with Michael Schumacher has been good to Weber, even if there are those who, for their own reasons, wish to challenge his position. His Stuttgart offices, with their elegant meeting rooms usually decorated with the helmets of his star racing driver clients Michael and Ralf Schumacher, or gleaming with the wide selection of merchandise that has been produced on the brothers' behalf – or perhaps even a Ferrari racing car – are comfortable. Weber glides around in expensive cars, often wears Versace suits or perfectly creased blue jeans, and exudes the aura of a man used to luxury and wealth. He has been married to Heidemarie, who is devoted to the protection of animals, for more than 40 years, and he is proud of his grandchildren. He would like to buy his wife fashionable cars and clothes, a Mercedes-Benz convertible for example, but she has insisted on her Volkswagen Golf. 'If I want to do something good for her, I'll have to buy a property for her saved animals,' he says with a smile.

He can afford a smile.

News of the ending of Weber's trial triggered a few wry grins in the Formula One paddock. Like many others, he was regarded as a bit of a rascal, in the nicest kind of way. He was sharp, tough, astute and battle-hardened in the ways of motor racing, the business around it, and the world beyond. He was also, inextricably, a part of Team Schumacher, a member indeed who knew the very core of the operation, had helped lay the foundations, and who had nurtured Michael himself from fledgling super-talent to world mega-star. In a long, entertaining and perceptive feature article for *Sports Illustrated* published on 28 April 1993, Jeff MacGregor described Weber as 'a flamboyant and divisive character even in the gaudy vaudeville of Formula One'. He went on:

Weber is Schumacher's peacock alter ego and his closest adviser, a smiling Father Confessor and best friend. A preening show boat to Schumacher's sometimes colourless technocrat, Weber is easing into his 60s as tanned as Aristotle Onassis and perfectly white-haired, and, from his bespoke loafers to his neatly creased jeans to his massive nugget cufflinks, altogether as sleek as an otter. A great deal of what gets written about Schumacher in the European press has more to do with how the reporters feel about Weber than Schumacher. 'He looks too much a pimp,' one German motoring reporter told me sourly. Weber's charming enthusiasm can be contagious, though, and he is a quite effective salesman too. In 1991, he talked Formula One team owner Eddie Jordan into trying Schumacher on a one-race basis for an absent driver. 'I told him Michael is *fantastiche* and to, what the hell, to try him.' Schumacher made such a splash that within a week he'd been pirated away to drive the rest of the season under contract to the Benetton team. A 900-horsepower Ruby Keeler! Who did the pirating, and just, what the hell, how, is still a sore point among F1 fusspots.

It is more than reasonably likely that Weber was influential in this deal that took Schumacher from Jordan to Benetton overnight on the eve of the 1991 Italian Grand Prix at Monza – a move that paved the way for the beginnings of Team Schumacher to take shape and be nourished to its initial pre-Ferrari fruition. Talks between all the interested parties took place in covert and bizarre circumstances at the famous Villa d'Este Hotel overlooking Lake Como. On the Thursday, when the teams arrived at the circuit and the race entry list was pinned on the circuit noticeboards, Schumacher was down as a Jordan driver; by the following day, however, his place with the homespun Silverstone-based Irish-owned team had gone to Roberto Moreno of Brazil, and the young German tyro, a veteran of one Grand Prix, had taken the likeable, nearly bald Latin American's seat at Benetton alongside three-time champion Nelson Piquet. By then, anyone in the sport who had not heard of Schumacher and Weber, who had come, seen and conquered in their own way within three weeks of being offered a first Formula One test, must have been sleeping on the dark side of the moon.

From an unknown, or virtual unknown, Schumacher had become famous, some might say infamous, thanks to two factors: his lightning speed in a car and his manager's lightning speed in securing the drive for Jordan and, more stunningly, the switch to Benetton. Everyone in Formula One was surprised. It is easy, in hindsight, to see that this was the work of a very sharp mind and a manager with a deft touch. It is also easy to imagine that this was a sign of what lay ahead: speed, sharp decisions, deft touches – and all done with a ruthlessness that lifted the sport to higher and unprecedented levels of competitiveness on the track and equally high levels of slick management, for want of a better description, off it.

The details of what later came to be known as the 'birth of the Piranha Club' became Formula One folklore. They remain the source of much speculation. The clandestine dealing, the long night of meetings at the Villa d'Este on 5 September 1991, is a subject that still stirs opinion and argument. Few who were there, as the drama that surrounded the 'transfer' of Schumacher and Moreno unfolded, knew the full story. Moreno was a reluctant mover and won a court action against the Anglo-Italian team, but finally agreed to move as many of the sport's most persuasive and important men hovered, talked and wheeled-and-dealed in the imperial foyer of one of northern Italy's most famous and spectacular hotels.

The story of Schumacher's switch from the blarney boys to the knitwear family stunned the paddock the following morning at Monza where Milan's beautiful people, including many models, several racing enthusiasts and soccer stars, had gathered with the regular circus of drivers, owners, engineers, mechanics, reporters, friends, cooks and motor home staff to prepare for work at the Autodromo Nazionale. The news triggered a howl of protest that fell on deaf ears. Ayrton Senna, who was heading towards his third drivers' world championship in four years, was so aggrieved he spoke out with passion at the way in which his friend Moreno, a fellow Brazilian, had been treated – like a pawn in a grandmasters' game of high-octane chess, with stakes to match.

Throughout the night before, as persuasive talking and

financial offers filled the hours downstairs in the foyer, Senna had slept above it all in his bedroom. Amid a flow of sandwiches and fine wine, men such as Flavio Briatore, Tom Walkinshaw, Eddie Jordan and Bernie Ecclestone, not to mention a Schumacher entourage that included lawyers from International Management Group (IMG), argued with other legal representatives and agents, including those working for Moreno, as Schumacher, barely ready to accept his mantle as the *wunderkind* and still growing accustomed to the place settings of his cutlery, and its purpose, at formal dinners, was moved from one team to another after just one weekend as a Grand Prix driver. It was cloak-and-dagger stuff, amplified by two applications for court injunctions (one in London and one in Milan), accompanied by many dire threats and wild reports of extraordinary behaviour, and completed by a late-night agreement, manipulated by many deft hands, that ensured the outcome was that which the sport's controlling interests had sought. The Piranha Club was born. So, too, was the long-term career of Michael Schumacher and the position of Willi Weber among the elite managers of the sport.

Eddie Jordan and his right-hand man Ian Phillips were at the heart of the action, and both were left with vivid memories. 'There was a lot of shouting and roaring,' said Jordan, who has never forgotten the pain he felt as Formula One's greatest driver slipped through his fingers. 'The meeting went on for hours.' The Jordan team had shone on the tracks in its first year, but was struggling for survival, financially, off it. When they'd arrived in Belgium in August 1991, they'd faced bailiffs, bills and threats of all kinds. The problems arose, according to Phillips, because money was owed to a Belgian driver, Philippe Adams. His claim resulted in the local courts approving an order to prevent the team from using their cars, or trucks, for fear that they would leave the country without clearing the debt. The bailiffs arrived on the Saturday afternoon, after Schumacher – who had tested for the first time immediately prior to the Belgian race and was installed in the Jordan in Gachot's absence alongside Andrea de Cesaris – had qualified seventh for his first Grand Prix. 'We found a way of clearing it up so that we could race,' said Phillips.

So they had 'found' Schumacher, thanks to some help here and there, and survived the legal and financial difficulties of racing at Spa-Francorchamps. But Jordan and Phillips were still deeply entangled in a desperate bid to keep the team going. They wanted to hang on to the dazzling talent of Schumacher – who through lack of experience had destroyed his clutch at the start of the race – and to try to find a new engine supplier for 1992. It was a juggling act, in terms of energy and resources available, every day for both of them. They had also to ensure that the true depth of their problems did not reach the ears of their suppliers, sponsors and creditors. They were especially keen to make sure that Schumacher and his manager learnt only that which was in their best interests. But within days they became so engulfed in their problems that they were sufficiently distracted from the more urgent need to sign Schumacher promptly, beyond agreeing a deal with heads of agreement in principle, and prevent him being charmed away in the night. These distractions, together with the information exchanges that are all part and parcel of the dealers' market that is the paddock in Formula One, undermined their prospects of keeping him.

Through those two weeks leading up to the Monza weekend, Phillips was busy trying to tie down Schumacher while Jordan was seeking engines as Cosworth, fed up with waiting for their bills to be paid, issued a winding-up order on Jordan Grand Prix. To make matters worse for Jordan, Weber was busy doing his level best for his protégé and client. Others with an interest in

Schumacher's future were adding their opinions too, and Weber had learnt enough about the operations of the Jordan team to know that their plans for the future were built on rocky foundations. He was fed information that suggested Jordan were in a bad way, information that was deliberately designed to persuade him to avoid signing any long-term contract with the Silverstone-based outfit. It was also pointed out that Schumacher, Weber and Phillips had shared a holiday chalet, and a bathroom, at the Belgian Grand Prix while other teams were prepared to offer him a top-class hotel room if he moved. Weber understood the scenario.

Benetton, owned by the Italian fashion chain, wanted to use Formula One for marketing their products, their image and the services of the other companies in their group. It was clear that they wanted Schumacher from the moment they saw how fast he was at Spa-Francorchamps, on the opening day of practice in the valleys of the Ardennes if not long before. Their director of engineering was Tom Walkinshaw, a man who worked in alliance with Flavio Briatore. He knew all about Schumacher. Walkinshaw, of course, had run Jaguar in the Group C World Sportscar Championship, so he had close-quarters experience of him. He had seen him racing for Mercedes-Benz and knew he was an exceptional talent. He was also in close contact with Jochen Neerpasch, an agent working on behalf of Mercedes-Benz as their competitions chief, as well as for International Management Group (IMG), and their drivers, particularly Schumacher, who remained under contract to Mercedes-Benz, where he had been developed as a junior driver. He also liaised closely with Weber.

Briatore, like Walkinshaw, saw Schumacher as a key figure in Benetton's future. 'The first time I saw Michael was in Spa,' he said. 'The first time I spoke to him was in London, a few days afterwards, in my house. He was with me and Neerpasch. We discussed Michael's position with Jordan and it was confirmed to me that there was no contract. It was only a one-race deal. I told Michael I was ready to put him in the car and that we didn't need any money from personal sponsorship, and that was how we did the deal. It was very important for him to get into the car immediately. For me, that was no problem. I felt it was important to find someone for the future of the team. We all felt very strongly that he was our driver for the future.'

Weber remained in the background, prompting and guiding as was often his style. 'I had a call from Weber on Friday afternoon [five days after the Belgian Grand Prix],' explained Phillips. 'Michael was due to come for a seat fitting on the Monday. Then, instead of Michael, Neerpasch and Julian Jakobi turned up. We wouldn't let Jakobi near the place. He was working for IMG then.' Phillips smelt a rat. He sensed something was wrong, and he was right, as events proved when they arrived in Italy. 'When Neerpasch turned up at the factory on the Monday before Monza, he presented a contract and said, "These are the conditions for Michael." He had, basically, taken the space on the whole car! So we worked all night on a version of the contract that we could sign. And then, in the morning, we were sitting around waiting for them to turn up when a fax came through from the lawyers with two lines from Michael: "Dear Eddie, I am sorry I am unable to take up your offer of a drive. Yours sincerely, Michael." At that very moment, Michael was at Benetton having a seat fitting. We knew because someone phoned somebody at Benetton.'

By the end of Tuesday, on the basis that they could prove he was having a seat fitting at Benetton, and after having agreed heads of agreement, Jordan requested his lawyers to apply for an injunction against Schumacher driving for Benetton. The case was heard in London the following day, Wednesday, 24 hours before they were due to arrive in Monza. It was not the first or last time a Formula One driver's future was to be decided by legal action. It was also an emphatic indication that Schumacher had a hard-headed manager to protect and guide his interests, a man who was not frightened of the threat of court procedures. 'We had heads of agreement, which under normal law would have been good enough,' explained Jordan. 'But what happened was that the judge said he could not restrict someone's right to work unless we had signed that other contract, which was unsignable. "On the basis that that contract is flawed, I cannot give you the injunction to stop him driving for another team until this contract is settled and signed," the judge told us. But they had no intention of signing that contract. So it was a mistake I will always remember. But, in the heat of the moment, no one was at fault.' It was a lesson for Jordan, and it was a deft move by Weber and the team around Schumacher.

'In Spa,' Phillips recalled, with a laugh, 'we stayed in a holiday camp. Five pounds a night. I shared a bathroom with Michael and Willi. It was a bit like a dormitory. And the next time I see Michael, he is in the Villa d'Este! They were all sitting there, having dinner, and we were outside! Eventually, Bernie [Ecclestone] came out. I'll never forget it. Eddie, Bernie and I, we went round the side of the staircase and there was this lovely glass cabinet there. We had told Moreno, "Don't settle, don't settle," but Bernie told us he had to settle. He said there was no money. I told him, "If nobody sits in that car by the time official qualifying comes on Saturday at one o'clock, then Benetton will be excluded from the championship. They cannot take *force majeure*. Moreno is going to sit it out. He isn't going to give in." Half an hour later, Bernie came back and said they had offered Moreno half a million dollars … So, at two thirty in the morning, Moreno took the money …'

Those events at Monza in 1991 that led to the coining of the phrase 'Piranha Club' as a soubriquet associated with the business of Formula One are an important part of the Team Schumacher story. They laid down their markers that night, and it was an early indication of what lay ahead for everyone. It also introduced Willi Weber, among others, to the Formula One paddock. If they had not made a note of his name before, they certainly did on the day when Michael Schumacher made his debut for the Benetton team. Weber had done his job with only one interest at heart – Michael Schumacher, and therefore himself. The two were entwined. That some people were left stunned, surprised and hurt by the process was, as they say, inevitable. In the new, hard world of the Piranha Club, Weber had guided events with guile in his client's interests. Omelettes cannot be made without breaking a few eggs.

Wilhelm Friedrich Weber was born on 11 March 1942 in Regensburg, Bavaria. His family name, according to the internet-based encyclopedia Wikipedia, is of German origin, derived from the noun meaning 'weaver'. After leaving school he chose to train in the hotel business, but he also got into second-hand cars as an entrepreneur, as cars were his passion. To widen his experience and polish up his qualifications, reported *Stern* magazine in a lengthy feature article, he also went to Miami to a test apprenticeship with Burger King. It was after this that he 'rolled up his sleeves' and set to work building his first business empire, renting pubs, hotels and restaurants around Stuttgart. He had seen musicians, disc jockeys, jukeboxes and gambling machines in the United States, and he cleared away the stale air of the early 1960s in southern Germany by introducing such features to his own properties.

According to *Stern*, he also rented a bomb crater in the centre of Stuttgart, filled it in with help from his friends, installed a ring of bright lights, and created a used-car sales yard from which he earned a commission from each sale. It was this enterprise that propelled him to his first million. 'At 25, he had made it,' the magazine said. 'At 26, he had lost it.' Weber lent money against bills of exchange, the biggest of which fell through. But his life slogan is 'never give up', and it reflects accurately his career and his attitude to setbacks. As always, he went out to show he could bounce back.

By the early 1980s, when he was approaching his 40th birthday, he was the owner of a string of properties including, reportedly, 30 restaurants and three hotels. He was comfortably well off, but there were rumours about the occupations of some of the tenants of those properties. In some sources, they are referred to as public houses or inns, and in others they are talked of as places where prostitution flourished, though Weber always insisted he was entirely ignorant of this activity, even if the claims were true. It is clear too that it was his intention and belief that he ran a successful and entirely lawful business. *Stern* reported that Weber was prosecuted for tax evasion in 1996, when he failed to enter in his account books the profits from the sale of a Ferrari car to Japan, and that he had been fined in 1988 for 'aiding and fostering prostitution'. He was made to pay 250,000 and 12,000 Deutschmarks respectively for these offences, the magazine said. Weber, it also said, remained upset by this latter charge against him. 'If you owned 30 properties like me at the time, how do you know what your tenants and lessees are up to without spying on them?' he asked.

He had pursued his passion for cars by racing. He was not a great success behind the wheel, but he soon learnt that he could satisfy his interest nearly as much by running his own team. In

1985, he launched his own Formula Three team, WTS, with his friend Jorg Trella. Then, after moderate success, he 'discovered' Michael Schumacher one wet day at the Salzburgring where the youngster from Kerpen was showing off his skills at the wheel in a Formula Koenig race. For Weber, his life restarted on that afternoon. He could, at last, wipe away the stigma of his past problems and set out on a new course with a clear sense of direction.

He had been looking for a replacement for Joachim Winkelhock, who had won the German Formula Three title with his team. Schumacher, the rising star, was impressing everyone as he drove to the title in the Formula Koenig series and to a runner-up position in the European Formula Ford 1600 series (behind the Finn Mika Salo, who ironically in 1999 stepped in and deputised with Ferrari after Schumacher broke his leg at the British Grand Prix). Schumacher also finished sixth in the German Formula Ford series that year. The Portuguese head of AMG Mercedes was Domingos Piedade, a man with a long association with and knowledge of Formula One and motor racing as a whole; he had worked with, among others, Michele Alboreto and Ayrton Senna. Piedade, whose two sons raced in the German kart series, knew all about Schumacher too. He told Weber, 'There is one driver who is in a class of his own. He is Michael Schumacher. He is the one you want.' Gerd Kramer of Mercedes-Benz supported this view.

Weber went to Salzburg, and he needed only one look. It was a filthy day. The conditions were diabolical, appalling. Heavy, incessant rain fell on the circuit. Schumacher was seventh on the grid. There was no doubt, in these circumstances, that Weber would be able to see what the boy from Kerpen could do, and what he was made of. By the end of the first lap, which he commanded with a bewitching mixture of precision and élan, he was leading the race. It was a portent of things to come. 'He had a clean line and he kept it, absolutely and identically,' recalled Weber. 'In every lap he had a complete mastery of his car and the conditions. The way he drove impressed me completely. It wasn't only that he was quick, it was the way he handled the car on the limit. He just pulled away as if nobody else was behind him. He was driving his own race. He impressed me so much. So I sent somebody to his team. He came to see me face to face and then we spoke and I asked him to race in Formula Three.'

According to Weber, this first meeting did not produce an automatic *fait accompli*. The young driver responded by saying yes, adding that he wanted to go to Formula Three, but he also wanted to know why Weber had chosen him to race for his team. The man who was to become his Formula Three team boss and later his manager in the most successful driver-manager relationship of all time supplied all the answers Michael needed to hear. 'He was completely out of control then,' said Weber. 'He was too happy. So we made a date for him to test the car and to make a seat. Then we met at the Nurburgring. And, again, the way he handled the car was absolutely unbelievable. We called him in to make some changes, and after an hour, only an hour on the track, he was already 1.5 seconds quicker than my regular driver! Afterwards, I asked him if he wanted to race for two years in Formula Three, but he said he couldn't do it because he had no money. I said, "Don't worry about that. You just drive the car." Under those conditions, we drew up a contract, and I said to him, "Help me get my money back." And we are still together.' The Formula Three deal was followed swiftly by a ten-year management contract, organised by a Swiss-based German television commentator and journalist named Burkhard

Nuppeney, in which Weber agreed to take care of Schumacher's career. It was a significant moment for all in the making of Team Schumacher.

Weber, having suffered some good and bad fortune in a chequered career, knew an opportunity when he saw one. So too did Michael Schumacher. They shared a love of racing and a resolution to succeed that brooked few obstructions. Neither was born rich. Both were prepared to work hard and endure what was necessary to achieve their goals. Weber's father, who was said to be a 'banking salesman', had been a survivor of the Soviet Union's POW camps. It was reported that when he returned home he had to support a family of five and a grandmother. The reports went on to claim that he became a trader of 'improvised goods', which in the normal under-standing of such things meant that he bought old United States Army stock and Wehrmacht clothing that he had his family refurbish at home to be sold on the civilian market. Willi Weber, therefore, grew up in the post-war era of austerity and depression, but also in an environment of adventurous entrepreneurial activity. He soon learnt how to fix a deal and, in the vernacular of the Formula One paddock of the 1980s and 1990s, how to 'duck and dive'. Yet he realised, too, as a young man that he needed to gain some respect and make his way in the establishment that emerged after the war.

Luckily for him, he was also in love with racing. 'I always had petrol in my blood, and I had fun with everything that bangs,' he told *Stern*. 'As a child I was the most dented soap-box driver you can imagine. I always had bloody knees and a swollen forehead.' He had first followed international motor racing when it resumed after the war by listening to Grands Prix on a transistor radio. Having worked tirelessly on his property empire, by the end of the 1970s he was rich enough to go motor racing. He bought himself a seat in Formula Three, but found that his seniority was against him by then. He discovered that 'the younger drivers did not want to be passed by us – under any circumstances'. His progress from ambitious but unsuccessful racing driver to team owner was natural. The association with Schumacher, another boy with petrol in his veins, was the same. Their partnership, which was to endure criticism, ridicule, envy, mud-slinging and strain, was the bedrock on which Team Schumacher was built. Yet, at times, it seemed that Willi Weber's career would never be allowed to run as smoothly as his protégé was allowed to drive.

One man who has triggered some of the most consistently irksome difficulties for Willi Weber throughout his long and rewarding relationship with Michael Schumacher is Burkhard Nuppeney. Nuppeney has claimed, consistently over a long period, that he is owed half of Weber's revenue from his original contract to manage Michael Schumacher. He bases this claim on the existence of a contract between the two of them, agreed on 23 October 1988, to split the work and the revenue relating to the 20 per cent of Schumacher's earnings that was agreed in the original ten-year contract. This led to a civil action against Weber being taken by the journalist in 1998. Weber defended himself by claiming that they had agreed to end the contract by mutual consent. He lost the case, but appealed. At the appeal, a key witness in the dispute, Udo Wagenhauser, testified that Nuppeney had told him that his deal with Weber was finished, so the appeal was upheld. But Nuppeney fought on, and he proved that Wagenhauser had lied. Wagenhauser was prosecuted and found guilty of perjury. Following this, it was claimed, but never proved, that Weber had bribed Wagenhauser to commit perjury, and it was this that led to Weber facing charges of bribery and corruption in Stuttgart in 2005, the result of which was a slightly ambiguous conclusion that left Nuppeney consulting his lawyers again. He wanted to establish if he had proper grounds on which to make a full claim for what he regarded as his money. It was estimated that Nuppeney might be owed up to 30 million euros.

In August 2005, during two long telephone interviews, he talked freely about the case from his point of view. He explained that he had been managing the affairs of another promising driver at the time, Frank Schmickler, who joined Weber's Formula Three team with his assistance. They had a seven-year contract, and this stated that Nuppeney would receive 20 per cent of the driver's earnings. When Weber's team identified Schumacher's talent, Weber asked Nuppeney to make the approaches and to draw up a similar contract for Schumacher to that which he had agreed with Schmickler – and then to share the work and the income for both drivers. Nuppeney said that Weber was reluctant to do this work himself in case Schumacher 'does not like my face'. Nuppeney at first protested, but relented and went ahead. In effect, said Nuppeney, this would mean Weber and he would share 20 per cent of the earnings of both drivers and in return share the workload in management, marketing and sponsor acquisition. According to Nuppeney, this contract was prepared and discussed at a meeting held at a famous golf club, Bad Ems, in September 1988. Before this, Nuppeney said, he had telephoned Jurgen Dilk, who was still acting as Schumacher's manager on behalf of the family, to discuss making arrangements for his graduation to Formula Three with WTS in 1989. Dilk, he said, knew all about the details of the contract.

Schmickler, invited to the meeting by Nuppeney because he wanted him to be fully informed of all the plans and the agreements, sat with Schumacher as Nuppeney explained everything. Nuppeney said he told Schumacher that Weber would pay to buy him out of his commitment to race for a Formula Ford team. 'Weber wants you,' Nuppeney told Schumacher at the meeting, according to his recollections. 'We signed the contract,' he said. 'It was a big chance for him.' Nuppeney added that he extended his seven-year management agreement with Schmickler, then nearly as highly rated as Schumacher, to ten years so they both ran side by side for the same period. 'It was all agreed, and Weber signed it,' he claimed. 'We were to take 10 per cent each from the two boys.' It was specified that these earnings were for 'out of car' activities. 'I did the contract, I drew up the contract, negotiated it, signed it and gave it to Weber,' said Nuppeney, adding, 'Then Weber got the money, Schumacher got the money, everybody was in the business except me. I got nothing.'

Once they began working, testing and racing together, it soon became apparent that Schumacher had the measure of Schmickler. Nuppeney, however, like Weber, represented the interests of both men and, he said, used his contacts to try to further their careers beyond Formula Three. He had an excellent relationship with Mercedes-Benz, and in 1989 he met the car manufacturer's representative Jochen Neerpasch at the Nurburgring to discuss opportunities for the drivers to step up to the Mercedes sportscar team, run by the Swiss privateer Peter Sauber. 'I tried to give him Schmickler,' he admitted. 'He was doing well then, at the start, and he said, "Let's give them both a chance."' Nuppeney said that Neerpasch asked him to keep their meeting private. 'Keep it quiet, don't tell anyone,' he said.

According to Nuppeney, a second 'secret' meeting was arranged one evening six or seven weeks later at his Koblenz home. Both drivers, Schumacher and Schmickler, were there, said Nuppeney, but when a chance to test for a works drive with Mercedes-Benz in sportscar racing's Group C was offered to them for the following year, they said they did not want to do it. He said they both wanted to go single-seater racing. Nuppeney argued with them and told them it was a 'win-win' situation with an international opportunity for them; he added that in his opinion it was just the step they needed to reach Formula One. 'I had to convince them to do it,' he said. 'I was successful, and they met Jochen Neerpasch soon afterwards at a restaurant at the Hotel Floride in Mainz. At this time, Weber knew none of this at all. I knew the place well because my sister-in-law got married there. It is a nice place, in a park, full of trees.'

Following this meeting, it was clear to Nuppeney that as the boys had then agreed to take the step into sportscars with Mercedes-Benz, it was time to tell Weber about it. When Weber was told, he made it clear he was against the move, said Nuppeney, and instead proposed moving to Formula 3000 with Michael Schumacher. They could not agree on the subject, despite Nuppeney's best efforts. 'He just said, "No way,"' said Nuppeney. 'We talked to everyone, including Dilk, and I pointed out all the advantages of going to Mercedes-Benz. Neerpasch was not impressed.' Finally, according to Nuppeney, Weber relented and agreed to attend a meeting to discuss the proposal with Neerpasch in Zurich. 'I flew there from Frankfurt,' said Nuppeney. 'Weber drove there from Stuttgart in a Ferrari Testarossa. We went to the Kronenhalle restaurant. It was very difficult. We worked so hard on him. Finally, he agreed. Then he drove me to the airport in his car and we talked. I still felt he didn't understand it.'

Schumacher's career was set for take-off. As Schmickler's waned, he prospered and shone. The following year he joined the Mercedes-Benz programme, took part in the young drivers' scheme, and moved into the Group C World Sportscar Championship. Again, he shone, and of course his performances led to his arriving, with some lucky twists along the way, in Formula One with Jordan at the 1991 Belgian Grand Prix. 'Michael was in,' said Nuppeney. 'He was so strong, so focused, and so single-minded. But Schmickler was not the same. He slipped back. He was lazy and had poor results. I talked to him. I told him what he needed to do, but ...'

As far as Nuppeney was concerned, his contract with Weber, and Schumacher, remained intact. But their relationship noticeably deteriorated. He found himself to be in a more remote position and lost contact. 'In the winter of 1990, I tried to phone Michael and I got no response,' he said. 'I thought it was very strange.' He kept trying to re-establish his position, but felt that since Schumacher was now in the hands of Mercedes-Benz there was little he could really do. Then, in the summer of 1990, he received a call from former Formula One world champion Keke Rosberg enquiring about Schumacher's availability to race with him in a Peugeot. It prompted Nuppeney to make some further calls.

One evening, as he was preparing dinner in his kitchen, Nuppeney said he received a phone call from Weber. He was cooking, so he switched on the hands-free loudspeaker system on his phone. 'When I mentioned the contract, he said, "Stop this,"' Nuppeney recalled. 'I was really shocked. Until then, I had never really found out anything about him.' Following this, he spoke again to Neerpasch. He claimed that Neerpasch told him that his 'biography' was not perfect. Neerpasch said more, according to Nuppeney, but the incident was a watershed in the story. Weber, who believed they had agreed to 'kill the contract', did not pay Nuppeney. 'He has never paid [me] anything,' he said.

In Nuppeney's opinion, Weber had taken a decision to split him from Schumacher. He said that he had one further private conversation with Michael in which the driver told him that Weber had asked him to 'act like that'. He said he knew no reason for it. 'After that it was very difficult for me to get any interviews with him,' he said. Hurt, disillusioned and angry, Nuppeney followed Schumacher's career until, after Schumacher had signed for Ferrari, he decided the time had come for him to pursue what he felt was the only course of action left to him – legal proceedings. But his personal relationship with Michael Schumacher, let alone Weber, was as good as destroyed before that. Schumacher, meanwhile, was reported to be on his way to becoming one of the best-paid sportsmen in history with a reported salary of more than 30 million euros from Ferrari and, by early 2005, career earnings of more than $229 million from retainers alone, according to BusinessF1. The story surrounding Nuppeney's and Weber's relationship continues.

Weber, resolute, supported throughout his tribulations by his star client, remained a frequent visitor to the Formula One paddock. As time progressed, however, he went from being a high-profile guest and superstar manager to a more out-of-the way role, regularly dressing in high-neck black clothing and most often to be found in the far reaches of the most private motor home in Ferrari's area of the paddock. Much the same had happened at Benetton, where during earlier difficulties it was reportedly deemed appropriate by Flavio Briatore, the then Benetton team chief, to distance himself from some of the more colourful rumours and innuendo that were reported at the time. Weber always protested his innocence, and he operated for a time as the main spokesman for Michael Schumacher. He then took a step away and rescinded that media responsibility to the Benetton media office. At Ferrari, Schumacher had an appointed, dedicated press-relations officer of his own, in team uniform.

Weber also, of course, managed the career of Michael's brother Ralf, guiding him through the jungle of the Formula One paddock with an experienced hand. His success with both Schumachers arguably established him, as Russell Hotten put it in his business book on Formula One, as 'the king of them all'. 'Weber has wet-nursed Schumacher through his career, even to the extent of sorting out his dietary requirements and moulding him for television appearances,' he wrote. 'The manager has built his reputation and wealth by devoting all his time to his clients. Weber sees his role as simple: to take the pressure off Schumacher's shoulders so that he can focus on driving. That means taking total control of the drivers' affairs. Weber is a big wheel in the Formula One paddock, and makes it his duty to know all the important people. He once explained his role to *Car* magazine: "I am the eyes and ears for Michael and Ralf. I have to know everything that's going on … and that means being trusted, listening and learning every day, everywhere."'

Unquestionably he has done his job well. A clever, resourceful and pragmatic man, Weber has negotiated fabulous deals for Michael in particular. One, according to Hotten, saw Schumacher sign a four-year extension worth $150 million in 1999, an arrangement that also included a proviso that offered Schumacher a job for life as a roving ambassador for Ferrari. This kept him out of the hands of McLaren Mercedes-Benz and their German title sponsor of the time, West cigarettes. The most extraordinary deals include the securing of Michael's original Formula One drive at Jordan, the switch to Benetton, his move to Ferrari, and the deal that allowed Schumacher to use the Maranello team's branding in all of his own merchandise. At the time, Ferrari were prepared to give Schumacher the world to move from Benetton and help bring about and sustain a massive revival in their sporting and commercial fortunes. In 1998, Schumacher was placed fourth in *Forbes* magazine's annual list of the world's richest sportsmen, with earnings for that year of at least $50 million. Much of this is thanks to the efforts of Weber. Schumacher's list of patrons, in various forms and at various times, has included a host of the world's best-known brand names, such as Omega watches and Nike sportswear. He has also had a long-term deal with the German vehicle service company Dekra and the financial institution Deutsche Vermoegensberatung. And then there is the Schumacher Collection comprising dozens of luxury items, and his property portfolio.

Weber has helped to make Schumacher very rich. In return, Schumacher has repaid his manager's loyalty and stood by him. And Weber, too, has become very rich. In effect, Weber was the architect of the foundations for Team Schumacher. He was the money man all right, and he has never forgotten how to do his job. Even as a disappointing 2005 season unfolded, Weber was still at work, still watching his and his clients' bank accounts grow by the day.

CHAPTER SIX

THE ALCHEMIST

There is a blind understanding between us.
We are more than colleagues. We are friends.
And that is rare in this business.

Michael Schumacher, describing his relationship
with Jean Todt in 1999

A refreshing moment: Fernando Alonso, on his way to becoming world champion for Renault, gives Michael a cold but sparkling reminder of life at the top.

No sense of humour? Michael pulls a face for the cameras as he lines up with Rubens Barrichello, Luca di Montezemolo and Jean Todt at the start of another season's tilt for glory.

Big man and little man: Ross Brawn, wizard of the pit-wall and master of Maranello technology, enjoys a joke with Formula One's commercial controller Bernie Ecclestone.

Family support: Michael and Corinna join Prince Albert of Monaco and brother Ralf and his wife Cora for a photograph that reflects their unity.

The most important person. No-one has done more to keep Michael Schumacher's show on the road than his lovely wife Corinna, here pictured with her husband in the snow-covered Italian Alps.

All together now: Michael takes a central role as the partying begins after another Scuderia Ferrari world championship triumph.

The trademark that has no copyright: Michael does his leaping starfish impersonation to celebrate victory in the 2004 French Grand Prix in a season when he and the Team were virtually untouchable.

Always thinking ahead: the alchemist, Jean Todt, in a typically thoughtful pose as he plans his and the Scuderia's next moves.

RIGHT: Happiness is a moment like this: nothing tastes so good as a victory.

A special bond: Michael and Corinna share a private moment inside the Ferrari garage.

Ready for the race: Nigel Stepney, the man responsible for so much of the Ferrari preparations, tunes into race mode again.

Here we go: Michael strides from pit-wall to garage with a look that says business is about to begin.

Watch him go: the red machine is human as well as mechanical as this group of mechanics prove during another Grand Prix session.

We work together: Jean Todt was Luca di Montezemolo's most significant appointment in the creation of Ferrari's spectacular era of success with Michael Schumacher.

Glittering rewards: Rory Byrne's design genius carried Michael Schumacher to glory – and brought him many awards along the way. [© LAT]

Long-term loyalty: Willi Webber has always managed Michael since he started his racing career and their trust is mutual. [© LAT]

Well, now, let me think: Michael has become an experienced media-savvy operator after years of championships and news conferences.

Jean Todt has almost everything in life, but he never has enough time. There are never enough hours in the day. He has two jobs, two offices, and enough responsibilities to make anyone else think he has been asked to run an army or a country. In a way, that is what he does. He runs Ferrari, the high-performance road car manufacturer, and he runs Ferrari, the Formula One motor racing team. He works every hour his body permits to achieve his goals, often from dawn to dusk, or so it seems. His work-rate is phenomenal, by any standards. To his colleagues, he is inspirational; to his employers, he is virtually irreplaceable. He is the man at the apex of the management group that has enjoyed years of sustained, unbroken success with the Maranello team. All of them, including Ross Brawn, the technical director, know he is 'the boss', to borrow an English expression. He is respected, admired and, perhaps, by some, feared. For Michael Schumacher, however, he is a friend, and sometimes, it has seemed, a surrogate father. Their relationship is so close that each of them has referred frequently, when talking of the other, to a family feeling in the bond that holds them together. They socialise, they spend some of their holidays together, and they share a set of objectives in their professional lives that ensure they work closely hour after hour, day after day, through each Formula One season. In the structure of Team Schumacher – a term Todt does not like because he believes his loyalty to the Scuderia is all-encompassing – he is there at the heart, alongside Willi Weber and Ross Brawn. He is the man who has moulded them all together, convinced people of his position, persuaded everyone that the direction they are taking is for the best, for them all. He is the alchemist who saw what it would take to turn Ferrari from also-rans into champions, and created the greatest team unit in Formula One history.

In March 2005, on the eve of the new season, as Ferrari basked in their supremacy but worked hard to pretend it did not exist, Todt flew to Melbourne. He had spent much of the winter in a kind of self-imposed political exile from the mainstream business of Formula One's often vexed administration. He missed meetings, found himself ostracised, and felt the envy of his rivals. He had helped to guide Ferrari forward as allies of Bernie Ecclestone's vision of Formula One in the future at a time when the rest were preparing to form a breakaway series. Ferrari, it was reported, were to be paid a sweetener of £55 million to stay on in Formula One, and on top of that another reported sum of a guaranteed £50 million annually to participate, regardless of their success. This meant they were being valued as twice as important to the show as any other team. And it helped explain why Todt, and his team, were not the most popular guests at parties and get-togethers. He had put a few noses out of joint, as the old phrase goes. Not only were Ferrari perennial winners of every prize in the sport, they were also being paid a handsome amount just to take part.

For Todt, it was all routine stuff. None of it was unexpected. He had, after all, been turning the baser elements he had inherited at Ferrari when he arrived in 1993 into gold for some time. He also understood the inheritance he had at Ferrari. He knew what it meant and what it entailed. 'Ferrari has always been special and tied to Formula One as Formula One is tied to Ferrari,' he explained. 'It is like in the movies when the stars are paid more. Ferrari is the star, and wants to be paid like a star. The others might be frustrated, but they would demand the same if they were in our position. It was easier for them in the past because we had no success, but now Ferrari is special and successful, and that is harder.'

It was an unarguable statement of fact and was delivered,

typically for Todt, with a soft and even voice that was not calculated or engaging. He played it straight. He cares little for his own popularity and he is prepared to take the criticism that comes, so long as it is reasonable, for being the man who does the unpopular jobs. Ferrari were winners, champions and rich – and that, certainly, made them unpopular with their rivals and peers who believed they deserved just as much back in return. But then, as Todt pointed out, why do the greatest opera singers, prima ballerinas, footballers and entertainers enjoy their financial supremacy? In short, it is about the box office. And Ferrari are hot – red hot, all over the world.

But it was not, and is not, always like that. There are times, as Todt has experienced, when it is tough to be a Ferrari man. If you are successful, you are reviled by your critics and opponents; if you are struggling, you are reviled by your own supporters. More than that, when you are at Ferrari and in the spotlight, every move you make is analysed. If you speak to someone, it is reported as a row; if you smile at a girl, you are about to launch into a love affair. It is very difficult, if not impossible, to have a private life, and it is very difficult to keep your public life under control so that it is reported reasonably. Todt has had to live through all of this.

In the paddock, he is often looked upon and described as a pocket Napoleon because of his stature, looks and nationality. The real truth is that his opponents, his rivals, find it hard to praise him, and, rather cold-heartedly, they begrudge him his success. In short, they are jealous. This has led to some problems and some tough decisions for Todt and for Ferrari. There is also the issue of Ferrari's style, both the image of the marque and the ethics employed by the racing team to ensure they or, in particular, their favoured driver win. This tradition, encased in those of Formula One as a team sport, was threatened and stamped on in the furore that followed the 2002 Austrian Grand Prix. For years, Ferrari had ordered their drivers to do as they were told; now, it seemed, they were being told not to interfere with the destiny of races in any way. Yet Michael Schumacher continued to win. This philosophy and code for racing lies at the core of the Scuderia and is a major reason why Team Schumacher, the 'dream team', was assembled at Maranello. Todt could build, with then team chairman Luca di Montezemolo's consent, a team of winners who would obey the old codes laid down by team forefather Enzo Ferrari and deliver the success they were designed to achieve, and which many of the *tifosi*, starved of success for more than two decades, had never experienced.

It is often convenient, also, in begrudging Todt credit for the renaissance of Ferrari to overlook his achievements. Formula One is, after all, a big business. To run a team like Ferrari is a huge challenge. To be the manager is a complex role, one that requires all sorts of skills, from those that are used to direct something like an aerospace business to those that are needed for man-handling and race tactics amid the hubbub of a Grand Prix weekend. Todt has done this and done it successfully for a decade, after walking into a team in decline.

In 1993, Ferrari was a prancing horse with a pronounced limp. Todt was headhunted for the job by Formula One's impresario-in-chief Bernie Ecclestone, a man who knew the real value of the Scuderia to his circus. A former champion co-driver in rallying, Todt had been a successful team manager for Peugeot. He won rallies, he won the Le Mans 24 Hours race, and he won the Paris–Dakar rally too – all very different disciplines requiring a refined approach to a general managerial role. He had proved his excellence as an organiser and leader in motor racing. Under the guidance of Ferrari's newly returned leader Luca di

Montezemolo, he set about building the 'dream team', bringing in Schumacher, Brawn and Byrne and then adding natural Italian and other Maranello-honed talent to the mixture, as well as the top Britons imported, as required and when available, from the Formula One corridor in central England.

Todt knew it would take time to rebuild Ferrari's fortunes and he never gave up his belief, not even after three successive campaigns for the drivers' championship had ended in frustration at the final race. His loyalty was invaluable to his men, and ultimately his patience was rewarded. When Schumacher won in Japan in 2000, it opened a floodgate of emotions. It also opened the way to Ferrari's domination, an era in which their combined talents saw them remain triumphant, sometimes ruthless and nearly always unstoppable. Todt's most fierce loyalty was to his German driver, the centrepiece of the new Scuderia, and he had no qualms in ordering Rubens Barrichello to move aside when it was required for Schumacher to win and keep his championship challenge vibrantly alive. 'I don't do anything on the pit-wall during the race except maybe to give the instructions nobody else wants to do,' said Todt, acknowledging his part in the Team Schumacher show.

The strength of his commitment to Schumacher was returned. Schumacher treated him, and continues to treat him, like family. This was a friendship of extraordinary strength for a business like Formula One, where few people had the time to do much more than make use of each other as passing acquaintances. 'When I arrived at Ferrari, at the end of 1995, I expected many things, but not that I would find a friend for life in Jean Todt,' Schumacher told the *Corriere della Sera* after winning his third title for Ferrari in 2002. 'With Jean, we discuss everything. Not just the obvious subjects of our work in Formula One. We spend a lot of time together, outside our professional lives. For example, in winter we often meet up at my house in Norway and go on skiing trips, stopping for the night in an isolated cabin, which is the sort of thing you only do with really close friends. The way Jean works is absolutely incredible. I don't know where he finds the energy. I could never imagine spending fifteen or sixteen hours in the office every day. Jean dedicates all his energies to the team and he gets involved in every single detail. He is never distracted. He is always 100 per cent motivated, ready to urge everyone on to reach our objectives. There was a time when the Scuderia was seen as a team riddled with politics. Now, however, it is known as a model of internal harmony, and that is one of the secrets of our success. This is mainly down to Jean, and it is the mark he has made on the team, with the constant support of our president Luca di Montezemolo. Jean and I have gone through good times and bad times together, and these are what have brought us closer. I have to say I am full of admiration for him.' The loyalty and the dedication worked. It brought six team titles and five drivers' crowns.

Given that he had proved he could win in any branch of motor sport, that he had an unrivalled knowledge across so many disciplines, and that he had the business acumen to handle enormous challenges, it was no wonder that in June 2004 Todt was being tipped to replace Max Mosley, the English president of motorsport's governing body, the Fédération Internationale de l'Automobile (FIA), if or when he left Ferrari. It was no wonder that when he became close friends with the former James Bond movie actress Michelle Yeoh, to whom he became engaged in September 2004, it was reported as major gossip news worldwide. Todt had been married before and was the father of one son, Nicolas, born during his earlier life in Paris, where he maintained a family home. The Malaysian actress was a film star, but he was the boss of the Ferrari racing team – a job that ensured he was always in the spotlight.

Jean Todt was born on 25 February 1946 in Pierrefort, a small Auvergne town close to the river Truyère in Cantal, France. His father, a Polish Jew, was a refugee who had escaped to France at the age of seventeen, according to grandprix.com. He became a local doctor and then did all he could to ensure his children had every possible advantage in life. Jean went to school in Paris, and after his primary and secondary education he took a place at the 'Ecole des Cadres' School of Economics and Business in Neuilly, Paris. There he became friends with fellow pupil Jean-Claude Lefebvre, who was keen on kart racing, and together they decided to go rallying. Owing to a shortage of funds, Todt decided to borrow his father's Mini Cooper S. Lefebvre drove it, Todt was his co-driver.

This adventure, initially nothing more than a bit of exuberant fun, led to a career in professional motorsport. In 1966, at the age of twenty, Todt made his professional debut with the NSU team as co-driver to Guy Chasseuil. At this time he dallied with the idea of becoming a driver himself, but his lack of success confirmed to him that he was better suited to navigating from the passenger's seat. He also decided that it was the future for him, his career. But to follow this decision meant he had first to persuade his father that he was not going to obey his wishes and become a professional man – a lawyer, an architect or a doctor – like him. Instead of learning the world from inside a university, a classroom or an office, he chose to complete his education – like Brawn, like Schumacher – in the outside world, away from academia. 'I decided that the years I spent as a co-driver in rallying would be my true education,' he says. 'It was going to teach me about automobiles and it would allow me to move internationally and to associate with foreign companies such as Ford, BMW and the Japanese.' Fortunately, for Todt and Ferrari, his father did not stand in his way.

'I was very successful [as a co-driver],' Todt adds. 'I did 30,000-kilometre rallies in South America, which were great experiences. One month, we did a thousand kilometres a day around South America – in Bolivia, in Peru, all over. I also raced in Africa and China.' By 1969 he was in international rallying in a Ford Capri, alongside Jean-François Piot. In 1970 he won the Tour de France Rally with Matra, co-driving with Jean-Pierre Beltoise and Patrick Depailler, and afterwards he was integrated into the Alpine-Renault team, scoring his first major victory as co-driver to Jean-Pierre Nicolas in the 1971 Portuguese Rally. In the years that followed he co-drove with some of the top names in the sport, including Rauno Aaltonen, Achim Warmbold and Ove Andersson, a man he would later come across as a rival in Formula One when Toyota joined the sport in 2002 with Andersson at the helm. Todt then began a successful relationship with Hannu Mikkola in Fiats and Peugeots, and eventually gravitated towards Talbot Sunbeam Lotus, where he partnered Guy Frequelin. In 1981, Talbot won the World Rally Manufacturers' title.

But in what can now be described as typically Todt-like decision-making, he had made up his mind before embarking on his rallying career that it would have to end when he reached the age of 35. As a result, in 1981 he decided to finish working as a co-driver and was promptly hired by Peugeot to create a racing department. 'It went very well,' he told Brad Spurgeon in an interview for the *International Herald Tribune*, with typical understatement. 'We won everything we raced in.' Indeed he did, and an invitation to set up a new competition department for Peugeot-Citroën arrived from Jean Boillot, the head of Automobiles Peugeot. 'I was 35 when I arrived at Peugeot to be their managing director,' Todt recalled. 'We started from scratch.' The result was Peugeot Talbot Sport, with a staff of 220. Todt axed the Talbot F1 programme and set about creating one to take Peugeot to victory in the World Rally Championship with the now legendary Peugeot 205 Turbo 16. The car won its first rally in the hands of Ari Vatanen on the 1000 Lakes in Finland in 1984 and dominated the World Rally Championship in 1985 and 1986 with sixteen wins and two WRC titles.

In the middle of 1986, however, the FIA announced that Group B rallying was being cancelled at the end of the year. Outraged, Todt took legal action against the federation. He lost, and Peugeot switched to rally-raids in 1987. Todt's battle with federation president Jean-Marie Balestre showed that he was not scared to take on officialdom. The two traded insults, Balestre mocking Todt's social ambitions and calling him the 'Napoleon of the Sands'; Todt fired back that he preferred that to being labelled 'the Emperor Bokassa of the Place de la Concorde' – a reference to the tyrant who was running the Central African Republic at the time. Todt took to the enforced switch with typical determination and his cars won several rally-raids, including the legendary Paris–Dakar. The team went on to take three more Paris–Dakar victories with the 205 and its successor the 405 – a total of three for Ari Vatanen and one for Juha Kankkunen. The cars also tasted success on the famous American hillclimb at Pike's Peak, won by Vatanen in 1988 and the following year by Robby Unser. Such was the Peugeot domination of rally-raid competition that in 1989, in order to stop his drivers racing one another across the desert, Todt settled a battle between Vatanen and Jacky Ickx with the toss of a ten-franc coin. Vatanen won, and he was allowed to cruise to victory to secure the coveted one-two finish. Sounds familiar.

Todt then made what would turn out to be a hugely significant move into the World Sportscar Championship. He took Peugeot into the category to fight for victory in the championship and the legendary Le Mans 24 Hours as his ever-developing motorsport team diversified and switched to the challenge of circuit racing. At the very same time, of course, Brawn was making his name designing Jaguar's challenger and Schumacher was racing with Sauber-Mercedes in their junior team. Thus, three key members of Team Schumacher were pitched against one another in the same category years before they all got together to begin their domination of Formula One.

The Peugeot 905s ran for the first time in the summer of 1990, and in 1991 the cars began to win, going head-to-head with Jaguar battling for the world title as Schumacher was plucked out of the category and thrust into Formula One. The following year there was no stopping Peugeot on their way to the title and a victory at Le Mans. Todt was now a national hero, a Chevalier de la Legion d'Honneur (the French equivalent of a knighthood), and the following year he oversaw a Peugeot one-two-three at Le Mans, but, almost incredibly, that was to be his last event with the team he had created. Peugeot management turned down his proposal to take them into Formula One, and when the offer came from Ferrari to take over the running of the famous Maranello team, he jumped at the chance. 'I had wanted to make use of the possibilities of a group like Peugeot to progress,' he recalled. 'Perhaps I would have liked to become the commercial director of the Groupe PSA. I left because Peugeot didn't allow me to evolve in my career and to profit by the enormous size of the group.'

At Ferrari, he found a more difficult job than he'd expected when he walked through the famous old gates for the first time in the summer of 1993. But he managed to convey calmness and keep the programme on course, and in the middle of 1994 Gerhard Berger secured the team's first win under his control. At first it seemed as if progress was being made, but Todt knew otherwise. When he saw the antics of Berger and Jean Alesi in road cars, once actually arriving at a test circuit in an out-of-control skid after the Austrian had grabbed the handbrake in the car park, he knew deep down that the Scuderia needed more than cosmetic surgery. It needed a deep-rooted change in its mindset.

When Michael Schumacher arrived in 1996, the team really started to come together with three wins. There were five victories in 1997, although Schumacher was later excluded from the world championship after driving Jacques Villeneuve off the track at Jerez in Spain during the infamous title-deciding European Grand Prix. Then, in 1998, Schumacher was beaten to the title by Mika Hakkinen, and the following year, when he seemed to be on course for victory, he crashed at Silverstone and broke his leg. Ferrari won the constructors' title, but second driver Eddie Irvine could not beat Hakkinen. Then, in 2000, all of Todt's disciplined work bore fruit. Schumacher, who had been spoken to by di Montezemolo the previous year to expedite his recovery, was back with a vengeance and scored nine victories. He took the drivers' title, and Ferrari retained the constructors' crown. The glory years had begun. 'To participate in the renewal of a team like Ferrari, which is a mythical team, and which was not doing very well, for someone who has loved racing since he was a child, and who had never done Formula One ... well, there were lots of great sides to it,' Todt reflected later.

Todt, Ferrari and Schumacher became linked, almost synonymously, with one another, and as part of the 'dream team' Todt created, as Schumacher acknowledged. 'At the time I came to Ferrari, it was clear it was not only a driver that was missing, it was technical people missing too,' he said. 'Jean Todt is 100 per cent the reason why we got those people. As a name, Ferrari sounds very nice, but when it comes to employing certain people from another country … They have families and everything, so you really need to persuade people and make them believe it's the right move to do, and make them feel confident. And that's what Jean is so fantastic at doing.' This power of persuasion, or conviction, is a Todt trait. He makes people think that what he believes is right, and inspires confidence. 'I like to convince people,' he explained, 'whether it be to convince a sponsor to come or a driver to race for us. When one likes to win, one likes to convince. To convince is to win.'

Sometimes, but rarely, in interviews, the subjects give something revealing away about themselves in unguarded answers. On Friday, 25 June 1999, Jean Todt gave an interview in which it is easy to detect his bristly determination to succeed and the faith he had built up in the 'dream team', and particularly Michael Schumacher, more than twelve months before they were able to start celebrating the initial drivers' title victory.

It was almost exactly six years since he had taken over from Ferrari, and that is a long incubation period for any team wanting to push ahead quickly, but Todt was still in control, still popular with di Montezemolo, and still plugging away to make his front-running team become a winning one. But despite still hanging on for a title – the constructors' one only months away, but the much-coveted drivers' crown still some way off – he acknowledged that the team had come a long way since the early days. 'It's best to look at the qualifying time-sheets and race results at that time,' mused Todt when asked to describe whether his improvements had so far been successful or slow. 'Very often back then we were fighting with very poor little teams and sometimes we dreamt of winning one point. So you can see how it was. Since then, things have changed a lot inside the team. Since then, we've reached a level where we are in contention for the world championship. If you're three seconds off the pace with an unreliable car, then you're just trying to see how you can finish a race or be among the first six. Then, once you're competitive, you're trying to be among the first three. And then you're trying to win a race, and then working out how to win a championship.' And that is the way Todt built Ferrari. Distinct targets and goals. Never any over-ambition, just slow and steady progress. 'I would say that since the 1997 season we've been in the situation where we can hope to win races, and be in contention for the championship,' he added. 'In a way, it was frustrating to be so close. Fifteen minutes before the end of the last race of the championship in 1997 we were there. We failed; then failed again at the last race in 1998. But whatever, Ferrari is now back at the highest level of competition.'

It was as a result of teamwork and the instillation of the slow-and-steady-progress ethos that Ferrari had clawed their way back into contention for the title. Missing out to Villeneuve and Williams in 1997 and then being beaten to the prize by Hakkinen and McLaren in 1998 left Todt bruised but not battered, disappointed but not distraught. He knew that if the team continued to believe in the plan, the masterplan developed by him and di Montezemolo way back in 1993 when they began searching for the men to fill the key positions within the team, it would come to them in the end. Even then he saw the positive side of losing, a crucial trait in a man who is determined to win. Formula One had been all about two teams in those last two years, but there was only one that had been in the race for the title on both occasions. 'The Big Two were Williams and Ferrari in 1997, and in 1998 and 1999 it's been McLaren and Ferrari,' he said pointedly. 'So in the last three years, only Ferrari has been consistent. This is a job where you need strong nerves. It's like an obstacle race: somebody keeps putting new obstacles in the way and you just have to jump them.'

Todt continued to tackle those problems head on with a personal determination that he instilled in the rest of his Ferrari workforce. The classic relaxed attitude of the Italian staff had been firmly replaced by commitment-based requirements. Again, it was all part of the teamwork that Todt realised was an essential part of turning those title defeats into title successes in as quick a time as possible, and in such a way that the first title would not be the end of the success, simply the beginning. 'If you have to deal with a problem, you have to be on hand to cope with it,' said Todt of his hands-on approach. 'You cannot cope if you're away. Even if there's nothing, you have to be there in case something happens. It would be very bad if somebody said, "I tried to see you but you weren't there." You have to be available all the time. If I'm not there, I must be in contact and able to react. I'm made like that. I wouldn't feel relaxed or comfortable if I wasn't there. It's the same if I have a list of ten people who have called me and I need to call them back. I couldn't look at that list and say, "I'll do it tomorrow." I can't do things tomorrow. I want to make sure that things that have to be done the same day are done. It's energy-consuming, nerve-consuming, head-consuming, whatever, but that's the way it is. Can I do more? We have a saying in French: only low-level people can reach their maximum. You never reach your limit. You can always improve.'

By the time the 1999 campaign began, with Schumacher, Brawn and Byrne all well settled into their seats in Maranello,

Todt knew he had pretty much all the pieces of the jigsaw. 'I feel that we have a very good team and I am proud of the people I've gathered around me,' he said. 'I like the people; I trust them at all levels. It's just a question of putting in reinforcements at mid-level. But the foundations are still there and need to stay there. It would be a big, big mistake to change the foundations. We have to try to reinforce at mid-level when we have the chance to bring in some good, new blood.

'I need to be the catalyst if people need to be pushed, but very often they push themselves. I make sure that they are working in the right conditions to achieve what they need to achieve. I give them the support they need. I ask a lot from the people in the team, but I feel that we give them a lot. Some problems are more managing problems than motor racing problems. We have a lot of motor racing issues. But I deal with it when it's a sponsor problem, a driver problem, an FIA problem, a technical problem, an engine problem. It's very varied. So it's important to have Ross deal with technical matters, Paolo Martinelli to deal with engine problems, and so on.'

And while Todt continued to push for success, he in turn was being pushed from above by di Montezemolo, the man who had hired him six years earlier to hand Ferrari the world title and put the scarlet Scuderia back on the motorsport, and ultimately motoring, map. 'Mr Montezemolo has his bosses too, who are the shareholders of Fiat, and I definitely have to answer to him so that he can answer to them. That makes pressure, but having said that, we get on very well. I think everyone understands the work and what we have to achieve. They are quite supportive.'

Schumacher was, of course, a key man in all of Todt's plans, and the thought of losing him, or indeed any piece of the jigsaw when it was so near to completion, did not bear thinking about. 'Why should I think what would happen if he wasn't at

Ferrari?' he responded aggressively when asked about Schumacher's position in the grand scheme of things. 'Michael's a great driver, a great guy, and he has a contract with us until 2002, so I would rather say, how could we achieve it with him, rather than could we achieve it without him. He's with us so I don't have to think like that.

'Thanks to the experience that we've gained, we've built up a very strong team. It's created a very strong link with some key people. We have a group of individuals who get on very well professionally and socially, which is very important. Michael is totally committed to the team as a driver. He's very important for the team, a point of reference on the driver's side. His approach is very strong, but I think the approach of the team is very strong for him as well. We are together for better or for worse; we are supporting him and he is supporting us. I think it's one of the great team–driver partnerships in motor racing. But he remains the driver.'

By the end of the following season, of course, Todt's faith in the team had been rewarded. His seven-year itch was over. His vision had delivered. His belief had been endorsed. Backed by Luca di Montezemolo, he had brought English know-how back to Maranello and made it work there, thus keeping the 'soul' of Ferrari in Italy. As Roger Horton, writing for AtlasF1, put it at the time, Todt had proved that 'Ferrari will never be "just another team". They are a team around which so many legends are entwined. If McLaren and Williams can claim to have brought the cold, hard logic of rational management to the business of winning Grand Prix motor races, then Ferrari can claim to have now matched them and yet still retained the passion for which the team is so famous … Almost certainly, the Ferrari of the pre-Todt days would have been torn apart by the media, and the politics that has surrounded the team for so long.

But the Frenchman's support for his number one driver never wavered, and this year, armed undoubtedly with the best car Ferrari have produced in a decade, Schumacher has romped to the drivers' title in some style.'

Horton also praised Todt for his work in rebuilding the team's technical base. 'He had inherited the rather clumsy arrangement [whereby] the cars were designed in the UK, as the team's designer, John Barnard, refused to relocate to Italy. This arrangement lasted until the end of the 1996 season, when Barnard departed and Schumacher's old partners at Benetton, designer Rory Byrne and technical director Ross Brawn, joined Ferrari. Crucially, it meant that now all the design and R&D work would be done in-house, in Italy. Last year's F399, only the second car actually produced by the current design team, might well have been good enough to take Schumacher to that first elusive title had his season not been interrupted by his Silverstone crash and injury. It was then that Todt's policy of building his team around Schumacher came under yet more fire. For so long the teams that were doing the winning treated their drivers as just employees – important employees no doubt, but their job was to drive the cars and essentially do as they were told. Yet Jean Todt stuck to his decision to maintain Schumacher as a virtual partner, consulting him about every important decision, team-mates included. So tight-knit did the team become that the phrase "win together, lose together", so often mouthed up and down the pit-lane, really did mean something at Ferrari. In the end they defied their critics and produced the results that counted. Perhaps only in their private thoughts did Schumacher, Brawn and Todt contemplate just how much longer they could have gone on together if they had suffered the pain of defeat one more time.'

Ross Brawn's words, uttered shortly after Schumacher's

triumph at Suzuka, summed up the feelings of all the Todt-recruited men. 'We've had four really tough years at Ferrari, and this hard-fought victory is a dream come true. When I came to Ferrari, this was my ambition, and to achieve this championship title is the end to that ambition at last.' The end of the beginning, perhaps, as Jean Todt might have pointed out.

In 2003, Todt celebrated the tenth anniversary of his arrival at Ferrari by guiding the team to even more glorious triumphs. By now the team was ripping the record books apart and leaving their rivals virtually tearing their hair out in frustration.

Early in that year, Todt gave another glimpse of himself, and his sense of pride with the progress made, in an interview with Peter Halley for indexmagazine.com. Looking back on the fantastic season of 2002 in which Ferrari won all but two of the seventeen Grands Prix and Schumacher took the chequered flag first on no fewer than eleven occasions, Todt admitted he found it difficult to focus on his achievements. 'Sometimes I have a hard time thinking about the success because I'm entirely focused on what will happen rather than what has happened,' he said. 'There's always some new problem to worry about. When I see people I've known for a long time and they express their admiration … then everything's all right, it's good. But just as quickly my mind switches to the next race, and I'm right back into the anxiety. For me, it's a way of life. I go from one obstacle to another. Sometimes I jump it, sometimes I fail, but I always look forward.'

In 2002, the 'dream team' and all of the Scuderia had proved that everyone involved at Ferrari was capable of a great team effort. Todt, though, was really the man of the moment. Not that he wanted to claim all the credit. After all, he was not a driver.

'There's more to it than the engine or aerodynamics,' he said. 'It's a combination of a great many things. We're a big organisation of about 750 people, so we have that many people trying to raise the bar. We produce the final result together. Still, I feel like we haven't gone as far as we can. There's always more to achieve, which is good: the day you realise there's no room for improvement, you retire. Ultimately, success is always about human beings. In Formula One racing, you need money to succeed, but money alone won't do it. You must have the right people, and you must get them working together. As the managing director, I'm sometimes a friend, a doctor, or even a fireman. You have to stay close to all the problems.' After a third championship double, Todt could also admit candidly that he was more concerned with people than machinery. 'We're working at an incredible level of technological sophistication,' he explained. 'But these huge advances are all because of people. The most important, the most complex, the most fascinating machine is the human being.'

And some of the most fascinating and intriguing human beings when it comes to Formula One are Todt and Schumacher. Their exceptional relationship has been built through a mutual desire for a challenge, but it has grown into something much more than that. 'Michael was already very talented when we took him on in 1996,' said Todt. 'He was a world champion two times over, and at that time everybody said he would never come to Ferrari because it wasn't a good team. But Ferrari is something special. Everybody in this business has dreamt about driving a Ferrari, and Michael enjoys a challenge. He and I have created a fantastic relationship, a real friendship. There's mutual respect and admiration. He's very professional and very talented. And he's curious. He wants to know everything that's going on. Also, he knows that his body has to be extremely fit.

He recognises that it's not enough to just be talented. Michael's also a very straightforward, honest person. He's humble and even shy, but strangers don't always perceive that.' In addition to highlighting this misunderstanding, Todt added that his number one driver was not keen on being described as a superstar. 'In a way, he doesn't like it. He's a very normal person. Michael's not spoilt, which is fantastic, because sometimes success spoils people. He is very close to his children. When he's at home, he takes his daughter to school. The best people, the most successful, they remain normal.'

If Todt sees himself as successful, therefore, he must see himself – a nervous, nail-biting observer of Grand Prix races – as normal. He is a lover of mathematics and would be happy to spend much of his spare time number-crunching if he had the chance. He was, no doubt, a keen observer of the Sudoku logic puzzle trend that developed through 2005, and will have been in some ways frustrated not to have had the time to take on the new style of mindplay due to his hours spent working to right the wrongs at the stumbling Scuderia. Even during the summer break he admitted he had no time for it, although he tried to fit in the odd game of backgammon. But in the high-pressure world of Formula One it is crucial to be able to switch off and relax, as Schumacher does so well in his winter and summer retreats, and Todt has learnt from his lead driver to develop some very normal interests that combine to make him one of those 'best' people he believes are so successful.

'I like spending time with old friends,' he said. 'But I don't so much like social events. They feel very artificial. At those kinds of events I try to protect myself a bit. Someone who doesn't know me might think I'm arrogant or presumptuous, but I don't really care. What matters to me is being with people I love and respect. Fortunately, in my professional and private life I've managed to surround myself with people I like. I'm very interested in contemporary art, but that doesn't mean I want to go to a gallery with strangers. I want to meet the artists who make it. I wouldn't think of taking a piece of art from somebody I don't know. I want the artist to explain it. I want to discuss it and understand it. So I'm more comfortable getting pieces from the few artists I know.'

Such personal strengths as these have helped to carry Todt through some difficult times in his first decade at Maranello. 'In July 1993, the company was at a low point and Formula One was a disaster,' he recalled. 'It was difficult for me to leave France and go to Italy, where Ferrari is a kind of national treasure. The fans and the media all immediately wanted to get rid of me ... People thought, "OK, they hired a French guy – it'll last a year." I took a lot of punches from the press. But I was determined. I set a goal, and eventually I achieved it. It's been ten years since I started and people have forgotten how difficult it was. They thought Ferrari would never succeed. Now they say we're too successful.'

Too successful indeed. Ferrari won its sixth consecutive constructors' world championship at the Hungarian Grand Prix in the middle of August 2004. A fifth consecutive drivers' championship was virtually secure by that stage of the campaign too. Yet for Todt, in his hour of yet another triumph, there were issues to explain and more jobs lying ahead. He had only recently taken over his new double role at Ferrari by adding the job of managing director of Ferrari to his original role as the sporting director for the racing team. A year earlier, at the same race, both Ferraris had been lapped, struggling in the only low point of their successful start to the new millennium. This time, the Ferraris had lapped all but the top five leading cars. 'It's simply that we've been working in the right direction and we have understood the problem that meant we weren't competitive enough last year, and that was mainly a tyre problem,' Todt explained. 'We have seen since the beginning of the weekend a very competitive Bridgestone-shod Ferrari, but we have seen that since Friday we had to do one quick lap as opposed to the race. I knew that we should be fairly competitive at Budapest, and that we confirmed on Friday morning. There are a lot of reasons for this, but clearly, with Bridgestone we have been doing a good job and it has helped us a lot to be competitive this weekend.

'But that doesn't mean it will be the same in Spa or in Monza. Every time it's a new challenge, which makes the thing interesting. Even if we know we have a good package, we know that the others are pushing like hell, because they hate seeing us in front, and we hate seeing them in front. That makes the competition. I'm never relaxed, but I think that's in my nature. It's easy to say that nobody will beat us, but believe me, they are all crazy about how they will beat us and when they will beat us. But we are going to fight as much as we can to beat them still. The secret is people – people and partners. Everybody has partners and everybody has human resources in their company, but maybe the way we handle it, the way we deal with the people – that's our style. Each company has its own style of management and of running a company [and] everybody is aiming to get the best out of it.'

And nothing was going to stop that from happening at Ferrari. Not even his new double role at Maranello would give Todt any reason to make excuses. Excuses, you see, are not part of his make-up. He even found time to make a joke about his workload. 'I'm organising my life slightly differently,' he said with a smile, 'but the distance between the head office of the sporting department and the head office of the commercial side is 300 metres, so it's easy to do both jobs.'

When you see Jean Todt in his big office, its walls lined with photographs of Ferrari triumphs, it is difficult not to feel he is a man of contradictions: open and courteous, but also closed and suspicious; pragmatic, but also passionate. But the one thing above all that defines his character is his determination to succeed. In the autumn of 2004, long since Schumacher had taken his fifth consecutive title at a stroll, it was not time for Ferrari to celebrate their success, it was time for them to approach the challenge of retaining their crown for a seventh consecutive season and leaving their rivals scratching their heads once again. It had become an annual ritual for McLaren, Williams, Renault, BAR and the rest, pondering just how they might defeat the power of Maranello and Team Schumacher, who had already comfortably secured 40 per cent of the new millennium's opening decade as their era.

Such dominance was something Todt could never have envisaged when he took the helm in the days when Formula One was in its formative years of the beast it has now become. A corporate explosion happened over that period, and Todt used the ready money of massive sponsors Marlboro and Vodafone wisely. Schumacher was his wisest move, of course, because that was the catalyst for him to secure the other key members of the title-winning team. But even now, Todt will admit it was never a given that Schumacher was the man who could do the job. He was just the man who could bring in the team that could do it.

'When I first came to Ferrari in 1993 we had Berger and Alesi as the drivers and they had contracts until 1995,' says Todt. 'We started to look at who could follow them, so, number one, we looked at the records of the drivers. Number two, we were trying to build a team that could win a championship. And number three, you needed a potential world champion in the car. In 1995, the potential of the team was improving and we needed some very strong drivers to improve on that even more. The strongest driver at the time was Michael. I remember speaking to his manager Willi Weber, and that was it. But when Michael joined the team in 1996 we were still missing key people, and it's true to say that in that situation, at Ferrari, we tried to get some people in, top people. Because of the politics and the fact that Ferrari was in Italy they all raised a lot of issues and stopped some things happening.' That is why Schumacher was key to the whole thing. 'Definitely having Michael on board was great, not just because we had a top driver, but because it made it easier to convince Ross and Rory to join. They already knew what it was like to work with him, but contrary to a lot of statements there was no collaboration. Perhaps Ross knew I was talking to Rory, and perhaps Rory knew I was talking to Ross. They both committed to Ferrari and I tried to make sure that we all had a very good understanding because we were working in a team. They have matured in their time here. We all have. Of course, I was also speaking with Michael, and Michael spoke with them and coaxed them into coming here because he showed them how big the potential was for Ferrari. I feel that he has been heavily involved in taking our package and making it higher.'

The one thing Schumacher can be said to struggle with on occasion is emotional issues. It proves he is human, and it was, no doubt, a part of his character he knew he should be able to control if he wanted to be the ultimate winning machine. His ability to overcome his mother's death and win just one day later at Imola in 2003 was astounding. But it is events on a global scale that affect him most, and it is teaching him to understand and come to terms with such issues that has been a key role of Schumacher's team. If he does not want to race, he does not have to race. Nobody is going to push him into it. He almost didn't after the 9/11 attacks on New York, and he was moved so much by the terrible Asian tsunami on Boxing Day 2004 that he gave millions to the appeals in a personal donation. Todt hasn't worked to subdue that part of his personality; rather, he has encouraged the family atmosphere of the team to help him. 'Michael is very emotional,' says Todt, 'and not many people will know him that way. When you see a dog hurt, it's emotional. A tsunami is much worse, and he's emotional about it. I can understand that and I can share it. For me, there is an emotion when I see people with Alzheimer's. I once took Michael with me to a medical institute for it. There are many more people who are suffering from that disease than we know, so many people, so we must be very careful not to overreact. I think it's important to guide your emotion. You need the right information, I would say, to run with your emotion because otherwise you could make wrong decisions.'

As a result of this fostering of family feeling within the team, there is a close bond between Todt and Schumacher. They continue to holiday together, and 2005 saw them spend part of the summer break in St Tropez along with Todt's fiancée Michelle Yeoh. 'Probably the relationship between Michael and myself is unique, even compared to other people within the team,' Todt admits. 'We became very close friends, and, to be honest, although we have disagreements, they are on a professional level and never impact on our friendship.' Nevertheless, Todt is charged with including in that atmosphere not only himself and Schumacher but every member of the Ferrari team to ensure that everyone feels as emotionally tied to the group as Schumacher. That way, if someone thinks about leaving, it will only be for a brief moment before they realise that their working life is a happy one. 'A family atmosphere is what we want to have,' insists Todt. 'We try to do a lot of things to put people together and we try to look after the people and answer their problems. There is no way that with so many people you can make them all happy, but still we try to support them as much as we can, so you have different levels. To make Michael happy is different from making a whole department happy. I think it's very important that each one of these is close to your own level so that you can all be happy. It's very difficult to achieve, but we try. We try to listen to what the people feel and what they say.'

'When they are happy at home, they are happy at work, and when they are happy at work, they are happy at home' goes the Ferrari theory. And while Todt will happily work his people skills to the maximum, he will only do so if his people are committed to the cause. They have to read from his own personal rulebook. 'I'm committed,' he says. 'Racing's in my blood. If I say something, then I will do it. I cannot manage or cope with not doing it. I don't know why, but I think you have your principles. I think you just try to achieve the goal, but I don't know exactly. I like to win. If you do something where you feel it's a challenge for you, then you like to succeed, and you have your own way to try to achieve it. If I did not have the same feeling now as I did at the start or all the way through, there would be no point to me being here. I love it, so that means always I need to keep the team together and protect them and do what I can. Sometimes you eat because it's time to eat, because you're very hungry, so you do things because you are used to doing them, in a certain way. I remember in 2004, before the start of qualifying and before the start of the race, you have a lot of pressure building up. But once we were champions, I was able to cool down in that situation, so that if you don't win, it's not a problem. But I think the natural feeling is that you want always the best.'

CHAPTER SEVEN

THE CAR MAKER

It was a great education. With Todt and Ross,
I learnt how a Formula One team should run.
Rory delivered the car to Ross,
and Ross ran the show …

Eddie Irvine, explaining how the chief designer
fitted in at Ferrari

He may not have designed them all, but Rory Byrne has a right to claim that he has been the creative source behind the cars that have carried Michael Schumacher to his unprecedented levels of success. He worked with Schumacher at Benetton during his two championship-winning years, and he followed him to Ferrari where he was involved in all the victories that followed. In short, when trying to evaluate Byrne's contribution to the Team Schumacher era, it is impossible not to say he has been integral and extraordinarily consistent. Yet he has also managed to retain a relatively low profile. Byrne rarely goes to the races, infrequently appears in the media, and makes few public appearances. His job is back at Maranello, in the factory, planning the next world-beater, not standing alongside the men with more glamorous roles who travelled the globe.

But Rory Byrne cannot be ignored, even if he might prefer to be. For, in truth, he is, like Ross Brawn, a rather shy and private man. Where Brawn loves to go fishing to relax and take his mind off Formula One, Byrne enjoys cricket and, in particular, deep-water diving, as well as a relaxing life near the sea in a very warm climate. He was, after all, raised in South Africa and had to be seduced to Ferrari from a new life he had planned for himself in Thailand after leaving Benetton. Indeed, it is most probable that he will return to his original plan and run a scuba-diving business in Thailand when his contract ends early in 2007. In his Benetton days, he would, as often as he was able to, take a long weekend and head off to the Far East to join up with a boat belonging to an airline pilot friend. Three days diving off Thailand or India, or in Micronesia, always enabled him to return to the office on Monday morning fully recharged. Between these trips, village cricket provided some exercise and a good reason for leaving the office. 'Scuba-diving and cricket, in the summer, keep me fit and sane,' he explained.

Born in An-Afraic Theas, near Pretoria in South Africa, on 10 January 1944, Byrne came into Formula One via Royale, who made Formula Ford chassis in the 1970s, and then the Toleman team, for which in 1980 he designed a Formula Two chassis. His design turned out to be for the championship-winning car, driven by Brian Henton, and a career that he had started almost by accident took a swift turn towards becoming serious. He stayed with Toleman when they progressed to Formula One, and in 1982 he found himself designing cars for Grands Prix. His first creation was made for a turbo-charged engine built by Brian Hart. The engine had previously been used in Formula Two. Understandably, it did not prove to be a great season for the Toleman team. The TG181 car suffered a series of problems, but Byrne learnt fast and, with the aid of some fast development, he and the rest of the team were able to turn a potential disaster into a reasonably satisfactory debut season. In 1983, therefore, Byrne felt more confident, and he designed a far more innovative vehicle, this time with two rear wings, which was to be copied by the majority of the field. Clearly he had made his mark, and in 1984 and 1985 he consolidated that impression by producing cars that provided great driveability.

In 1986, Toleman was taken over and renamed by Benetton. Byrne's 1985 chassis became the basis for a new car powered by BMW engines, and Gerhard Berger, later to earn a reputation as one of the most popular and consistent drivers in the sport, delivered his first victory at the Mexican Grand Prix in Mexico City. When BMW were succeeded by Ford, Byrne remained involved before he was lured away to the nascent Reynard project for a year. He returned to Benetton in 1992. Making the most of his knowledge, he created the B192, the first of the high-nosed Benettons that were to dominate Formula One for a period in the mid-1990s.

Byrne's creations carried Michael Schumacher to his first two drivers' titles in 1994 and 1995 and enabled the Benetton team to lift the constructors' title in 1995 as well. They were the glory years for the Enstone-based outfit, but when Schumacher departed for Ferrari at the end of 1995, the atmosphere changed. Ross Brawn followed Schumacher to Italy a year later. After initially deciding to leave Benetton and start a new life in Phuket, Byrne changed his mind when Ferrari called, and he joined them in February 1997. The 'dream team' was up and running.

Byrne has always been his own man. During his career he had been offered work by Colin Chapman, the creator of Lotus, and praised by Patrick Head, and had also been made an offer by Peugeot. He rebuffed most of them, but not Ferrari. However, it needed what he called an indecent proposal to persuade him to leave his scuba-diving school on the sunshine island where he had prepared himself for the hardships of peace, quiet, perfect beaches, warm sea and watching the sun go down every evening hand in hand with his fiancée. 'It happened that Jean Todt called me and asked if I would be interested in working for Ferrari,' he explained. 'Ten days later, I was in his office. When I said yes, we had not even spoken about money or contracts. To work for Ferrari, the most famous Formula One team in history, alongside Michael and Ross was a unique opportunity not to be missed.' Luca di Montezemolo, the chairman, recalled the day when Byrne turned up for work for the first time, looking for all the world like a holidaymaker, tanned and relaxed in a short-sleeved shirt. 'You will soon see that Maranello is much better than Phuket!' said di Montezemolo.

Byrne's first car for Ferrari was designed for the 1998 season. It proved to be a season that took Schumacher close to glory, but not quite far enough. His F399 for the 1999 season was another step forward, and it delivered success in the form of the constructors' world championship. Had it not been for Schumacher's accident at Silverstone, they might have won both titles. Eddie Irvine gave it his best shot in the second half of the year but was unable to prevent Hakkinen from lifting the drivers' crown for McLaren Mercedes-Benz. Byrne, a meticulous and ambitious man, finally achieved his goal for the team in 2000 when his F1-2000 carried Schumacher to the drivers' title and the team to the constructors' championship again. By then Rubens Barrichello had replaced Irvine, and that year he and Schumacher scored a record 170 points. It was the breakthrough that led to five successive years of unprecedented success.

But this brief outline of Byrne's career and achievements only hints at the man and his story. It also throws up several intriguing questions and coincidences. One in particular: how can it be that Byrne, like Brawn, made his way to the top to design, create and run world championship-winning Formula One cars without a formal mechanical engineering education and the usual armfuls of certificates and degrees? The answer is difficult to pinpoint, but it has as much to do with people management and judgement as it does with qualifications. Their success shows that it is the people that count, not their curriculum vitae.

Byrne is the son of two academics, teachers, both hard-working and meticulous people. His father was still working an eight-hour day in 1996, when he was 80 years old. This attitude to life was passed on to his son, who in a 30-year career in the motor racing business has proved that it is possible to be self-taught and to reach the top providing you have a natural understanding for mechanical engineering and a feel for the best design work required for racing cars. It also helps to have a hobby related to speed or design, and in Byrne's case this was provided by his special interest in designing and building model gliders. It fired up a competitive spirit too, and pushed him towards aerodynamics and lightweight structures. 'When I was at university and early on,' he explained, 'I was into model aeroplanes, especially gliders, made out of balsa wood and tissue paper, but I did design my own glider, so I got into the routine fairly early on of buying a kit, a given design, building it and then understanding where it could be improved on aerodynamically.' He won three world championships for hand-launched gliders.

His early education career is interesting in itself. 'I went to about five or six different primary schools,' he revealed, 'because my father, who was of Irish stock, was an auditor for one of the big mining houses in South Africa, so I moved around all over the country. But all of my secondary schooling was at Queens High School in Johannesburg, where I graduated in 1960 with distinctions in mathematics and science, I think, with chemistry and physics. Then I went to Witwatersrand University and I actually took industrial chemistry, in which I have a BSc degree – not engineering. I've had to pick up the engineering as I went along! But along with industrial chemistry, we did applied mathematics. The methodology is similar. I think that has helped me.'

Most modern Formula One teams would not take a second glance at Byrne's profile if he, like Brawn, was to submit it today and ask for a job. Byrne knows this, and has the humour to enjoy the joke. 'If I submitted my CV, as someone of 25 years of age, to any of the racing teams nowadays, I wouldn't even get an interview,' he said. But of course his unusual early education and interests did help him start out with a job. 'When I graduated in 1964, I spent about four years as chief chemist at a chemical manufacturing plant called Colchem in Germiston, about fifteen kilometres east of Johannesburg. Then I decided that this wasn't for me so I started up a speed equipment business with a couple of friends of mine. We used to import Weber carburettors and sell racing camshafts, branch manifolds and modified cylinder heads for all the road-going boys to make their cars go faster. It was quite a lucrative business.' This early spell in his career demonstrated not only a good technical mind at work, but also a smart business brain.

It also led him naturally into motor racing, an interest first fired when he fell in with a group of motor racing friends while he was at university. They mostly followed local saloon car racing. Byrne modified his own Ford Anglia 105E and raced it, and then did the same with a Ford Escort. His enthusiasm, in effect, took him away from his job at the polymer manufacturing plant near Johannesburg. But he soon found he was not born to be a world champion driver. 'I can put one reasonably decent lap together,' he said with a smile, 'but I can't keep it up lap after lap, and I soon discovered that.' This discovery accelerated his interest in the technical side of racing. He asked a friend to be the driver while he worked on the car and its preparation. They finished their first race second, took the lap record on the way, and established that Byrne knew more about the work outside the car than in the cockpit.

'I had the speed equipment business for four years, and during that time I designed a Formula Ford car [the Fulmen] which I built, with a couple of friends, for Roy Klomfass to campaign in South Africa. At the end of 1972, Roy finished second in the South African Formula Ford Championship and we decided to go to England with him to help him further his career. So I sold my business and went to England and helped Roy through 1973. But we ran short of funds, so we had to stop racing. It was much tougher in England than it was in South Africa. For a start it was more competitive, and secondly, it rained a lot too. I was fairly fortunate really, because we'd bought a Royale RP16 – it took us six months to learn to understand it! – and Bob King, the Royale technical director, had some sort of major health problem which meant he had to relinquish the company, so he sold it to his accountant, Alan Cornock. Alan wasn't technical and he asked Bob who he thought should design the cars, and Bob said, "There's this South African guy who's come over and from what I've seen of him he's got half a clue, so why don't you give him a chance?" And that was my chance.'

Like so many young, enthusiastic, car-mad racing people of the period, Byrne was short of money but rich on energy and ideas. He was also determined and motivated. 'I started with Royale in 1974,' he continued, 'designing all their single-seater cars, initially Super-Vs and Formula Ford 1600s, and later Formula Ford 2000s. I spent four years there, which were really exciting and proved quite rewarding. Geoff Lees won all the major championships in 1975. Rad Dougall won the Formula Ford 2000 Championship the first year that was run, I think in 1977, so it was a very successful time. During that time I also met Alex Hawkridge and Ted Toleman, of the Toleman Group, who actually bought Formula Ford 1600s to race themselves. They felt that they would like to set up their own racing team, so they started Toleman Group Motorsport on a more serious basis in 1978, and they persuaded me to join them. We campaigned the European Formula Two season, initially with Rad Dougall, in a March 782 – an excellent customer car. In 1979, we campaigned Ralt RT2s quite successfully for Brian Henton and Rad Dougall, and Brian narrowly missed winning the championship. And the following year we campaigned in Formula Two with a car, the TG280, that I and John Gentry designed, and we finished first and second.

'That success, first and second, led us to believe we were ready to move on into Formula One. In fact, we had been lucky. I had exploited a loophole in the regulations in which the height of the edges of the bodywork was defined relative to the driver's backside. So I lowered him through the seat and well into the bottom of the monocoque, reducing the ground clearance at the sides of the car by around fifteen to twenty millimetres in the process. By the time everyone else had caught on the Pirelli tyres were developed to a stage where they were superior, and it really was all too easy. It lulled us into a false sense of security. When we arrived in Formula One, we were in for a massive shock. But still, 1980 was a really successful year.'

As with so many teams, Byrne found the step up to the top echelon of motor racing extremely demanding. 'We took a ridiculously big step with a new engine [Hart 415T], a new chassis [TG181] and new tyres [Pirelli] – the whole shooting match,' he told Peter Wright, the former Lotus designer, in a technical insight article for grandprix.com. 'It was a brave step, and a tribute to Alex Hawkridge's and Ted Toleman's commitment to stay with it. It took us several months even to begin to get to grips with it.' As Wright put it when he reflected on this 'educational' part of Byrne's career, he had certainly done it the hard way, going from industrial chemist to Formula One designer without working for any other designer in any class of racing. 'Credit is due to those who gave Rory the opportunities along the way to reveal the inbuilt talents that the years at Benetton amply demonstrated.' There, under the guidance of Ross Brawn as technical director, Byrne was given all the proper support and organisation required to succeed. 'Ross is a proper technical director,' Byrne said, 'setting procedures, establishing systems, race engineering and overall engineering programmes. He takes the final decision on how big a technical risk we are going to take, and we seldom seem to disagree – he seems to accept most of what I propose we should do. I don't feel as much ownership of the cars now, but I don't really miss it as it has happened so gradually that I have adapted.'

At Benetton, Byrne also had a special professional relationship with Pat Symonds, who was Schumacher's race engineer and who was recommended by the departing Ross Brawn as his successor in the technical director role. Symonds also had a chance to move to Ferrari but chose to stay and take up the challenge at Benetton. Byrne had also worked with Symonds at Royale, where the Englishman succeeded Byrne as chief designer. Their association was a long one, and in some respects it seemed that Symonds was always destined to become a long-term part of Team Schumacher, rather than a man who played only a significant role, during 1994 and 1995 in particular, but in the end preferred to remain apart and independent.

Symonds, of course, faced a special difficulty in 1996 and 1997, in the immediate post-Schumacher years, in persuading Jean Alesi and Gerhard Berger to drive to the limit a car that had essentially been the vehicle that carried Michael Schumacher to his championships. In their own ways, they both found it virtually impossible. 'I was very interested to hear Rory's views on Benetton's development policy for the 1995 race car and whether they had set out to produce a car from which only Schumacher could wring out its ultimate performance,' commented Peter Wright after his interview with Byrne in 1996. 'The combination of good response and marginal stability either caught out the unwary or persuaded them to stay clear of the limit in fast corners. Only Schumacher came to terms with these characteristics and was able to exploit them to the full.' Byrne explained, 'That was not something we worked out directly. It was more of a development programme that happened after I rejoined Benetton at the end of 1991. We developed a car that gave the best performance and Schumacher adapted to drive it. It was a continuous process. There was no conscious decision, as such, but it's an inevitable consequence of his driving ability and style, and it enabled us to develop the car to maximise performance.'

Byrne, of course, worked in his early days in Formula One with another of the sport's great drivers, Ayrton Senna. He suggested that only he and Schumacher had the all-round ability to lift themselves and their cars beyond their rivals, from his experience. They taught themselves things, as he did. And, of course, he learnt from them. At no time during his racing experiences with different people and teams did Byrne find the time to return to a classroom and collect qualifications or degrees. His was a classic case of learning as he went along, becoming a self-made man – a quality that is common to so many of the people in the Scuderia's 'dream team', and particularly those within the Team Schumacher group itself.

But the growth in the volume and quality of the technology that came into Formula One had a profound effect on the work of both Brawn and Byrne. Byrne was always aware of this, and admitted that his role at Ferrari had changed: he had gone from 'hands-on' design into a more managerial and supervisory role. 'As technology advances, there is so much scope that I really have to spend all my time thinking about where the next step is coming from,' he explained. 'What you can do is limited by the budget, time and the ability to manage people. It's quite difficult to expand and retain efficiency while motivating staff and keeping them focused. But at the end of the day, I still get the same enjoyment out of this role. The last time I actually engineered a car at the track was in 1993, and I seldom go to races now as there is so much support and research work to do here at the factory. These days, with data transfer down phone links and modern communications, it is not so necessary. It may not be quite as good as being at the track, but it allows me to keep abreast of things on a continual basis while still being able to carry on my function here. It is really much more efficient for the company. At a test, the actual amount of useful testing relevant to the research I am doing is minimal. It is mostly reliability running, which has no direct relevance to performance, but does determine success at races. I don't need to be there for all that.

'By far the most important aspect of my job now is coordinating all the research activities. I've got five key people who report to me, who are in charge of structures, vehicle dynamics, aerodynamics, R&D and design – the actual design. My most important job is to bring all those activities together to make the design. As far as designing is concerned, occasionally I will get on the board. I can't design on CAD [Computer Aided Design], so the only drawing board in the place is in my office, and there I might draw something out and then I'll go and discuss it with Aldo Costa, who is in charge of all the design, and then someone might pick it up. But that's really a small part of the activity.'

These days, the emphasis in Formula One design is on specialists, but Byrne pointed out another basic requirement. 'You need mechanical engineering for a start. You need a lot of disciplines, but to actually design the car itself, I think you need to be a mechanical engineer. Obviously aerodynamics are very important, and so are the electronics. But it's fundamentally an exercise in mechanical engineering to actually produce a car. You have to have someone to lead the team who physically designs the pieces these days. Still, it's a huge field. Some of them are specialists in composite materials, some of them are specialists in metals, some of them are specialists in electronics and electronic systems, and some of them are transmission specialists. Nowadays you require specialists in every field.'

In 2002, Rory Byrne was credited with being the designer of the near-invincible F2002 car that proved to be a record-breaker. In it, the 'dream team' delivered fifteen victories, nine 'one-two' finishes, 221 points and their third successive world championship double. It was universally declared to be the greatest Grand Prix car of all time. Tributes, some of them washed down with a bitter taste, poured in. One critic, Will Gray, writing for AtlasF1, wrote, 'The supreme attention to detail that has allowed Ferrari to shoot into orbit at a rate their rivals cannot cope with has been as awesome to witness as it has been upsetting to endure, and their final run of five consecutive one-twos in the final five races of the year has shown a team in a state of absolute perfection. So depressing has that been for the fans as well as their rivals that when Michael Schumacher and Rubens Barrichello parked their cars up at the end of the Japanese Grand Prix, the rest of the paddock breathed a collective sigh of relief. Phew. At least we won't see that again ...' But it was not to be Ferrari's final supreme triumph because they went on to win again in 2003, this time after a tumultuous struggle to beat down a fightback from their rivals, and then walked clear of everyone again in a dominant 2004.

Byrne deserved to be declared a genius for his achievements. For six successive years, Ferrari won the constructors' championship title. He was at the heart of their team. He was at the heart of Team Schumacher. And he did it by working and working until he found the car to perform to his satisfaction. His attitude never changed: he was only interested in creating

The F2002 car, as Byrne said, was at that time seen as the ultimate Grand Prix machine. Designed to the same rules specifications as their rivals, and to the same regulations as its predecessor, the F2001, it had a three-litre engine, was constructed mainly of carbon fibre, had a seven-speed semi-automatic gearbox, and push-rod torsion spring suspension. Others had similar cars, but not as fast. When asked exactly why his cars were so superior, Byrne admitted he had no easy answer. 'I find it hard to answer that question,' he said. 'I don't know where our rivals are. But I think one of the biggest improvements we have made over the last year has been our straight-line speed relative to our main opposition. Last year, relative to Williams, we were generally a bit slower. This year, I would say, we are generally a bit quicker. The two main things that affect straight-line speed are engine power and aerodynamic efficiency, and, you know, I think you would be fairly hard pushed to differentiate what was better. But overall, everything on the F2002 was new. The gearbox was completely new, even to the way we produced the casing material and the way of making the casing. All the internals, the way the gearshift operates – all of that was fundamentally new. The back end was totally new, the cooling system was totally new, the way we constructed the chassis was totally new, the way we constructed the suspension was new. So although it didn't look a lot different, there was a lot of fundamental new stuff on the car.'

Ferrari had introduced their new car at the end of March at the Brazilian Grand Prix, the third race of the year. As they had only one ready, it went to Schumacher, not Barrichello, because he was ahead in the championship. He used it well, survived a first-lap clash with Juan Pablo Montoya, and went on to claim his second win of the year. By the end of the season it had been beaten only once in fifteen races, and Schumacher won the of both cars this season I am not sure it is actually any better than the finishing record of both cars last season or the season before.' Looking back, he was right. In 2002, Barrichello retired five times, Schumacher none. In the previous year, together they posted six retirements, but the honours were split with Schumacher having two car failures and Barrichello having two, with another two crashes for the Brazilian making up the numbers. 'We have a philosophy of how we operate to make sure our cars are reliable,' Byrne continued. 'Really, I think reliability is down to hard work and having good systems. There is certainly no magic to it. I think for the last three years our reliability has been at what I would call a good level. It is still not perfect by any means, but it is at a level that I think is acceptable.'

If Ferrari's overall reliability record was both very good and consistent, Schumacher's was excellent. At that time, Ferrari had finished on the podium in 53 consecutive races, but it was the fact that Schumacher, due to his astonishing consistency and the team's metronomic perfection, had finished on the podium at every race in 2002 that highlighted their impressive reliability. 'Michael had an incredible year,' Byrne said of that 2002 season. 'Rubens had quite a few problems, certainly in the first half of the year. But I am a firm believer that there is no luck; at the end of the day it all balances out. Whether it was Michael's car or Rubens' is totally random. It is nothing to do with the engineers, the way the car was run, the chassis, the engine, the gearbox or anything. Certainly Rubens' finishing rate in the first half of the season was, by our standards, totally unacceptable, and really I think Michael was fortunate not to have had some of the problems that Rubens did. The fact that there was a problem – that wasn't bad luck, there was a reason for the problem. Certainly in one or two of the cases that problem could have afflicted Michael's car just as easily as

Rubens'. Michael happened to be lucky. Maybe it will even out next year.'

That prospect, however, was not of great concern to Byrne. He is a man who likes to win, and to ensure that he stays winning. From his armchair, at home, he admitted he felt anxiety about reliability and had no desire to see more exciting racing – and championships – provided by any misfortunes. 'It's not that I am afraid,' he said, 'but you are still nervous. When you start from the front and you are leading the race it can only get worse. You sit there dreading that something is going to go wrong somewhere. You spend an hour and a half just praying that nothing is going to go wrong. It's not as exciting as if there was a race going on with the competitors. That would be more exciting, but I am still just as nervous whether there is an exciting race going on or they are controlling the race from the front. It doesn't alter the possibility that something could go wrong.'

Like most traditionalists and most *Ferraristas*, Byrne also holds an old-fashioned view on teamwork and strategy. When asked about the furore over the 'team orders' finish at the Austrian Grand Prix of 2002, he gave a measured response. 'I think the way Ferrari has operated the team in the past and has continued to do this year is a team policy, not an individual driver policy. The drivers are members of the team, just the same as I am a member of the team, and if the person I am responsible to lays out a plan and says this is the way he would like things to be done, then I get on and do it. And the drivers, in that respect, I don't think are any different. To be honest, I adopt the professional approach that matters of that ilk are really discussed and decided between Ross and Jean Todt. In my opinion, in hindsight, it obviously wasn't necessary because Michael won by a country mile. But if, at the end of the day, that team order hadn't been used and he had lost the championship by two or three points, I think our chairman might have asked some questions as to why we didn't apply a different strategy.' He had an insight, however, into the way Schumacher 'gave' victory at the United States Grand Prix to Barrichello. 'To be honest, there was much less of a fuss there,' said Byrne, referring to a general feeling that it was something to be accepted. 'It was probably Michael's biggest driving mistake all year, but I don't think it was even an issue inside Maranello. Really, at that stage, whether the order was reversed or whatever, it would have made no difference to the outcome of the championship or anything.'

In summary, it is obvious that Byrne created a wonderful winning machine in 2002 regarded as beautiful by many people, but that was of no additional pleasure to him. 'I don't consider beauty first because only efficiency matters,' he said. 'A winning car is always beautiful! Moreover, the concept of beauty is very subjective: what I think is nice probably doesn't suit everyone. The whole shape of the car comes from research and wind-tunnel studies. When I look at this car, I don't only see its external shape; I see how well integrated it is, I consider the amount of work and resources allocated to its design. Every single element of the F2002 was carefully studied. This, also, is beautiful.' Add a driver like Michael Schumacher to a car like the F2002, however, and the results guarantee that even as harsh an art critic as Rory Byrne knows he has seen a masterpiece.

On reflection, it might be said that the success of the Ferrari cars designed by Rory Byrne from 2000 onwards had as much to do with the introduction of the Scuderia's new wind tunnel as anything else. Until it was introduced, the team had failed to win the drivers' championship; as soon as it was put to use, they started to take control. It is pertinent, then, to look back at how Byrne handled the media launch questions on the day when his 2000 challenger was revealed at Maranello, the day when the final step towards Team Schumacher's long list of achievements was made.

'The 2000 Formula One car is the first to be conceived entirely in our new wind tunnel,' explained Byrne. 'It incorporates a fundamental revision of the placement of the main masses, including a new V10 engine, to optimise the weight distribution. We have also achieved a significant reduction in the height of the centre of gravity. This helps tyre wear in a race. In 1998, the overall width of the car was narrowed another 200mm, and the narrower the regulations make the car, the more important it is to reduce the height of the centre of gravity. The effect on tyres is one of the most important aspects, but there are others such as reduced roll, improved aerodynamic efficiency. It's one of those areas where you lower it as much as you practically can. We have also incorporated a number of characteristics which will be obligatory for the coming years, to improve driver comfort and safety.

'The transmission is all new and incorporates new materials and processes. Its lubrication system has been revised to save weight and improve efficiency. On the suspension side, we have a new system for the springs and the height adjustment, and for the first time all the main components are made from carbon composite. The power steering system has also been revised. We are using torsion bars with the suspension, but the fundamentals of the suspension are different this year. The fuel system has been completely redesigned to improve performance in both qualifying and the race, when it will be possible to reduce the time taken to refuel. In terms of fuel capacity, it's something we review from year to year, and we've reviewed it for this year, but I'm not prepared to say what we've done. In terms of the fuel flow, the FIA regulates the flow delivered at the nozzle, but there are other areas where you can gain a small advantage if you're careful. You can certainly lose it if you're not careful. Then there is a new Step 9 Marelli electronic system which improves the management and data acquisition system on the engine and car.'

Pretty standard comments for a launch – the sort of 'lower, leaner, meaner, faster' principle employed by all teams. But when pressed, Byrne soon revealed the secret to Ferrari's upcoming success. 'The main improvement in performance comes from the aerodynamics,' he said, 'because in this area we have made the biggest step forward since I joined Ferrari.' It was a bold statement for any designer talking about the most vital part of modern-day Grand Prix design. 'I think part of the improvement is because we've done all the development in the new facility rather than the old one, and it's due partly to the effort the aerodynamic department has put into this car. It was started a lot earlier than last year's car, and that's paid off. We're mostly running a 50 per cent model in there at the moment, but there is provision to run a full-scale model and we'll review that in due time. We have two models at the moment, but we're constantly reviewing that and upgrading our facility and capability. That may increase in the future.'

It certainly has. In fact, under the eye of the latest chief aerodynamicist, John Iley, a man who made his trade at Jordan and Renault before hitting the big time, it has increased significantly in line with the rest of the teams. And it is still in that wind tunnel where Ferrari makes its mark, with the modest and unassuming Iley a crucial part of Byrne's design group and a snug fit within Ferrari's incredible team of minds, a team that has grown more impressive as the names of the men further behind the scenes filter out. Engine guru Paolo Martinelli and statistician Luca Baldisserri have both been brought out from behind the red curtain, along with the reclusive Iley, who is at home in his control room.

From that wind tunnel, where the 2000 car was created, and the associated design offices and model shop, Iley, guided by the experienced and ultra-knowledgeable Byrne, helps a huge team hone Ferrari's sleek scarlet machine closer and closer to perfection at an astonishing rate. Bleary-eyed aero engineers work in shifts as the wind tunnel in Maranello whirrs on 24 hours a day, day after day after day, creating, testing, modifying and re-testing relentlessly to ensure that every two weeks or so Ferrari can continue their pursuit of success on the track. Other impressive facilities help Byrne to hone his racer to perfection. Not content with being the only team to own their own test track, Ferrari own two of them, Fiorano and Mugello, where drivers pound around testing the latest designs from the pen – or in more modern terms the 3D CAD drawings – of Byrne and his team. But Byrne believes it is the wind tunnel and not the test tracks that are key to the biggest gains in performance. 'Whether we test at Barcelona or Fiorano or Mugello I don't think is going to make very much difference on our first-race competitiveness,' said Byrne at the car launch back in 2000. 'We're going as hard as we can, and we're going to be introducing updates and modifications during this test programme to give ourselves maximum competitiveness for Australia. Whether we test at Barcelona or Mugello will not actually test our performance. We feel it is much more important to be close to base so that we can attend to any problems much more quickly; the whole logistics is much easier. But there's still scope for development. There is always scope for development.'

In May 2004, Rory Byrne told the Scuderia that he did not intend to extend his contract when it expired at the beginning of 2007. He did say, however, that he was prepared to take up a consultancy role.

There had been hints that Byrne would step down. Not only is he past his 60th birthday, he is also the father of a young son. At one time, when asked about the downside of working in Formula One, he replied, 'Probably the worst part I find is that it's virtually all-consuming. I never seem to be able to get much free time. That's the main thing. In 2000, the year my son was born, I had a total of eight days off in terms of holiday. Last year I probably had about ten or twelve. I think that's the worst part of the job, actually not being able to find the time to go scuba diving in the Galapagos for a couple of weeks. I just can't do it. It's something I would really like to do. I can do it – my contract says I have 25 days' leave a year – but if you actually want to keep improving and keep at the front, I find that the job is just so intense and there's just so much do. And having more resources doesn't actually make the job easier, it makes it more difficult, because you've actually got to take more time to think how you are going to use those resources properly. It doesn't mean less workload, it means more workload.' At the same time, he gave an insight into what else he might do with his time, if he had more of it on his hands. 'I'm going down to Mugello – we're testing there still. I hardly ever get time to get out of the office and be there for a day's testing, so I'm taking tomorrow as a nice opportunity to get in the Ferrari and give it a blast down the A1, which is good fun. I've got a 360 Modena. I've had it about three years. I've done 30,000 kilometres in it. It's a nice car, it really is. It's practical: I go shopping in it, I use it every weekend. I park the company Fiat in the garage, pull out the Ferrari and use it all the time. It's brilliant fun. When you get to all those high-speed turns through the Appenines mountains on that autostrada it's incredible. Just really good fun.'

Diving, driving, Ferraris, and sunshine time with his family. It was easy to see the way Byrne's mind was drifting as his cars swept towards another constructors' title. It was the first sign that the 'dream team' was breaking up. Team Schumacher's invincibility was no longer to be taken for granted. The results of 2004, in a car overseen by Byrne during 2003, were unlikely to be affected by the decision, but it remained an unanswered question as to whether or not things would be the same in 2005, for it was clear that Byrne was no longer in the mood of earlier days – a time when, as he plotted the design of another championship winner, he could say, 'There's not been a day since I started when I've not got out of bed raring to go, raring to get into the office. We've gone through some bad patches, and even then I can honestly say I've always got into my car really keen to get into work. So from a job satisfaction and personal motivation point of view I think it's fabulous. Like any professional sport nowadays, it's not without its risks; there are downsides. The satisfaction comes from enthusiasm, and from that comes commitment. I generally do a twelve-hour day, and when we have setbacks I just get my head down and keep going. If I was ever going to give up, I would have done so in 1981 with the TG181!' When he spoke those words, he did not know what the Ferrari years would bring him. But even after such sustained success, he was tired and ready to rest.

CHAPTER EIGHT

THE SCUDERIA

Stand outside the Ferrari factory and you wonder why Ferrari doesn't win every race. Stand inside, and you wonder how they manage to win any.

Gerhard Berger, reflecting on life at Ferrari
before the Team Schumacher era

Many good men with fine reputations perished amid the internal bickering at the Scuderia Ferrari. They came in hope, if not belief, but departed in distress. Often bitter distress. Some shone along the way. And then came the men who built Team Schumacher, sweeping away decades of decline and politics. Their reward was Formula One motor racing's greatest spell of sustained success. The disappointment of so many other evocative names who attempted to rekindle the glory of Jody Scheckter's championship triumph of 1979 – a list that included trumpeted heroes such as René Arnoux, Michele Alboreto, Gerhard Berger, Nigel Mansell, Alain Prost and Jean Alesi – was forgotten. So, too, were the more forlorn figures who failed to make an impact with Enzo Ferrari's team, drivers whose passage through the rituals of life at Maranello left them struggling for the competitive oxygen that sustains careers. Before Jean Todt came and rebuilt the team, life at Ferrari as a Grand Prix driver could be as brief and brutal as it was glamorous and inspiring.

When Michael Schumacher joined, he knew little of this. His confidence was high. He had so much self-belief that he feared nothing. He knew success was not going to be automatic at Ferrari, but he was prepared to work and to wait. He knew his own talents, his own achievements, and therefore his own value, thanks to an effective bidding war between his old team and the Scuderia which the latter won with a then astonishing estimated $20 million investment in his services. But he knew little of the history, glamour and magic that made Ferrari the most-loved Grand Prix team on earth. Nor did he know much about the story of Ferrari's drivers, their fabled treatment by the *tifosi* and the reverence in which they are held by most of Italy's ordinary citizens.

Ivan Capelli, an excellent Italian driver who drove for

Ferrari in 1992, was brought up to worship the team. That knowledge, which was not to concern Schumacher, was overwhelming for him. 'I realised it the first day I was presented as the new driver,' Capelli told Christopher Hilton, as reported in *Inside the Mind of the Grand Prix Driver*. 'Going down from Milan to Maranello, I stopped at a petrol station and nobody recognised me. Nobody asked me for anything. Coming back, in the night, when the radio and television had been saying, "Ah, Capelli is now a Ferrari driver," I stopped at the same point of the highway, but on the other side, and they wanted autographs and pictures of me. Just twelve hours of difference ...' Capelli had driven 78 Grands Prix for AGS, March and Leyton House before joining Ferrari. His dream turned into a nightmare, and he was sacked before the year was out after collecting three points from fourteen races that were marked by ill fortune. 'It was difficult,' he recalled. 'I had some overstress, let's put it like that. It began to really affect me. All the pressure of the team was on me. I was living in Monte Carlo at the time so I didn't face it every day, but when I went back to Milan to see my parents I did.' When asked if life became more difficult for him after this experience, Capelli revealed his humour and Ferrari's standing. 'Well, I wasn't able to pay in a restaurant,' he said. 'They wouldn't let me. Before Ferrari, I had to pay. During Ferrari, I didn't. And afterwards, I had to pay again.' His confidence shattered, Capelli drove in only one more Grand Prix, for the Jordan team in 1993. Later, he became a pundit on Italian television. On reflection, much later, he said he had been 'too soft' to survive at that level. 'People that are going to the top are so tough and they are not looking at anything else – they are just tough.'

The year in which Capelli suffered, Schumacher shone at

Benetton. At the 1992 Belgian Grand Prix, where the sad Italian driver suffered an engine failure, Schumacher won his first Formula One race. By 2000, and the heart-stopping drama of the decisive Japanese Grand Prix at Suzuka, Capelli was forgotten. He was a man destined to work in the media, no longer a Ferrari driver, and he must have felt a deep sense of pain mixed with natural emotions of joy as the Scuderia revelled in their red wigs and their victory. He knew that nothing in motorsport could equal the feeling the Maranello men were experiencing that day, that evening and all that night. By the time they triumphed again in the final race of the season in Malaysia, they were the first Ferrari team to win both championships for 21 years.

This was a big story for Italy and an historic day for Ferrari and Formula One. 'Red Wigs Everywhere as Ferrari Do the Double' was the headline on the Reuters report. It captured the moment:

McLaren congratulated Formula One rivals Ferrari on Sunday as the Malaysian Grand Prix paddock filled with champagne-soaked people dancing and celebrating in scarlet wigs. McLaren driver David Coulthard also donned a red wig at news conferences after Ferrari completed a rare double of the drivers' and constructors' championships in the same season.

Triple world champion Michael Schumacher, who won the drivers' title two weeks ago at Suzuka in Japan, took the race to secure the constructors' title for Ferrari as well. Briton Coulthard was second in the race, with Brazilian Rubens Barrichello third for Ferrari. It has been 21 years since the Italian team last won both titles.

Ferrari sporting director Jean Todt, a plastic beaker of champagne in his hand, said it was a moment of great personal and professional satisfaction for him. 'I came here to build up the team, to put the pieces into place and to achieve this success, and for me it is a very satisfying and very special feeling to have done it. The season could not have finished better than this. Two drivers on the podium. The statistics are fantastic this season: ten wins, nine for Michael, one for Rubens. A record year. This time we only needed three points, but we did it properly,' said the Frenchman, whose team arrived in Malaysia knowing one title was won and the other was assured if they took just three more points.

Schumacher drove in typically bold style on a remarkable afternoon twelve years after the death of Ferrari founder Enzo Ferrari in 1988 – the last season in which all the race victories in one year were taken by only two teams. The German was slow away from pole but made up ground after Finland's Mika Hakkinen in a McLaren was handed a ten-second penalty for jumping the start.

'We wanted to win the constructors' championship and we have done it, not just by getting three points, but by winning and by coming third. It was a very tight and a very tough race, and DC [Coulthard] was pushing me all the way,' Schumacher said. 'It is a shame, but all the guys in the team are flying out tomorrow with everything so they are going to be packing up most of the evening now. But then, we will have a big, big party and we can go into a winter holiday which the whole team really deserves.'

Barrichello, who finished third despite suffering with a heavy cold in the high temperatures and humidity, said he had enjoyed the race and the season. 'I am so pleased,' he said, also wearing a red wig. 'Now we can start next season in a really strong way too.'

Ferrari president Luca di Montezemolo, one of the most superstitious of the team's supporters, had flown into Malaysia on Sunday morning to be present on the big day. But instead of watching the race at the circuit, he chose to stay away and follow it on television from his hotel room. 'But he wants to join the big party tonight back at the hotel, and we will all enjoy ourselves with him,' said Todt. 'That is why he came. For us all, it has been a long time coming to achieve this, and we will have a real celebration.'

Ferrari were big news again. They were winners. It meant, too, that every member of the team was newsworthy and that the 'dream team' at its core would be followed everywhere. It was the price of success. And with more and more success came more and more media pressure and intrusion. Everything had changed. The public wanted to know more. Every thought and comment from any of the Team Schumacher men was important. Even though they were all media-savvy, battle-hardened and experienced, it took the pressures they had known to a new dimension. Yes, Ferrari were special – not just to Italians, but to everyone who took an interest in cars and motor racing all over the world.

This team, which had come into being over several years of honing, was finally back at the forefront of a sport they had been involved in from the beginning. It was like England winning at rugby or cricket again, something that to the traditionalist should have been happening for ever but, due to internal problems and heightened external competition, had somehow not happened for what seemed like an age. In many ways it had been Luca di Montezemolo, the steely-faced front of Ferrari Corporate, who had created Team Schumacher, a business-based and well-structured racing team often accused of lacking passion, through the introduction of the mathematically minded Todt and the subsequent agreement to invest in Schumacher, a Germanic genius renowned for his hard-nosed determination but thought, fairly or unfairly, to lack the spirit of excitement for victory. Schumacher jumped for joy every time he won at Benetton, and he took the same, staged and well-formatted trademark two-footed podium leap with him to Ferrari. It was the same celebration in 2000 as it had been in 1994 and 1995, a celebration that di Montezemolo, back in the Benetton era, just had to bring on board.

His initial tactic, to bring in Todt, sowed the seeds for the years to come. 'When I brought Jean Todt into the team in 1993, it was a controversial decision,' he recalled when Todt renewed his contract some years ago. 'He was a Frenchman. He didn't know F1. Now Todt has re-signed to stay with us until the end of 2004, which means he will then have been with us eleven years – something of a Ferrari record.' Make that thirteen years by the time his latest contract comes to an end at the conclusion of the 2006 season, a longevity only allowed by his careful planning to put the right men in place to create an unprecedented era. The Scuderia is ruthless, after all; even Todt's head would have been on the block had he not achieved this personnel positioning with perfection.

Todt arrived just before the French Grand Prix, his home race, and his brief was clear: he needed to make the team sing, and make it sing quickly. He needed to turn an apparently unstructured outfit into a slick operation in tune with itself and its overall goal of world championship success. 'People who are good at their jobs and at the top of their professions are usually strong characters,' Todt remarked. 'They need to be listened to and to be loved. Ferrari has men of this level of talent throughout the team, but a man who is not prepared to listen to good advice is stupid. Ferrari is no more complicated than any other team. It is a team of legend and mythology. I am convinced that it needs stability, and once we have that the whole team will be able to relax and it will operate better. President Montezemolo has given me enormous support, and the morning I left Paris for Magny-Cours I was delighted to receive a gift from him: a Ferrari prancing horse emblem engraved with my name, and a card wishing me good luck.' He saw his role as being like a conductor in an orchestra. 'It is not my job to play around with the instruments,' he said on his arrival, 'just to lead and direct.' That said, there were several members of the orchestra who were not quite playing the same tune, and a few outside whom Todt believed would fit in better.

The prancing horse had always been a symbol of something beyond a motor racing team. As Todt said, it had the legend and mythology created by no other team, and it was that enticing aspect, as much as the pure challenge of the task, that lured first Schumacher then Brawn and Byrne to come and play for di Montezemolo's orchestra. 'For me, Michael is by far the best driver in the world,' the president mused. 'As a person, somebody who is very close to the team, very correct and reliable, particularly in difficult situations, I like him very much. Ross Brawn is a first-class man, loyal and strong. He has done a very good job to put together the English method and Italian creativity. Rory Byrne is a fantastic person. He has let grow up a lot of young technicians, on the track and behind the pits. Together they all approach their jobs very well. Just look at the results.'

But while Ferrari's results were proving that Team Schumacher was indeed the success di Montezemolo had expected it to be all those years ago, its very achievements would soon begin to break up Formula One. Ferrari had become, to outsiders at least, too well structured. It lacked flair; it lacked the passion of the marque. It was achieving results, but it was doing that in such a controlled manner and such a dominating fashion that viewers were starting to turn away. Formula One was in trouble. Rather than muscle in together to solve the problems, Ferrari were accused by some of thinking only of themselves, not the future of the sport. And it was di Montezemolo who, several years after he began the creation of the all-conquering Ferrari Formula One empire, was heavily involved in thoughts of taking all that away from the place where Ferrari had grown up. Ferrari was thinking of leaving Formula One.

That almost happened in the winter of 2004/05, when the sport was in the grip of a political crisis and many feared for its future. It was stunning news: Ferrari, after five successive drivers' titles and six constructors' championships, had contemplated abandoning Formula One. Ferrari, after all, were the only team with a name and a value that was bigger than the sport itself. 'World champions Ferrari discussed leaving Formula One before agreeing last month to remain in the series until 2012, according to team boss Jean Todt,' said one of the newswire reports, again from Reuters. 'Ferrari, the sport's glamour team and the only one to have competed in every championship since the first in 1950, were persuaded to stay by a $100 million sweetener from Bernie Ecclestone, *The Times* newspaper said later. "We are a small company and we have to cover the costs of Formula One," Todt, also managing director of the Fiat-owned Italian carmaker, told the paper. "We discussed very often leaving Formula One because it was costing too much money. Ferrari could have been in a position to stop being in

Formula One. Yes, that is sure. The trend of the evolution of rising costs without extra revenues put the question on the agenda," added the Frenchman. Ferrari stunned carmakers planning for a possible rival series from 2008, when an existing commercial agreement with Ecclestone and the sport's governing body expires, when they agreed to sign on for another four years. Todt said there had been no betrayal, despite the determined opposition of the other nine teams. "Sooner or later the reality and the logic will take over," he said. "I understand that, for some, it doesn't make sense, but it will. We needed to agree the future for the sake of security. We couldn't just go off blind in a new direction, and it was up to us to secure the future of Ferrari inside Formula One."'

Formula One without Ferrari? Impossible to imagine. As Jean Todt said after signing that 2012 agreement, 'At the end of the day, we have to act in the interests of Ferrari.'

Nigel Stepney has worked at Ferrari since 1993, and is thus as well placed as anyone to comment on the set-up and mentality there, and to muse on the key to the Scuderia's success. He was born in Leamington Spa, in Warwickshire, in 1958. 'My dad was an arable and dairy farmer,' he says, 'so I was driving tractors from the age of four. I can drive them, lorries, combine harvesters – anything. I did take my driving test. I only had one lesson, but I passed first time.' He was very active in a number of sports too, and succeeded in playing football for the Warwickshire county team before succumbing to the full-time lure of working with fast cars.

As an Englishman within the almost mystical heart of the Ferrari team, he has the job title of 'team coordinator', but admits, with typically down-to-earth candour and humour, that he almost prefers to describe himself as 'a glorified chief mechanic'. Nevertheless, he has a very comfortable office in the racing department's headquarters close to the Fiorano test circuit at Maranello where, as a totally dependable and very experienced and consistent member of the team, he has been involved in the long slog from disappointment to glorious, sustained success. His beginnings in motor racing may have been modest, but he has vast experience, and he has put it to excellent use for the Scuderia.

'After I left school, I went to Southam, which is a small town about ten miles away from home, and I worked at Broadspeed, where Ralph Broad used to do Triumph Dolomite Sprints,' he explains, glossing over the fact that Broadspeed at that time were one of the best preparation shops for successful touring car teams of the era, including Ford Capris and Jaguars to run in the European Touring Car Championship. 'I did my apprenticeship there. I was seventeen when I started. Then, after two years there, one of the guys left Broadspeed and it started to go downhill, so I went to join Shadow in Northampton. They needed people. I've done pretty much the same job for various teams ever since. It is a blinkered life but has got less blinkered as the years have gone on.'

The Shadow Formula One team was in decline when Stepney arrived, but he gained valuable experience there and worked with the rising Italian driver Elio de Angelis. They enjoyed each other's company, and when de Angelis moved to join Lotus, in 1980, Stepney joined him in Norfolk. He went on to become the Italian driver's number one mechanic, until de Angelis moved on again and went to Brabham, only to be killed in an accident at the Le Castellet circuit in 1986. Stepney remained with Lotus and began work with another young driver of great potential, Ayrton Senna. As a result of that, and his many years at Ferrari, he can claim to have worked closely with arguably the two greatest drivers in modern Formula One history.

When Lotus fell into decline in 1988, Stepney joined Benetton, the source for Ferrari of many of their successful 'dream team'. However, Stepney was only with the team until the end of Schumacher's first brief debut season in 1991, at which point he became involved with Nelson Piquet's Formula 3000 team. This was not a success, and in 1993 he accepted an offer from John Barnard, with whom he had worked at Benetton, to go to Maranello and organise the Ferrari racing team. The move suited him. He had the experience to do the job well and he introduced an English approach that was needed in Italy. 'Generally it changed my outlook on life because I knew I was restricted in what I could do in England,' he says. 'Coming from an English team to Ferrari is something you would always dream of, if you're into motorsport, especially Formula One. Coming to Ferrari was the place to be, from the history point of view especially. When you actually walked in it was a bit of a shock in terms of the amenities of the place, the size, and what was available to do the job. I'd come from Lotus and Benetton where the resources were nowhere near, so it was staggering. Also, they were the first team I'd ever been with who made their own engine. So that was completely different. Because you had the engine there, you didn't have to go anywhere else, and there was no outside interference like that between Benetton and Cosworth. Everything was in-house.

'It took me a while to take it all in. It must have been eighteen months or two years before I got a footing in the place, here in Ferrari, where we could work together as a group of people. Before that it was very much individual groups in those days. It wasn't really amalgamated as a group working towards the same goal. When Jean Todt came along in the middle of 1993, he started to collect people around him and put people in positions that could start working in a supportive way. Whether those were the right people at the time was not the case. What was [the case] was having people in an organisation in positions where they could start working in an organised way. Some people carried on working and some didn't. I was one of the lucky ones because me and Jean got on. But those first two or three years were difficult. Also, there was John Barnard, who had a group here and a group in England. It was the second time he was with Ferrari, but designing and building a car in two different places just doesn't work. You have to have it under the same roof. Though for sure it was a step in the right direction because the technology John Barnard was bringing was great. Lots of the stuff on the cars now, like semi-auto gearboxes, rear wings, steering wheels – the things that overran the primitive technology of that time – is stuff that John invented.

'It all got streamlined a lot more when Rory, Ross and Michael joined. It was Rory and Ross who got the design office started here. They were confronted with a big group of people who had struggled to work together. I'd worked a little bit with them at Benetton, where everyone had to follow an organisation. It took many people a while to conform. Everyone would try to find the easiest way out of it – the work they didn't want to do – but they just continually repeated what they wanted you to do, and finally, once they could trust some people, they put the procedures in place and a design structure which made the whole thing go in the right direction. At the time we needed the step up to the top level. We had the car, we had the engineering, but not necessarily the organisation or the drivers.

'Michael came along and brought a big change in terms of trust. The previous drivers were very good at having the ears of the press, or going to the president and having a word that would cause undercurrents. Then Michael came in and, yeah, he was doing the same thing, but he was not doing it in front of everyone, but behind closed doors, talking to Jean Todt and Ross. He had respect for people and he wouldn't say anything out of context. He didn't want anyone to have the ammunition of "Michael said this, Michael said that". He was very professional in his approach and that helped to give a balance and support to the directors and the engineers. He gets friendly with people but he doesn't tell people things they don't need to know or need to work with.

'Drivers are powerful here. They can get anything they want – almost too much so in the earlier days. Before Michael came in they expected to be treated like gods, even if they weren't the best. At the time Michael came, he was one of the best around because he was competing with the Prosts and Sennas in a Benetton. It was quite a competitive era, and he brought an air of confidence. He showed us what could be achieved if everybody pulled together. To try to get to the top you can have everything, but unless you have a driver who can put it all in place, you're not there. Eddie Irvine came in too, and he was also a professional guy, but he was a completely different animal! Still, he gave a good feeling to the team and they both worked well together and formed a very strong pairing.'

Having worked with Senna and Schumacher, Stepney is in the almost unique position of being able authoritatively to compare the two. 'When Ayrton was at Lotus,' he says, 'everyone respected him and knew what he was capable of – just like they do with Michael now. It gave everyone a big motivation to take the team to the next level. Ayrton would also do a lot of the work behind closed doors, with Peter Warr, Gerard Ducarouge and Honda. Honda respected him very much for that. He never bad-mouthed the engine. Obviously there were problems, but he worked behind closed doors to solve them. He gave vent to his anger, but he did it professionally. Guys like Colin Chapman and Warr would have been very pleased with that. He used to get upset and blow off some serious steam, but never where the press or the photographers could see it. I remember one incident, at Monza in 1986 or 1987, when he was so pissed off with himself when he was leading and he went off, and we were quite good in the championship at the time. I think he finished second that year. He went behind the trucks and broke down. But if it hadn't been for him we'd never have been so high up anyway. If he had been in a Williams, he'd have won easily in the Nelson Piquet era, but it was character-building for him and he hated to make mistakes. Michael is the same. When he makes a mistake he just goes red. Once at Imola, with a struggling car, he made a mistake in qualifying, but he had a sensational race and was able to pull it all back. He could run a strategy that no other driver could run because they just don't have the capacity or the ability. Michael responds to a challenge.

'Senna was very clever too. The teams weren't the same size as they are now. When I was at Lotus, the whole team was about 60 people. You didn't have the same available technology as now, but he was very clever and he used to do a lot of things that drivers now take for granted because a computer does it for them. He did it by himself with the engineers. Michael, though, gives the engineers the ideas to go and make the technology happen, which Ayrton couldn't do because the technology simply didn't exist back then. It's two different eras, so you can't really compare that well. You can look back, for instance, to when we had a fuel limit and drivers always had to watch their fuel consumption. Ayrton used to be perfect on that. He'd watch his gauge so that if he was 0.1 of a litre down by a certain point he'd ease off for the rest of the lap, and vice versa. He used to use marker boards and bridges as his reference points for fuel and braking. One year we were testing at Estoril and they'd taken down the bridge so he hadn't a clue where to brake and ended up going off.'

Stepney often enjoys a laugh when recounting old memories. His words are a reminder that in modern times, Schumacher and Ferrari enjoy not only a fabulous budget but also vast technical and human resources. For Stepney, however, the key to the Scuderia's success is subtler than that: it owes far more to a special team spirit, built up gradually over the last decade or so, than most people realise. 'I don't think we've necessarily got the 150 best people in Formula One working within our structure,' he explains, 'but we have got 150 bloody good people who can all work together. If you had the best, maybe they couldn't work together because of their egos. Everybody has respect for each other among the top twenty guys here, in terms of management. Nobody treads on anyone else's toes. There's Stefano Domenicali and Rory and Ross. If Michael or someone needs to talk to someone about the car or whatever, they know where to go. We don't overlap; we know where our limits are in our work. We don't try to do somebody else's job, and if you have doubts you go to Ross. Michael's the same. He stimulates you. Everybody can improve because you never know everything and we all make mistakes. It's just important not to make the same mistake twice. The main thing is that the people below you in the chain trust you. That's an ethic that wasn't here ten years ago. Back then, if you made a big mistake you'd be sent off to the foundry or be relegated to the tea-boy.'

One of the other Ferrari traditions of the past that was dispensed with was the drinking at lunchtimes: mechanics were treated to a glass of slightly sparkling red wine, as served in the local ristorante, with their meal. 'Barnard put a stop to that in

1993 when I came,' says Stepney. 'He stopped the Lambrusco at lunchtime at tests and races. You wouldn't accept it now because the idea of people drinking while working on potentially dangerous cars is a bit off really. You need to have your wits about you; you need to be able to concentrate hard. But it is part of the culture of Italy, and you have to take culture into account. Give English guys a few beers at lunchtime and they'd be off their heads, but in Italy it's a perfectly acceptable family thing. Everybody does it. I do it myself. You go home for lunch and have some pasta and a glass of wine. [The ban on drinking] was blown up as a big drama at the time, but it wasn't really.'

After twelve years at Ferrari, Stepney has been virtually assimilated into the team, the culture and the lifestyle. He is a part of Team Schumacher too. But he admits he found it difficult to immerse himself thoroughly in the Italian way of life, to succeed in bridging the two halves of his life. 'Coming from England, you have to mix in,' he says. 'It was very hard: a new team, a new language, a new mentality. I knew people here, but I didn't know the culture. You needed to know the culture. If you only come here for a race weekend, three or four days, and go to the odd restaurant, you'd hardly understand. But now, to go anywhere else would be very difficult. You have such a good lifestyle here, and it's a very good place to work. To work for Ferrari is to be right at the top of the sport.'

Here, Stepney has touched on the essence of the Scuderia: their unceasing competitive drive. Once you have become committed to the racing mentality of Ferrari, it is in your blood. You would not, for instance, even countenance accepting a comfortable job down the road from Maranello with the Minardi team at Faenza, just to be able to stay in Formula One and in Italy. 'No,' Stepney says, 'I'd need to be in a competitive team. I'd want to go where I thought the best possibility was to beat Ferrari – because if they booted me out, I'd want to kick their arse. Even if I can't be the best, I am still competitive. Michael is the same. He wants to perform to the maximum level in everything he does, whether its skiing or football. He's not afraid to do it. We all share that drive. Look at Ross when he goes fishing. He has to be competitive to stay at the top in this sport. If he wasn't, someone else would walk all over him. Sometimes the drivers being so competitive is a little bit detrimental to the team, and you end up with one group supporting Michael and another supporting Rubens, and you have to be careful that it doesn't split the team. But we're quite good at that. It doesn't and hasn't happened to us, as has happened before at Ferrari, and at McLaren when Senna and Prost were there. That's the kind of thing that breaks down a team. That doesn't happen here now, and it makes us stronger. Ross is excellent in this kind of situation. He says, "Look, guys, you work for Ferrari, not yourselves. Drivers come and go, so remember that."'

This competitive instinct that suffuses everyone at Ferrari in the colour of red is easy to see, but harder to understand. Not everyone is born with it, so it must be developed. Stepney thinks not. For his part, he believes it is just a part of his personality. 'I never followed groups,' he explains, 'I just wanted to do my own thing. When I started in Formula One, the first year when I was with Shadow, I looked at all the big teams like Brabham, Ferrari, Lotus and McLaren and I just thought, "OK, that's what they have, this is what we have. I want to get there." But I didn't want to just walk in there. I wanted to be competitive with what I had at the time, and I worked very hard with a lot of people who supported me. Jo Ramirez used to be team manager at Shadow and he gave me a lot of support when I was there. Success can be a word-of-mouth thing. If people respect you, then Formula One is a small world, and if you are prepared to put in the work then the rewards are there. It never comes easy. People might say that with Michael it comes easy, but he puts in such a huge amount of effort. Michael does so many sports all the time – he never stands still. Formula One is a very hard life as an engineer or mechanic, especially in these nineteen-race seasons. It's not an easy time for families. Finding a weekend off is great, but Michael just lives for activity. If you're physically fit then you're mentally fit.' Competitive drive in a nutshell.

Typically, as with anyone involved in the team, in the summer of 2005 Stepney remained bullish about Ferrari's ability to recover from their poor progress in that year's campaign. 'We have had some years when we came from behind to win,' he pointed out. 'In 2003, we needed to win the last three races to be certain of it, and we won in Monza, the United States and in Japan – and won the championship. We have put ourselves under a lot of pressure now, but we can come from behind. And we know that we have to win. Look at the last two races [the Canadian and US Grands Prix in June]: we've taken 32 points, which the other teams have not been able to do. That should be soul-destroying for them. The car's coming on, the drivers are motivated, and I think the second half of the season they'll all be struggling to keep up with us. Renault should have won the last five and haven't, so that will mentally damage them.'

His optimistic words may not have borne fruit, but they were well intended, and spoken with the belief that permeates the Scuderia.

No man in Italy is ignorant of Enzo Ferrari. He died in 1988, but he left a light that has not yet stopped burning. His reputation has gained mythological status, and he is still loved for what he did, what he made and what he represented. His name is synonymous with cars, speed and power, but also with a sense of elegance, simplicity and style. There is energy and beauty about the word Ferrari. It embodies a combination of qualities that sit at the heart of the team and beat within the fibres of the modern Scuderia. Almost without consideration, those qualities inform the thinking of the men who run the racing team in this millennium, and they live too in the philosophies that are referred to regularly by Ross Brawn, Jean Todt and Rory Byrne. The 'dream team' respect their obligations to the traditions of Ferrari, and for that reason it is impossible to peel away the skins of the extraordinary onion that is Team Schumacher and not find at its core Luca di Montezemolo's modern interpretation of the Old Man, the *Ingegnere*.

When Michael Schumacher took his number one away from the Benetton team's rural headquarters at Enstone in Oxfordshire, England, where the factory was surrounded by green meadows, leafy lanes and damp pastoral landscapes, to the arid, ceramic-making, light-industrial centre of Maranello, under the beat of the high Italian sun, he was forewarned, severely and often, of what the challenge would entail. It was not only about results but about a style of triumph. And it was about ending years in the doldrums for a team that had been living on past glories but which had been slowly dying as a result of in-fighting, stories leaking almost systematically to the media, ancient political bickering and a lack of leadership and direction. But Schumacher had a gut instinct about motor racing, and he appreciated too what might lie ahead if the greatest driver in German history could combine with the legend of Ferrari to deliver victories and championships. Maybe he could not articulate his feelings in pretty sentences, but in his heart he knew that with the right people around him he could make Ferrari roar again.

It took time, of course. Schumacher listened closely to di Montezemolo, who knew the Scuderia Ferrari legend better than anyone, having once been a close associate of the Old Man himself. Di Montezemolo had taken over an ailing Ferrari F1 team in 1974 and turned them into a team that won six of the nine constructors' championships between 1975 and 1983. The transformation of Niki Lauda was an indication of di Montezemola's powers. The 24 year-old Austrian had arrived at Ferrari with a big wallet and a big mouth but no real reputation; under the ruthless new team boss, Lauda became a champion. But Schumacher was no Niki Lauda. Oh no. Even greater things were expected of the German double champion.

Di Montezemolo left Ferrari in 1984 but returned in 1991, after organising and managing the 1990 World Cup finals in Italy, again to do the job of rescuing the F1 team. His big moves were the appointment of Jean Todt as head of racing and Schumacher as number one driver. The German would be earning more than the rest of the drivers on the grid put together, but di Montezemolo was a winner, and in Schumacher he had clearly seen a kindred spirit – someone who hated coming second as much as he did, and who would make Ferrari live up to its reputation. Alongside the words of wisdom, di Montezemolo also made it clear just how high his expectations were for his star driver. In September 1999, for instance, just two months after Schumacher had broken his leg at Silverstone, di Montezemolo demanded in no uncertain terms that he must turn up to work immediately and earn his salary. If Schumacher was hard on himself, the episode showed, the Ferrari president was even harder.

Schumacher had also listened to Jean Todt. Behind it all, whether he could see and hear it or not, he knew lay the destiny of a team created by arguably the greatest man in the history of motorsport. The ghost of Enzo Ferrari hovered over them, and it remains there. Anyone who visits Monza for the Italian Grand Prix and watches as the Ferrari cars ease out for their first run of the day in morning practice will feel the hairs on the back of their necks stand up and tingle as thousands of *tifosi* cheer aloud. They are not just applauding their team and its history, they are revering their country, for Ferrari is tied to the nation's history. As James Allen wrote in his revealing book on Michael Schumacher, *The Quest for Redemption*, Ferrari is far more than the name of a car manufacturer. 'Ferrari is not just about cars and motor racing, it is part of Italian culture. Frank Williams and Ron Dennis, though deserving of great respect, are not part of Britain's history. But Enzo Ferrari is very much part of Italy's.' Thus the myth of Ferrari is a part of the Schumacher success story.

When it was announced that Schumacher had signed a binding long-term commitment to remain with the 'dream team' at Ferrari, it was news well received by those who had known the Old Man and understood the traditions and the myths. Schumacher drove to win, sometimes in a near Machiavellian fashion. He wrung every drop of performance from the cars. He was a driver Enzo Ferrari would have enjoyed employing, even if in this modern era it meant that the driver introduced an entourage that in effect built a team within the team itself. Writing in *La Gazzetta dello Sport*, the hugely respected veteran motor racing correspondent Pino Allievi commented: 'The news is beautiful. And important. Schumacher is the guiding force of Ferrari, the man who has constructed around him the family team. Ferrari is the prisoner of Schumacher. But Schumacher is the prisoner of Ferrari, which pays him well and gives him the freedom of action which he would not find in any other team.'

In 1977, when the slim and speedy reed of a boy that was Michael Schumacher was learning his lines on kart tracks in northern Germany, Keith Botsford, a British journalist based in Italy who worked for the British newspaper the *Sunday Times*, travelled from his home near Rome to interview Enzo Ferrari. Botsford, like Allievi, was an experienced motor racing correspondent. He spoke fluent Italian and he understood both Italy and the myth of Ferrari.

At that time, the Old Man was regarded as a recluse. He was 79 years old, nearly always seen wearing dark glasses, and lived a life that restricted him to a tight geographical area around Modena. His office at Maranello was simple, possessing a near-empty desk, a sculptured glass version of the famous Ferrari prancing horse – the emblem was taken from the plane of an Italian war ace – a portrait of his son Dino and little else. (To anyone who has visited the modern Maranello and the offices of Todt and Brawn, there are echoes, but no great similarities; the best likeness, in my memory, is of the office di Montezemolo kept inside the old factory after he had taken control again in the early 1990s.) Botsford found there a man who understood perfectly what it meant to be a racing driver and how fragile the glow of success could be in a sport of death and vast financial rewards. He also found, magically, the man behind the myth that has sustained a brand name across decades of prosperity. 'There is simply more to Enzo Ferrari than any other figure in the world of motor racing,' he wrote. 'But little of the inner man is ever revealed to the public. The man who is God to most in the sport has private sorrow to match public triumph, and for 25 years since the tragic death of his only son Dino, who at the time of his death suffered from terminal muscular dystrophy, he has consistently refused to become public property ...' But for

Botsford, Ferrari broke his rule, meeting him for an interview, and then lunch over the road from the factory gates, almost certainly at the Cavallino because the Montana – favoured in modern times by the race and test team, and run so warmly for so long by the welcoming Rosella, who Schumacher describes as 'my second mother' – is slightly further away. Only a rare few journalists had been privileged to enjoy such close contact with Ferrari.

In his report, Botsford stated that there had been only two passions in Ferrari's life: cars and Dino. One gave him joy, the other had given him grief. 'The shadow of that death, and his own, obviously hangs over him,' he wrote. 'His talk, from the start, was about "the hallucinating fragility of life" and his daily visits to his son's grave.' 'Suicide is an act of courage,' Ferrari told Botsford. 'No man who takes a journey into the unknown is cowardly or vile. A man is nothing until he is dead. It is death that puts a stamp on his personality. Death has led me to constant self-examination, but I know life is an illusion, mainly the illusion that we are something. So when people talk about my fame, I know better than to be taken in by it. I am a man who has pursued an adventure. But it is probably an error to say who I am; if I am unable to see the defects in the machines I build, how can someone else judge me?' This complex series of ideas and considerations populated only the hinterland of Ferrari's mind. Botsford was steadily drawn deeper.

He described Ferrari as still a big man of formal, eloquent speech, with almost colourless eyes withdrawn behind a nose and mouth that were fleshy and prominent. He had been ill with a lung infection (due probably, he suggested, to a lifelong inhalation of noxious engine emissions that left him weak and spent), but he was in his mind as alert and as categorical as ever. He said that Ferrari's talk was of almost brutal frankness, and concluded that the heart of the matter, for this man, was egotism. Nothing else. 'No one loses anything or does anything for someone else,' Ferrari said. 'We live in a vast prison, like Kafka's. The world is a penitentiary, and we are the inmates; caught in an instinctive egotism, we have to depend on our own force and nothing else. Whatever we pretend, we value others not for the good they can do us, but for the evil they might. The man who might kill us receives our full attention. He requires it, for we live in a cruel world where violence has taken the place of reason, a world where the only positive element is fear, the chief instrument of power.'

The Old Man's words apply strongly to several members of Team Schumacher. Gian Paolo Ormezzano, a journalist and Ferrari expert, wrote in *Ferrari World* magazine in 1992, 'If a qualifying adjective were to be applied to Montezemolo which explained the man, I would say that he is a sportsman: competitive, tactical, dynamic and capable of sprinting. He is someone who even thinks of choosing a menu as competitive. He is above all a fighter, a tactician, a man of the scrum who also enjoys card games. A sportsman in the way he excels, not someone who heroically enjoys others excelling. He is not, it must be said, a sportsman according to the gospel: the world champion boxer does not turn the other cheek when he has been smitten on one.' It is impossible, too, not to see flashes of Todt, Willi Weber and Schumacher himself running vividly across one's inner cinema screen as Ferrari's thoughts are read again in modern times. Introspective, obsessive and analytical are the words that connect them, fair or not. Todt is a man of obsession and routine. Weber, besieged by rumour and innuendo, has lived a career that has seen him, at least metaphorically, apparently fleeing the wolves on more than one occasion. Schumacher has a self-confidence, albeit one that appears fragile at times, that borders on arrogance, revealing an ego that is often misunderstood.

He can also be extraordinarily superstitious. In particular, let us recall what Schumacher admitted after he had won the drivers' title for a third time with Ferrari at the 2002 French Grand Prix. 'I had a premonition and I was convinced that I would take the championship only in Hockenheim [the next race],' he said. 'The way the race was going I didn't think this was my day. First, Rubens had a problem, then Montoya was in front of me for a long time, and then I made a mistake after the first stop when I crossed a white line and got the penalty. That happened because I was concentrating on Montoya, who was chasing me, and I was watching my mirrors. From the pit-wall, Ross told me about it, so I tried to push hard to build up an advantage so that the penalty did not affect me too much. When I was back on track, I was surprised to find I was second behind Kimi. There were ten laps to go and I decided to give it my all again, to put him under pressure. Then Kimi skidded on the oil. There was nothing he could do. I had been warned about the oil from McNish's Toyota so I was able to react a bit. He was unaware of the danger and went off the track. The last few laps were the worst of my career. I could feel the weight of an enormous responsibility. I was so scared of making a mistake and ruining everything.' How the Old Man would have understood that confession, and how he would have lauded his driver for bringing home glory under such pressure. Men such as Schumacher, Todt, di Montezemolo and Weber survived and flourished in Ferrari's vision of a Kafkan prison.

The creation of the cars, according to Enzo Ferrari, is 'another Kafka labyrinth'. He said: 'You are in an endless corridor, along which every door is closed. You want to get out, but you can't.

You have to find a solution. I find it sometimes in the night, sometimes as if in a dream. When I see a possibility, it is like a blinding light, like lightning. In my head, I say, "Why not a machine like this, or like that?" I become a thinking instrument. I guess at a concept, I formulate a theme. But the constructor is not free. Not as the poet is free. To realise a dream is the work of a team, like the birth of a superior mind. A new motor comes into the world with the cry of a newborn child; raw material is transformed into a living being with a voice of its own. Machines bear the marks of their makers' minds, but also of conviction, otherwise how to convince others that your dream is possible?'

It is clear why Ferrari once dallied with the idea of being a journalist. He had a love of words and imagery. Instead, as he later explained, poverty persuaded him to go into the car business, and to go racing. There, in the motor industry, he learnt to disregard all talk of misfortune and to accept the hard, pragmatic realities of sciences and race results. 'I think of myself as a promoter of ideas,' he said. 'My task? To explain an idea to those who must realise it; to argue until they find the right thread; to persist, keeping the thread in mind, until a solution comes. But I am a constructor. I remember all my errors. I think there is no such thing as luck. Ill luck is what we didn't know, or failed to foresee. In such collaborations there is an ascendant curve; its peak is a moment when this common effort works, its base when it breaks down. It's elite work, not made for most. Two of my oldest collaborators are ill. I put in young men. But as soon as young men acquire cultivation, they acquire personality. Will they then work together? It is my job to choose people. And then to give them total confidence.'

The language apart, if you close your eyes you can hear Jean Todt talking. Or, in a less profound fashion, Ross Brawn. The same grasp of realities, the same feet on the ground, the same suspicion of emotional interference, and the same disdain for all qualities other than the pure facts of racing. After Schumacher's historic 2002 season, Brawn denied that Ferrari were living in a fairy-tale where everything worked automatically to perfection, as if it was preordained by some kind of destiny. 'It is more a case of meticulous preparation,' he insisted. 'In Formula One, a lack of problems is not down to miracles or luck. There's no secret. Reliability is the key to winning. Our first objective at the Hungaroring was to win the constructors' title. We got it, and with the one-two finish Rubens has moved into second place in the drivers' championship. Now we are working on maintaining that position to the end of the season. It would be another wonderful result for Ferrari. We can do it, and Rubens' determination is the best weapon we have in that respect.'

How Enzo would have approved, for he was a manager of men, a team-builder. After talking about his poor family background in Modena where he received 'very little formal education', and after mentioning his self-acquired though modest erudition, he remarked, 'But I am surrounded by people who have more than I – that is my secret.' He argued that he was not, nor did he need to be, an engineer or a technician; instead, he was someone with a passion for cars, a man who knew enough about human beings to harmonise the ambitions of his colleagues. 'Aren't all conquests ultimately the consequences of superior and technical capacities?' he asked.

What Ferrari really loved were committed drivers. He was often seen as having scant regard for the men in his Ferrari cockpits, but that was more down to his resolute determination for them to win every race they were in and his absolute dismay when they did not achieve that sometimes impossible goal. Still, most of the drivers on his favourites list were Ferrari drivers. He told Botsford and anyone else about a few of them, including the one he respected the most – Stirling Moss. The list also featured Tazio Nuvolari, Gilles Villeneuve, Alberto Ascari, Mike Hawthorn, Phil Hill, Juan Manuel Fangio, the ill-fated Wolfgang Von Trips, Lorenzo Bandini, John Surtees, Chris Amon (one of his greatest favourites), Jackie Stewart, Mario Andretti, Jacky Ickx, Clay Regazzoni, Ronnie Peterson, Niki Lauda and Carlos Reutemann.

He revelled in talk of drivers because he identified himself with them. He said he could understand their problems because he had been one himself until his son was born, at which time he bowed to his wife's protests that he should give up racing and remain safe and out of danger. 'But,' he said, 'they are no longer of the race I knew. Today they are athletes who hire out their capacities for profit. They have been assimilated into their surroundings. The old drivers didn't risk their lives for nothing, but the sport came before the cash.' He went on to describe what he called 'the parabola of today's driver'. In this, he said a driver's objectives were, in order, to prove he is better than his team-mate, and then to prove that he is better than any other driver. 'To prove that, he has to extract economic and technical advantage from the constructor, and having obtained that, he reaches the top. He risks his life, yes, but it is a glamorous death he faces, and all racing drivers are volunteers. There is no justification for death, even in war, and we constructors have a responsibility, which is to determine the causes. These are seldom single. But man is presumptuous. No driver thinks he will be next. Not only that, each thinks he's too good to make the mistake his dead colleague made. They don't reflect. If they did, would they take unacceptable risks?'

Ferrari, of course, lived through the years when some saw Formula One as a kind of glamorised slaughterhouse. He witnessed, too, the work of Jackie Stewart and Louis Stanley in improving safety standards and reducing the death rate, but he was gone before the black weekend at Imola in 1994 when Ayrton Senna died and Michael Schumacher won a sad and hollow triumph in his absence. 'I've had dead drivers,' Ferrari said. 'They were psychologically in an anomalous state, or ambiguous about death. Drivers need quiet private lives; how to reconcile that with burning the candle at both ends? Egoism tells them, "Make a living, get rich, go out again, do not become a creature of regrets." That is the world today – one is first, or one is nothing. The modern world creates idols, which is cruel, when the intent is then to destroy them. Because today, the great hunger is for emotion. It is ego which rules us all.'

CHAPTER NINE

HOME FRONT III

*Sometimes when I look at him, I get a tremendously
deep feeling of happiness. I look at him and think,
'That's my husband.' It's a marvellous feeling.
Michael is so strong and so tender, so full of energy,
and so profound. He is a good man and a completely
devoted father. The four of us make a great team.*

Corinna Schumacher, talking about
her husband, Michael

'Corinna Betsch was born in Halver, Germany, in March 1969. A former office worker, she was a friend of Michael Schumacher from 1990. They married on August 1, 1995. They have two children: Gina Maria, born on February 20, 1997, and Mick, born on March 22, 1999.'

One bare factual paragraph. Of course, there is more information available, but it stands as something of a tribute to how well Corinna, Michael and their family have done in trying to keep their home life private. Corinna has not become public property. She does not give interviews. She is Michael's wife and that is as far as it goes. Close the door, leave her alone, and let her be. And to most of us that is right and proper.

Some of us have been fortunate enough to meet both Michael and Corinna through working in Formula One. They are a fine couple. It is easy to see that they are a very close pair. It is also easy to see that they have a happy, natural family life. Corinna, from the start, before she married Michael, was always a very easy-going girl. She had a good sense of humour, adding a light-hearted touch to the sometimes austere way in which Michael could behave when he was in racing mode. And she loved to sing and dance and party when he won a championship. But then, who can blame her for that? In truth, it may be that she deserves the glory and the money just as much as Michael. She has, after all, sat and suffered, her nerves no doubt doing their utmost to undermine her confidence, through each of his many races, not to mention test, practice and qualifying sessions. She was the one who had her heart in her mouth when he crashed at Silverstone in 1999. In *Schumacher – The Inside Story of the Formula One Icon*, Corinna revealed that she is almost as superstitious, or at least ritualistic, as her husband. 'When I am not at a race, I always go upstairs to my room at 13.10 to be on my own,' she said. 'I know that Michael is ready then. And at

13.15 exactly I ring him on his mobile. I always call to wish him luck, and it drives me crazy if I can't get hold of him. But this hardly ever happens, and if it does, he calls back. He knows that I have tried to speak to him.'

Theirs is an inspiring relationship that is an example to other people. No matter what is said or written about other aspects of the 'dream team', it is clear that in Corinna, Michael has a partner and friend who will never let him down. This stability, built on deep trust and mutual love, has given him the security to go out and race to win. He knows she is there, and she knows he is there too. The photographs in the *Schumacher* book show a tenderness in Schumacher that has not often been seen by the public, and in just a few words Corinna makes clear her feelings for him. What comes across most clearly is her utter commitment to him as a human being, her respect for him as a husband and father, and her faith in his total honesty. 'The wonderful thing is that nothing is too much for him,' she told Sabine Kehm. 'Never mind what, when or where – it's always OK. I have never heard him groan, roll his eyes, or say, "Later, no more now." Michael is a doer. He simply gets on with it, as if nothing creates difficulties for him. That is a great feeling. It gives you a sense of security to know that when he takes something in hand, it will get done. He'll manage it. Everything will soon be sorted out. I love that.'

She said that she could go to him with anything, and ask him anything. If there are certain things she is unsure about, she just talks them through with him, and somehow he always has an answer. Michael, she said, never assumes the role of the stronger sex. He always wants to hear her opinion, and if she finds things are getting on top of her, he just says, 'Calm down, I'll deal with it.' It is one of Michael's great strengths, she maintained – his willingness and ability to listen to another person's opinion. 'He accepts that in many areas other people know much more than he does,' Corinna added. 'And then he seeks out their opinion. He is interested in loads of things, particularly when he has never had much to do with something before and therefore knows next to nothing about it.'

Together, Michael and Corinna share a love of animals and nature. This is one of the main reasons why they chose to make their home in the green hills overlooking Lac Leman, near Geneva in Switzerland, where on their small estate near Gland they are able to enjoy a rural and carefree life. 'We're going to realise our dream of owning a farm,' Schumacher was quoted as saying in the Lausanne daily newspaper *Le Matin* in July 2002 after spending a reported $10 million on the 32-acre estate. The move, to their delight, meant that Corinna could ride her horses every day, Michael could take the dogs for long walks, and their children could explore the area in privacy. Having faced opposition in their original desire to move to an estate in German-speaking Switzerland, the decision to stay among francophones meant that Michael could also continue playing as a striker for local village team FC Aubonne, and then, after a switch of clubs, FC Echichens. Like most things, he treats it seriously. It is also one of the few things, apart from work or taking the children to school, that he accepts as a necessary reason for leaving home. For him, home and family are at the heart of everything.

It is impossible, of course, for Michael and Corinna Schumacher to live a totally undisturbed life. Since he won his first drivers' world championship with Benetton in 1994 he has been in the glare of the media spotlight. Their marriage, for example, just a few days after Michael won the 1995 German Grand Prix, was part of a scrambled week of publicity in which they were due to be united by civil ceremony in Kerpen-Mannheim while being besieged by media reporters. This was followed by a private wedding ceremony in the chapel of the German government's guesthouse at Petersburg in the hills above Bonn, a place chosen for its excellent security.

His mother Elisabeth's death, too, was turned into a public affair. Michael and Ralf were competing at Imola in the San Marino Grand Prix when she fell seriously ill and lapsed into a coma. That Saturday evening, after qualifying, they left the circuit in a Maserati coupé, drove to a helicopter landing pad, flew to Bologna airport and thence flew to Cologne, in Ralf's private jet, to be at their mother's bedside in hospital. It was a chance to pay their last respects. Early on Sunday morning she passed away, and fewer than twelve hours later, having returned to Italy, the brothers raced in the Grand Prix. Michael won the 65th victory of his career, but there was no leaping with joy and no champagne. It was a podium of grief. Michael wore a black armband around his fireproof overalls. 'My mother loved to watch us racing,' he said afterwards. 'Everybody in the team has given me the feeling on this terrible day of how much they back me.' Jean Todt had words for the occasion too. 'Michael has proved again, even to those who do not seem to accept it, that he is a special man,' he said. 'Despite being in mourning, he wanted to take part in this race for the sake of the team, and he wanted to win it. I think that as well as showing what he is as a driver, he showed what he is as a man.'

Another important incident in his life, long before either of these two, taught him something about his own mortality. It too was played out in the public domain, because as soon as it was over it was reported as a news story all over the world. It happened in early 1995 in Brazil, where he was acclimatising in readiness for the Grand Prix at São Paulo. He nearly died, but, for a racing driver, in a completely unexpected way. 'This,' he told *Sports Illustrated*, 'may tell you something about my character.'

Schumacher was scuba-diving off the coast with a crew whose ineptness he did not discover fully until it was almost too late. The crew absent-mindedly allowed the boat to drift while Schumacher and his companions were underwater. Willi Weber, who dislikes diving, and Corinna, who was seasick, remained on the boat and had no idea of the danger that was unfolding. Schumacher said that he and two other divers 'were down for 30 or 40 minutes with a diving teacher who wasn't thinking about the boat drifting away. So when we came up, the boat was gone. I looked around and finally saw it, far away on the horizon.' According to some sources, the waters were shark-infested – sometimes, at least. This detail may add drama, but it had no real part in the story as it unfolded. 'In the beginning, I tried to keep all of us together,' Schumacher continued. 'I said, "Come on, boys, hand by hand, let's swim in the direction of the boat." But after ten minutes, two of the guys were finished. They just couldn't go any further.' Thanks to his excellent physical condition, Schumacher knew he had to be the one to swim to the boat, if he could. 'I kept thinking, "You do one of the most dangerous sports and nothing happens to you, you're never afraid. Then suddenly you're in the water doing something that everybody does, and now you have the feeling." It was strange. It was the first time in my life I've thought, "That's it [for me]."'

Finally, when he was within 200 metres of the boat and screaming at the crew, which was enjoying some loud music, he was seen and he and the other divers were rescued. 'He wasn't exhausted, and he wasn't panicked, just very angry,' Weber recalled.

'That was the first time I have seen myself so very upset,' said Schumacher. 'I threw the goggles into the boat, and I was close to throwing the tank, but then I thought, "If you throw it wrong, we're going to have another disaster." So I cooled myself down. [People] say I am a machine and that I never get out of control, but that is my personality, to be under control in all situations.'

But sometimes, even for Michael Schumacher, there are times when he cannot control everything, including media coverage of his home life. His family and close friends rarely give interviews, but others do, even if they are modest affairs, and these can fuel all kinds of speculation about his life, private and public. It was for this reason, and some attractive tax arrangements, that he chose to leave Monte Carlo and live in Switzerland. That region of the country within reach of Geneva airport had long been favoured as a base by several motor racing and other sports and entertainment stars. 'My wife couldn't even go out to the supermarket without being pestered by fans,' Schumacher recalled. 'I had been told that Switzerland was the only place where celebrities can live without being bothered, and it's turned out to be perfectly true.'

Michael, Corinna and their children Gina Maria and Mick chose to live in a large, modern but in no way flamboyant house near the centre of a wine-growing village, Vufflens-le-Château, whose previous main claim to fame was an imposing castle and a well-known top-class restaurant. Schumacher established friendly relations with the villagers and with the municipality, which granted his request to construct a large covered garage for his car collection. He was so pleased with having obtained the planning permission, which he had suspected might be difficult to gain, that he offered to pay the 75,000 Swiss francs needed to create a games area near the local school. 'He heard about the project from his gardener and made a spontaneous gesture, which we accepted with pleasure,' said local official Fabienne Siegwart. 'It had nothing to do with a deal.' It earned Schumacher a place in local hearts, and, after his liking for a natural and open life, a nickname. In Vufflens, he became known as 'Schumi – le chouchou du village' (the village pet).

In Switzerland, Schumacher lived a normal life. According to *Swiss News*, he would often drive to the local pizzeria in a four-wheel-drive car, after telephoning ahead, to collect his favourite pizza, with spinach and onions. It became known as 'The Schumacher'. The fact that he loved Italian food spread though the district, and for pasta producer Raphael Giannini's Loretta label, that was fortunate. Giannini discovered that Schumacher loved his product, wrote to him, and received a reply offering to endorse his goods. As a result, the pasta featured in the Michael Schumacher Collection and reportedly enjoyed an 85 per cent sales rise in a year.

His enthusiasm for playing football, on the right side in attack, for FC Aubonne is well documented. He would fly home for training sessions from anywhere, whenever it was possible. His presence also increased the attendances for a small club that played in the Vaud cantonal third division. He once contributed five goals in one spell of fifteen matches, describing one he scored in a key encounter as 'better than winning a Grand Prix race'.

But in Switzerland, more than football, Italian food and friendships, it is probably the peace and anonymity he is afforded that he values the most. 'When I'm at home,' he explained once, 'I am back in a normal world, jumping on the trampoline with the kids and things like that. It helps me be balanced, and that's important.' To his neighbours, he is regarded as simple, shy, affable and polite, a man who is almost embarrassed by his celebrity. In 2001, it was reported, while

Schumacher was out riding his bike, he stopped to chat with another cyclist. The biker asked what he did for a living.

'I race cars,' Schumacher replied.

'What kind of cars?'

'Ferraris.'

'And what is your name?' continued the cyclist. When he heard the reply, the unimpressed biker responded, 'Well, I have to be on my way. Have a good day, Michael.'

Corinna met Schumacher for the first time when she was seventeen and dating another German racing driver, Heinz-Harald Frentzen, who later became one of Michael's major rivals in Formula One. They had split up some time before she took any serious interest in the man who became her husband. Schumacher made a romantic proposal to her in Monte Carlo and she accepted. She has always felt that their romance continued to burn brightly after they married. 'We sometimes laugh ourselves silly over nothing,' she said. 'It is like the way the smallest things can be funny for young lovers. It is still like that for us. It's crazy – we've known each other for half our lives. On a free weekend we will often get into the bath together and tell each other about our days. The wonderful thing with Michael is that everything is so harmonious. There is this link between us. We are always touching – it's automatic. For example, when we are eating we sit very close to each other. Sometimes I have to laugh because we are so close we can barely eat.'

Michael has said he knew he would marry Corinna from the moment their relationship began. 'I look at it as fate,' he said. 'I was sure about Corinna from the start. When she and Heinz-Harald split up, and we got together, I knew straight away that I would marry her. We both knew that you can only expect something of others if you are willing to give something yourself.' It is an ethos that has worked for them both, and it is the same ethos that has made Team Schumacher such a success.

CHAPTER TEN

LOYAL PARTNERS

Bridgestone has been an absolute intrinsic part of winning the championship and us being able to dominate in the way we have …

Ross Brawn, at a news briefing in July 2002

When Jackie Stewart, now Sir Jackie Stewart, was in his racing heyday, he made a point of cultivating very close relationships with his sponsors and his teams' technical partners. It was common sense. It meant that he stayed on good terms with Goodyear, for example, enjoyed a healthy relationship with Ford, and became an ambassador, after his driving career ended, for famous marques such as Rolex and Moët et Chandon. Stewart's example proved that multiple Formula One champions needed to enjoy loyal partnerships to sustain and make the most of their successes.

It has been just the same in Michael Schumacher's career. His business manager Willi Weber has done some sterling work in maintaining a fabulous portfolio of income streams from off-track sources, but it is the way in which Schumacher has made the most of his racing talent and work ethic to squeeze the best out of the technical partners who helped carry, power or fuel him and the Scuderia that has been the key to Team Schumacher's success. Just as with the people recruited to the team, the key word has been loyalty. And it has worked both ways.

For most prestigious companies, an opportunity to be associated with the red cars from the prancing horse stable has always been regarded as one to take – swiftly, if possible, and for as long as possible. That is why internationally significant brands such as Marlboro, Vodafone and Olympus have done their utmost to maintain excellent relations with the team. Ferrari carries them into international markets and gives them superb brand development opportunities. For the privilege, they pay substantially. It is not a cheap deal to be a sponsor at Ferrari. But on the track there are other factors at work, and companies such as the Japanese tyre suppliers Bridgestone and the fuel and lubricants giant Shell are deeply involved in assisting Ferrari and Michael Schumacher. Success is not the work of one man, or just a few from within Maranello; it is the product of a deep cooperation at all levels with many partners.

Central to Ferrari's title-winning years has been their relationship with Bridgestone. With its different mindset, the Japanese culture has often been a difficult one to intertwine with the European set-up at Maranello, as has happened in previous collaborations – Williams and Honda, for instance – in the past. But the team has been wise enough to realise that the relationship is a vital one, and has nurtured and developed it. Jean Todt's continual reference to his 'friends' at Bridgestone throughout a difficult 2005 season was not simply done as a public relations exercise, it was a genuine suggestion that together they stood and together they would remain.

Schumacher has always made time to develop ties with all his colleagues at Bridgestone, and for that he has earned the respect and friendship of the company's head of tyre development, Hirohide Hamashima. Their relationship stretches back into the distant past of Schumacher's career, way back to one day during a very brief spell in Japanese Formula 3000 racing, when he finished second at Sugo in his only outing. 'I first met him in Japan, at Sugo, in 1991, I think,' Hamashima recalls accurately. 'At that time he had no experience of a qualifying tyre, so he wanted to know how to use it. After the practice session he came to the Bridgestone garage and he was asking, asking, asking, for a very long time. But it was quite good because he knew who the right person was to ask about the tyres, and also he liked to make his own mind up about the tyres. The key point was how to use the tyre, but that was only the starting point for many, many practical points he asked me. After that he understood everything. He went back to his garage after about one and a half hours. At that time his team-mate Johnny

Herbert was already back in the city to maybe have some dinner or something, but not Michael!'

Hard work has always been a Schumacher trait, and so has curiosity. He wants to win, and he knows that with knowledge comes speed, and speed wins races. That is why he asks so many questions. 'He has always been very inquisitive, and that is one of his most important qualities,' Hamashima confirms. 'That and his work. He is always very motivated, through good and bad times. In 2003, though it was better than some recent times, it was not a good year for us. Of course he did not complain. He demanded a good specification from us, but he always took care of me. He said, "Hammy, you are a little bit bigger on the stomach because the stress makes you bigger, so be careful!" When we meet at the circuit he always asks about how the family are and so on. He is always very interested. He has a very good attitude and appreciates everyone. Last year [2004] he was very busy at the Belgian Grand Prix, but he came to our garage to express thanks and to give the championship to our people. Basically he is very, very kind, and he takes care of his team, his family and everything.'

To a suggestion that this concentrated, hard-listening Schumacher may be the possessor of a mind like a computer, there is no denial. 'Yes,' says Hamashima. 'And that is very useful. When he feels a lack of knowledge he finds the right person to ask the questions to, so that ability is very nice. When he attends technical meetings, with Ferrari and Bridgestone for example, he is quiet during the meeting, but after the meeting he will ask good questions. He asks the right people, he has a good ear, he is good at listening, and he also has an excellent ability to understand. And he always works so late. He is working night and day because his motivation never stops. Once, for example, when he was testing at Jerez, he had a question and he called me in Japan. He will do that any time – four o'clock in the morning, whenever – and that is no problem because we understand his attitude. He motivates everyone around him and pushes them to his level.' After so many years of doing this, surely Schumacher must be ready to design his own tyre? 'No, he is not at that level, but he gets enough knowledge to drive, and also if he feels a strange feeling from a new-concept tyre he will ask us. He has a professional level of knowledge about the tyre.' And that is Schumacher to a tee. He gains enough knowledge from whatever area to get his job done, no more, no less, because to learn more than you need is useless, a waste of energy, an overuse of storage space that could be used for a more beneficial purpose.

Schumacher's thirst for knowledge crops up in many conversations about what makes the man, and as someone who has known the German well through years of hard work, Hamashima has developed his own insights. He believes Schumacher finds his main job, driving, a relaxation compared to the work he puts in outside the cockpit. 'I think that maybe taking the interest in driving out of him would leave him highly stressed,' he says. 'Of course, he said that he likes to stay at his house with his family, so maybe that makes him relax, but also driving makes him relax too. When he is at the track he is there to work. Other drivers might go off and have a nice meal or whatever, but he loves working things out. He loves working, he loves to win.'

Away from the track, away from the areas that directly assist his pursuit of glory, Schumacher doesn't neglect his sponsors either. He works positively with them because he knows that doing so will make them more inclined to help him. Schumacher's willingness to support Bridgestone's commercial and marketing activities is unequalled. He shows the right kind of qualities, and never lets them down. 'For example, we always have a press meeting before the Japanese Grand Prix and he usually attends that meeting,' says Hamashima. 'Sometimes he tells the media about when he was driving as a young man. At that time, for example, a Bridgestone go-karting tyre was very expensive, but his grandfather bought it for him and he was very happy. He speaks very carefully and thinks about what he says with different people, and it makes the press very impressed.' According to Hamashima, the same attention to detail that has impressed race engineers for more than a decade is applied by Schumacher to the relationship between team and partner. 'I think he has great respect for our long-term partnership,' he continues. 'He is a professional. Sometimes his demands for a new-specification tyre are very difficult for the factory lead time, but once we have made a new specification and he has tried it and given us a good result, after that nobody can refuse his demands or his requirements! He respects our engineers too, like Kees van der Grindt – respects them and collaborates with them. Kees has been with him in Formula One since 1999, but their relationship together goes back much further than that. Sometimes I watch their discussions, and when they are speaking together they get on well. They respect each other, and that is excellent for us.'

The motorsport-mad Dutchman Kees van der Grindt joined Bridgestone in 1977 after leaving his first job in a go-kart factory in the centre of Holland. Karting was his first real love, and it remains a passion to this day. It drove him to the extreme lengths of jumping on a train to make the two-hour journey to work every day for six years. 'In Holland we didn't have any major racing industry apart from a kart factory,' van der Grindt recalls, 'so I started to work there as a schoolboy during holidays. I was eighteen, still studying, and I travelled every day by train in my spare time to the factory. You could just about survive financially, but that was not important because it was very good experience.' It also provided him with the opportunity to meet a young German named Schumacher, and begin a relationship that now sees him working as Schumacher's tyre engineer in Formula One.

It wasn't too long after learning his trade in karting before van der Grindt's ambitions took hold and he started looking to take his skills to a higher level. 'Tyres were already of some interest to me,' he explains, 'and I had some background from my studies, so I wrote a letter to two major tyre companies about karting, and Bridgestone was the one who replied. Suddenly, two Japanese people interviewed me. It was quite an experience to get to know people from another culture.' Van der Grindt worked his way through the ranks at Bridgestone, and was involved in Formula Three, DTM and Le Mans projects. He was paired with Ferrari when their tyre company, Goodyear, quit Formula One at the end of the 1998 season, leaving Bridgestone as the only supplier of rubber in Grand Prix racing. But it was not until he was reunited with Schumacher – van der Grindt is now solely responsible for the world champion's tyres – that he achieved his ultimate aim. With tyres playing an ever-increasing role in the make-up of a successful team, it was vital that their partnership flourished. It did, and the Dutchman became a crucial part of Schumacher's multi-person world championship-winning collaboration.

'During the race weekend I am the one who is probably closest to Ferrari and the cars when they are running,' he says of his role. 'My job is to collect as much data as possible to be able to answer all of their questions. If everything is going well there are maybe no questions, but I need to collect as much data as possible because I need to be prepared to give advice.' He shares Ross Brawn's view that the engineering side of any Formula One team should be departmentalised, with each section responsible for its own products, so as not to allow important decisions to be made without expertise. Brawn's role as the man who oversees the departments and integrates them in a non-confusing way is, van der Grindt feels, a major reason behind the success of Bridgestone's partnership with Ferrari, and therefore, of course, with Team Schumacher. 'In my position it is important to have a good idea of everything,' he continues. 'It is important to understand the car as well as the tyres, but in Bridgestone we have specialists who have much more knowledge about their areas than I have. This is what Hirohide Hamashima calls "Bridgestone Power". We are very strong in that. Bridgestone knows how to use the people in the right position. There is no point having a guy who is an expert in chemicals being involved in chassis set-up, but in order to develop compounds he does need to know the requirements. I would say in my case it is more all-round knowledge and less specialised.'

Bridgestone's work was central to Ferrari's successful run between 1999 and 2004, and it is a relationship the Italian team has worked hard at. Their strategy was simple. Why should the team share any of the parts that make it so successful? Not content with having the fastest car on the grid, they wanted the fastest package, and to do that they could not share any one of its components. Team Schumacher was an exclusive club, and Bridgestone had to be part of that. Ferrari worked hard to steer Bridgestone into that mindset, impressing on them the importance of designing a car to fit a tyre, and vice versa. To do that, the tyre manufacturer needs focus; so long as they were supplying other teams, there was bound to be a loss of that focus. Eventually, team by team, Ferrari's rivals defected to a rival brand until ultimately they were left with exactly what they wanted – a virtually exclusive relationship. By the 2003 season they were sharing tyres only with backmarkers Jordan and Minardi, mid-grid runner Sauber, to whom Ferrari also supplied engines and with whom they enjoyed a special relationship, and BAR-Honda, who were their biggest threat among the Bridgestone runners. By 2004, however, BAR had defected, and when Bridgestone got it right, Ferrari's rivals were left far away in the distance.

'What we have achieved with Ferrari and Schumacher is amazing, and one of the most impressive years was 2004,' says van der Grindt, recalling the utter dominance that followed a tough season in 2003. 'It was good not because we won again, but because it was a great achievement after realising some of our weaknesses in 2003. That year we had to fight very hard to win the championship, but we were very happy about the confidence Ferrari, and the drivers of Ferrari, had in our capability to improve. They gave us the confidence, and we improved, which was a big reward. When we saw the quick lap times of all our competitors in the winter testing we had to keep that confidence in ourselves and think, "Look, with one quick lap you are not going to win a race. You need quick and consistent lap times." When we got to the February [2004] Imola test where everything came together, we were suddenly extremely competitive. We thought we could look to the future with some confidence and were sure we would win some races. After the races in hot conditions in Sepang and Bahrain [in March and early April], then we could say not only in theory but also in practice that we had done a good job. What was a little bit surprising was that the gap between us and the opposition was much bigger than expected. But we always look to ourselves, rather than our rivals, to measure our performance. Our target is always to win the next race. Hiroshi Yasakawa [who had begun the company's motorsport activities outside Japan] always says the next race is very important because you are only as good as the last race. But other people also want to win, so there is a fight. We want to win the first race, the second race, the third race. It would be wrong if that was not the target and we said, "OK, now we have won twelve or whatever, that's enough." No way.'

Van der Grindt embodies this Bridgestone attitude, which itself betrays the Ferrari influence. Every word seems to reveal his competitive streak, and his sentiments could have been uttered by any one of Schumacher's inner sanctum at Ferrari. He does not, however, seem as inclined to heap praise on Schumacher as some others, perhaps because he understands and appreciates the idea of Team Schumacher more than other partners who are or have been as closely involved as he. 'If you have the best driver, the best car and the best tyres,' says the Dutchman, simply, 'I think you just add them together and you win.'

Team Schumacher has also benefited from its relationship with Shell, which again enjoys an exclusive Formula One relationship with the Italian team. Shell has always been one of the companies most keen on maximising Grand Prix racing's opportunities for product development and extreme testing, as well as for its numerous advantages on the promotional and public relations side. Again, Schumacher has recognised that if he provides what the supplier requires, they will provide him with what he requires, which in Shell's case was a refined, ultra-powerful fuel designed within the FIA's stringent regulations and constantly being developed to provide more performance and improved reliability.

Because of this good relationship, it was a wrench for Shell's F1 director of communications from 2001 until 2005, Peter Secchi, when he fulfilled a boyhood dream and tore himself away from Ferrari to take up a media post at English professional football club Tottenham Hotspur. His experiences with Schumacher reflect the astonishing degree of professionalism and dedication that have been part and parcel of the German's dominance from the earliest days of his career, and they once again show that when Schumacher puts his mind to something, be it for his wife Corinna, his family, his friends or his team's sponsors, he does it to the best of his ability. Always.

'I first met Michael in 2001 when I joined Shell's PR department, having come from a background in touring cars and rallying,' recalls Secchi. 'The first time I met him was at a photo-shoot at Mugello, in Italy, for Shell, in February 2001. It was a really cold day, and pretty dark by that time. The team had been testing all day, since about eight in the morning. You could even see the lights from the steering wheel reflecting off the drivers' visors. When they got to the end of the day, we had to do the shoot. Shell wanted all sorts of poses: we wanted Michael filling his car up at the petrol pump, Michael holding oil cans – all that kind of stuff. Michael came bouncing over to us, looking fresher than any of the camera crew, and that was despite the fact that he'd just driven round and round the track for the last ten hours. He was incredibly professional during the shoot: you only had to tell him to do something once and he would do it. That attitude he showed then, on that day, didn't change at all, not once, right up to the day when I left Shell after the Monaco Grand Prix in 2005.'

Ask any sponsor who has required Schumacher to cooperate in a promotional or marketing project and the same comment is always made. Contrary to some perceptions, created inaccurately by people without close knowledge of how he works, he has no problems at all in handling that part of the business. 'Someone once told me that the trick with Michael was simply to tell him exactly what you wanted beforehand, over a bottle of water or something, and he would do it,' says Secchi. 'And that's exactly what happened all the time. I don't know if it's a typically German thing to be so efficient because I've never worked with any other Germans, but he certainly does fit the popular stereotype, if you like. In fact, it gets to the stage where you work with him and you wonder if he's really human after all! He's the best driver, he's super fit, he's an excellent footballer – he's always the first one out with a football in the paddock during breaks in testing – he talks well to the media, he has a gorgeous wife and a lovely family, and he's an absolutely brilliant bloke too. You think, "Come on, mate, you must have a flaw there somewhere." But no! OK, he had the odd mullet haircut in his younger days, and he's worn some dodgy shirts in his time, but that's about it.'

All those aspects that Secchi described underlie Schumacher's phenomenal ability to deliver with consistent professionalism both on and off the track. In terms of his status as a racing driver, he is the ultimate competitor, a man who combines the inherent skill to control a racing car on the outer limits of its performance with sufficient technical sympathy and intuition to make a major contribution to its evolution and development across a season. This is supported, of course, by his understanding that for him to succeed he needs the support of everyone around him, from mechanics, engineers and technicians to sponsors' representatives, catering staff and management. He gives them all his time. They are all part of his team. That is why, when called upon to give a service on behalf of a sponsor, he responds with 100 per cent commitment, as he has always done throughout his career. He was brought up that way, and he believes in it. And it has paid off handsomely for him.

'I don't think it's really fair to say that he works harder than other drivers do on all sides of the job,' Secchi continues, 'but you do hear the stories about Michael. For instance, I heard that he did a test around Imola for a whole day, with a public relations appointment during his lunch break, and then he ended the day by running two laps of the track just to keep up his fitness levels. And, like everyone else I am sure, I can't say he ever turned up late for a media call, or any other event that he had with us. The thing with Michael is that there are very rarely any surprises. If he says he'll be at a certain spot at a certain time, you know he'll be there. If he ever does surprise you, it will be in a good way. I got so used to seeing groups of kids hanging around track entrances looking for autographs and having to say to them, "Sorry, guys, not today because we have a press call or a meeting we are already running late for." But Michael is not like that. If he sees them, he'll quite often say, "Come on, Peter, just five more minutes," and he'll go and talk to them. It really makes their day. Small things like that make such a difference.'

And it is not only the fans with whom Schumacher has shown his natural touch for communication. He also brings it with him into his job on an everyday basis. 'Shell has an on-site laboratory at every test,' Secchi explains, 'and at every race Ferrari go to. Often, after a race, he'd stick his head into the tent and just say something like "cheers" or "hard luck, guys" or something like that. He also comes down just to say hi sometimes. He learns everybody's name too. Maybe it's his intention, or maybe he's just good at remembering names, but he learns them. I know there wasn't a single person there who wasn't star-struck during their first meeting Michael. It's hard work in an F1 paddock, and absolutely everyone involved with Ferrari, Shell and Bridgestone, and all the other teams too, work flat out all the time, but having Michael do things like that makes it so much easier to work hard because you know that he appreciates it. He shows it more than some other drivers might.'

It is easy to see that in his support for technical partners, Schumacher has lifted the 'game' to a new level. As he did with fitness, preparation and work ethic, he set a new standard. There are few drivers who can claim to match him. But of course those same suppliers were expected to rise to the occasion. 'It was a huge move when Shell joined up with Ferrari for 1996,' says Secchi. 'And it became even bigger and better when Michael joined too. I was shocked when I found out how much work Shell put in for technical development, rather than for the brand association and the logos. But it was all because Ferrari put so much pressure on them to do it. Jean Todt is an extremely tough man to have to answer to because he sets his standards so high, but I guess that's why the team is so successful. They just keep demanding improvements all the time. But it's worth it, because when you have success you savour it more because you worked harder for it.'

In his years with Shell and Ferrari, Secchi had an opportunity to see, from the inside, how the Scuderia and its 'dream team' worked and rose to the challenges laid before them each year. 'It's not just a Ferrari team really,' he says. 'All the major technical partners are integrated together. It was really difficult when I started because the Ferrari people at Maranello don't just say, "Come in, you're wearing red" – you have to really earn their trust. That's something Jean Todt is particularly fussy about. He thinks you have to earn trust before you can be let in to their circle. Of course, you're privy to some seriously confidential technical stuff and they have to know you aren't going to blab about it outside. Once you're in, though, and you've gained that trust, it's a great place to work, and it can be astonishing the kind of things you are given access too. When Michael took his seventh drivers' title in Spa in 2004, we had a massive party in the team hotel. It was behind closed doors, of course, but it wasn't just Ferrari, it was Bridgestone, Shell, all of us. There is such a team atmosphere at Ferrari. I don't know if it's built around Michael, but you can see the support he gets and the support he gives. If something breaks and you have a bad race, you never hear Michael, or anyone in the team, say to the press, "It was Bridgestone's fault – their tyre blew" or "It's Shell's fault – the fuel wasn't right". Compare that to the culture at Williams between them and BMW, where it seems there is always someone pointing the finger ...'

When Luca Badoer pounds around the testing tracks of Fiorano or Mugello, his consistency and reliability are also a vital part of team development. The Italian, who failed to live up to the promise many felt he possessed as 1992 International Formula 3000 Champion, became Ferrari's test driver in 1997, replacing Nicola Larini, who had grasped his chance of a return to a Grand Prix race seat with the Sauber team with both hands.

After a Grand Prix career that took in three under-funded Italian teams – Scuderia Italia, Minardi and Forti Corse – Badoer decided to take on the role at Maranello in a bid to rebuild his reputation. It was a role he would have been looking to fill for a couple of years at most before working his way back on to the Grand Prix grid, much the same way as Larini had before him. But that never really happened, and it never really happened because Badoer knew that where he was was better than anywhere he could go. When Schumacher broke his right leg at the British Grand Prix in 1999 Ferrari elected to put unemployed Finn Mika Salo in the hot seat rather than Badoer, who had by that time achieved his goal of returning to racing but was deemed such an important part of the Ferrari group that he had to combine a Minardi race seat with his test role at Ferrari. Since then, he has never left.

Badoer has used the inspiration of Schumacher to knuckle down and increase his stock within the team, and he admits that his attitude, indeed his technical aptitude, is largely down to the influence the German has had on the team. 'Working alongside Schumacher,' he says, 'I have learnt so much from a technical point of view, and about his mentality and application to the job. The secret of his success? He's a little bit better than the rest in every area. In races, it's crazy. No one can manage three hundred kilometres at qualifying pace the way Michael can.'

Badoer thinks that the constant striving for self-improvement is typical of the current Ferrari set-up, and he attributes some of that to Schumacher, even though it's highly unusual for a driver, who is after all subordinate in rank to the team boss, senior engineers and designers, to be the one who inspires a team to follow in his mould. Badoer thinks the team has benefited as a result, and that now there is a 'perfect' working environment at Ferrari, with the right people heading up the right departments and everyone working together to achieve common goals. 'When I'm asked to define Ferrari, all I can say is that it is the perfect team and the perfect company,' he says. 'During testing, the atmosphere is always very professional. Win or lose, it

CHAPTER ELEVEN

AMICI DEPORTIVI

That's what I love so much about Ferrari:
the warmth of the people connected to the team.
This is not purely a working relationship.
It's like coming to visit friends.

Michael Schumacher on life with the Scuderia

Footballer, Formula One driver and family man, though not in that order – these are just some of the parts that make up the whole of Michael Schumacher. But he is not just a Formula One driver, he is a Ferrari racing driver. He is also a sportsman, a motivator and a full-time, paid-up member of the fun club at the team – but only when the work is over. At Ferrari, before Schumacher, there were as many media leaks as holes in a colander. There was a lack of discipline, and a fraternity that was growing stale through misuse. The new Ferrari, fired by the dream team, is a different beast. Discipline and order are taken for granted, and the fraternity is vibrant. The family is smiling. It really is like working with friends.

To discover how this happened, and what part Michael Schumacher himself played, meant a visit to the office of the team's sporting director, Stefano Domenicali, a man much the same age as Schumacher, a friend and a colleague, and someone who has grown through the same experiences in the same timeframe at Maranello. He was charming, fluent in English, happy to talk. 'In 1995,' he begins, 'when we first met Michael, we were pretty sure about getting a great driver – a great, talented driver. It was unusual for a guy at that age to show that he was not only the number one in terms of success but also from the technical point of view, not only on the track but also in the way he was preparing the car: from a set-up point of view, preparation and use of the tyre, from the point of view of the behaviour of the car. Also in the way that he was able to handle racing with all the pressures that are on the shoulders of the racing driver. That was, for sure, already clear. He was a guy who was able to listen and to understand the people who were around.

'Still, he was a little bit closed in the beginning. Maybe he was different in approach because he is a German. He took a slow first impression of our Italian environment, even if we already saw ourselves as a multi-cultural and multi-language team. It was his way. And maybe this kind of approach, like a teacher who may have come into this different world to teach, was just something we got from first impressions. But as things progressed, he was able to understand and to integrate with the people he was working with. Of course, it's a learning-curve approach. When you work and live with a group of people, then you start to understand and rely on the people around you. It is the same for us all, and the more you live together, the more you understand. Maybe that is the reason why he came in here with a certain air of responsibility.'

That is part of the Schumacher persona. Already by the mid-1990s a double world champion, he was aware of his worth to the team but also aware of the importance of the team around him. Like any newcomer in a new job, it took him time to work out who he liked and who he didn't like, who would be key to his success and who would be less important, or not even a factor in the team's future. He soon worked out who his main allies and his main men were. 'Michael was really good at understanding the people who were around him,' says Domenicali. 'He knew they were good people – a little different of course, but good – and he was able to catch little bits and pieces from everyone. Being Michael Schumacher and racing with Ferrari meant he not only had to be able to drive but he had to do all the other jobs too.'

It had been the same at Benetton – less so, but the same idea. He had to learn the Ferrari way, and at the same time develop with the world of Formula One, a sport that was at the time going through a significant step change, from what was still effectively a gentlemen's race series to one dominated by major motor manufacturers and all the corporate associations such businesses brought with them. Demands from sponsors increased, professionalism grew, and Schumacher now had to be a perfect PR man as well as proficient in the technical side of the job. He also, of course, had to drive fast. But that came naturally. 'When he first came here it was a lot to think about,' Domenicali sympathises, 'but I would say now that Michael is a very mature person who can manage himself, and he is a real professional in the Formula One world. He is professional with the media, with everything. Maybe in the old days a driver would perhaps only concentrate on driving. Full stop. But now the life of a driver like Michael is very complex. It's full of meetings, full of engagements with sponsors, and full of activity.

'I could clearly see that in that first year of working together and living together he grew and changed a lot. This was because it was his intention. A person who is not intent is not able to change his mind and change his approach when he's living different experiences. Certainly what I can say after living with him in that way is that our personal relationship has grown year by year. I would say that he completely relies on me on the things I am responsible for. If I say something, he understands it 100 per cent. Of course, sometimes we have to discuss things, but that's part of the game. You become authoritative because of what you're doing, the skills you have. People around Michael know that he deserves his position. It has nothing to do with anything else. It is not because of a gamble, or racing lines, or racing strategy. It is his authority. This is something he has earned, and it is something that I've noticed.'

Given his experience and position, Domenicali is well placed to discern if Michael Schumacher had a more profound effect on Ferrari than the other way round. In other words, in the team's evolution from also-rans to champions, was Team Schumacher's influence the decisive factor, or Scuderia

Ferrari's? 'I would say that both changed, but not one more than the other,' he says, delivering a straight, unequivocal answer. Perfectly politically correct. 'Where Ferrari were when Michael joined us, we had already decided to move, to change the organisation of the team. It was already something that was decided. I'm sure that Michael helped the organisation to change in a certain way, in terms of methods and the technical approach to the business of racing, but it was really the team that was able to create the success [pre-1996]. The way of working at Ferrari changed when our president Luca di Montezemolo made Jean Todt responsible [in 1993], and then we created the group of people who have been in certain positions for some years. We should remember that the people who were in charge when the first choices were made to restructure the management and steer this group of people in a certain direction, they are still here now. Luca is the man. We have to be very grateful to our president. Not just in Formula One, but also in terms of the industry side of the company. So we had already defined what it would take for us to be a winning team, though for sure Schumacher was an essential element of this puzzle.

'There are certain things you can have a feeling for when you live with a certain person. Apart from the fact that he has become more experienced in racing, and that's part of the normal nature of his life, Michael also proved that he knew the proper way to integrate with Scuderia Marlboro Ferrari. That is to his credit, I think. It is a real credit to him, because he was ready to understand the best way to integrate with our team – and not all drivers are like that.' In short, Schumacher was prepared to invest more in personal relationships within the team than others might have done before him – the 100 per cent commitment in all areas theme again. 'Yes, Michael is very good at all this,' confirms Domenicali. 'Michael really understood the needs of the Italians who worked with him. We need to create an important link between the personal stuff and working together – it's an Italian characteristic – and Michael was very good at that. He knows, for example, that my family is very important to me, and he knows how to create a personal link to use to speak to me about those things.

'We play football together because we know that it's a great way to create a group feeling – and, of course, we enjoy it as well. We want to play together every weekend. We do something on Thursday evening usually, because we go out together with Michael. We play football. We just have fun, though we protect him. Our number one rule is "no tackles" – we don't want his career destroyed. He gets frustrated he has to do more running than us, but he's a good athlete. We can say, "Michael, run up and down because it's good training for you!" And he loves it. A team is created this way, not by speaking only about Formula One. It means we can go out together, we can stay together, we know each other, and this is very important.' Though such sporting activity has worked for Schumacher as a means of bonding with the men in the team, it has not been the same for Rubens Barrichello, despite the fact that the Brazilian's father was once on the books for Santos at a time when the great Pele was there. 'He doesn't care so much. He is not really so interested, but Michael is always playing with us on Thursdays. Michael passes, tackles and runs. When we have these moments when we are all together, you can create something, not only because you enjoy yourself, but because you can start discussing a lot of other things from it. But you have to know how to do it. You know, we, as people, have a different relationship among ourselves to other teams.

'Michael has a high work rate in everything. We are not just talking about setting up the car or technical stuff or business, but just relaxing. Knowing each other, year by year, we discover these kinds of things, and with Italian guys this is very good. And I must say that Michael always thanks his guys, so they are always grateful to him. He is very open. He always gives everyone a gift at the end of the season to say thank you for his hard work. This, too, is something that creates the right atmosphere to work together. In this way, Schumacher is really a part of the team, and he knows how to lead the team in that respect.' This is a portrait of the man that would come as no surprise to graphologist Andreas Franz, who once discerned in the 'thick, rather than thin' signature of the champion 'human warmth and generosity'. But, Domenicali goes on to point out, while the team appears to revolve around Schumacher and his many talents, it is not only concerned with him. The other driver in the team, he insists, is also very important, not only for points-scoring but also for team spirit. 'Michael is a very, very important member of our team, no doubt at all,' he says, 'but it's part of our job to help the other driver too, so that he is merging well within the team project. Otherwise you'll destroy the team.'

Still, the Schumacher factor at Ferrari is so influential that it is difficult to measure the strength of the rest of the operation without him. One way would be to imagine seasons 2001 to 2004, the ones that followed the team's first double in 2000, being contested without Schumacher, as if he had retired. 'It is difficult to say what would have happened,' muses Domenicali. 'Who knows? It's hard to say whether or not we would have won those titles. To say we would have been a winning team or not a winning team is very difficult. All I can be sure of is that if Michael had gone, then we'd have lost a very important member of our team.'

Not only is he important, he is inspiring. Stories abound about Schumacher's punctuality, discipline and organisational skills.

While men in Domenicali's position at other teams have been known at times to go grey with worry at the lateness of their drivers, particularly for early-morning calls, Domenicali claims he has not once had to make a phone call to remind Schumacher to wake up. One famous story, from his early days at Ferrari, concerned the example he set in the mornings. At the team's first pre-season test at Estoril, he was at the circuit long before the mechanics and was in fact sitting waiting when the catering staff arrived. 'If you want to win world championships, you have to get up in the mornings,' was his first explanatory comment to those team members more used to an easier routine. 'When he is on the job, he is really on it, and we learnt a lot from him,' Domenicali admits. 'But I don't really want to say it like that because it implies that we are lazy, and that's not true. We are very professional. We always plan something at least the evening before. We discuss it, and then we do it. But I can guarantee you 100 per cent that Michael has never been late for a morning meeting, and for me that's incredible.'

It is an insatiable appetite for work that drives Schumacher day in, day out, be it testing, racing, PR days, or even days at home with his family. Moreover, to him, time is precious. 'We have nineteen Grands Prix and Michael is travelling, he's moving, but he wants to test, he wants always to be there,' says Domenicali. 'I think being a champion is in his DNA – his body belongs to the car! He doesn't want to stay out of the car too much because that's his job, and that's how he likes to work. This, again, is incredible, I have to say. If you take other drivers, I would say that no one is like him in that respect.'

Does this legendary professionalism extend to learning Italian? Domenicali dismissed the belief that Schumacher has not picked up the language, despite ten seasons racing for an Italian team. 'It's not true, not at all,' he protests. 'Some people accuse him of that and say, "Why do you not speak Italian?" But, unfortunately, the rest of the team doesn't necessarily speak Italian either, so that's just something that is part of our environment. We are international, and English is the first language in the team, so we are used to it. He speaks Italian with the Italian mechanics. Of course he's not fluent, but it's good enough to speak with the mechanics. He is so professional that when he wants to speak with someone in a formal way he doesn't want to show any form of weakness. When he speaks in Italian he gets a bit lost sometimes, but he understands.'

Having made friends with the German through work, football and fun, Domenicali has learnt to appreciate the Michael Schumacher the world does not usually see. He believes, too, that their friendship will survive when Schumacher is no longer racing for Ferrari. 'I'm pretty sure it will be like that,' he says. 'We have known each other for so many years and we have such a strong relationship that I'm 99.9 per cent certain we will stay friends. Nobody can be 100 per cent sure of anything.' In spite of their close friendship, Domenicali has never been a visitor to the Schumacher home in Switzerland, though he did stay with him at his apartment in Monte Carlo one year during the Monaco Grand Prix. Again, this is all part of Schumacher's life-sectioning, intended to keep his private life as private as possible and his public life focused on the specific job in hand. 'That's something I like very much,' Domenicali insists. 'I am really 100 per cent one of the first supporters of this, because for me, in this business, it's important to keep the two things separate. We have personal lives. Full stop. He knows that the media and everyone is interested in his personal life, but that's just part of our world. I like the person who is able to keep the two things separate. It is what I like to do myself. He has a way of seeing things that is very different from many people in Formula One. I think it's the way he creates energy for himself, and others. Keeping it all separate is part of his life. I think if he chooses to talk about his family in public, then fine, but it should be his choice. He should not be pressured into it. We often speak about our families, but privately, and that's very good.'

A typically passionate Italian, Domenicali was virtually born to be the sporting director of the Ferrari team. His early life, it seems, was designed to take him to Maranello. 'I was born in Imola,' he says, 'and they say that if you are born there, you smell the fuel when you come out of your mother! So I could not escape from motor racing. And during the first year of my studies I used to go to the track at the weekends to work the whole weekend of the racing. I used to help the organisers in the paddock, or in the media centre, or wherever. Then, when I graduated from the University of Bologna, in business administration and economics, I sent a CV to Ferrari, as it was always something you did in the business environment.

'I was called here, and my first job was to be responsible for the fiscal administration business. During the same period I had my licence to be the clerk of the course at Mugello, the track owned by Ferrari, so since 1991 I have worked for the race team. From 1992 to 1994 I was the race director at Mugello, so I did MotoGP, DTM, all the international races. I started to get some experience in the racing world. Then I was moved, so I was responsible for cost control here. Then, step by step, I was in control of human resources and sponsors, and then I became sporting director. I ran the organisation – human resources, budget control, finance, sporting regulations, logistics and the track. It is a lot of work, but my family respects the job I'm doing. It's difficult because a lot of the time you're out of the home, but they know that this is part of my life and they respect it. Sometimes you have to compromise, because when you are living with a person who has a baby you want to stay more with them.'

Like most people at Ferrari, the idea of working for any other team rarely, if ever, enters Domenicali's head. If he was offered a job at Minardi, on better pay, he would not go. 'I am not a person who is doing a job and wants to do other experiences as well. That's a personal choice. So, for me, it's Ferrari and only Ferrari. It's something on which I'm completely clear in my own mind, even if the market is interested. I believe it's a personal decision that if I have to work in Formula One, I cannot ask for more than Ferrari – even if a Roman Abramovich or someone else came in and offered me three times my money.' This feeling of loyalty, almost as if an Italian oath had tied them to the team, is common at Ferrari, and it's unforgiving. Domenicali admitted he found it difficult to explain. 'It's something about the Ferrari myth,' he says. 'When I joined Ferrari, it was a very difficult period. They were losing every single race. It was like betting on a horse with three legs. But it's something that is part of the myth; it's around this company. It's difficult to explain because you may say that you could go to McLaren for more money and a different environment. Personally, it's emotional to me, and I would say no. I'm not interested. But I don't have a completely rational answer for this question. It's something irrational, because it has to do with far more than Ferrari's working environment.'

The cynical mind immediately senses a bit of pride, perhaps a touch of arrogance. It is, after all, easy to say you want to stay with a team that is winning all the time. But, as we have seen, at Ferrari this loyalty seems genuine and profound, as became clear when Domenicali was reflecting on the golden moments of the current era. 'The most important thing is the sum of it all,' he says. 'In a sport, no one has won so often and in such a consequential period of time as we have won in these years. So, certainly, it's something that is part of me. That is for sure the first big thing. The second one is that even if we won many things in the last six, seven, eight years, the motivation of winning again is always very strong at Ferrari. Of course there are certain races or certain moments that are in my mind because of certain factors, both negative and positive. This is just part of the memory stock that everyone has in his mind. I think it is fantastic to be with the people who work with me in this company.'

Understandably, Domenicali is a particular fan of both Schumacher and Todt. 'This is a serious job,' he says. 'The problem is that in this environment you see so many different angles, from everywhere, from inside and from outside. You have to be functional about it. If you can't be this way, then you have to be mathematical. If you don't elaborate when you put things in order, then your priorities are lost, and you run the risk of forgetting a lot of things. This is the approach we have to use in this work. Always remember what you are doing, why you are doing it, and if there is something urgent, do it straight away.' And at Ferrari, if there is one man who can deliver fast results on cue, it must be Michael Schumacher. 'If you ask him to do the next five laps in 1:23, then he will, and this is incredible,' Domenicali continues. 'Only if you are a driver, or a sportsman who understands just what a tenth of a second is, can you appreciate seeing a driver on the same time for five laps, ten laps, an hour. It seems easy from the outside, but if you convert those tenths into centimetres on the track, you can begin to understand how difficult it is to be so consistent. And now the car is full of sensors, so if you're speed goes down you can't just say that something is wrong, as some drivers used to, because it would show up on the data. Add in that speed on the track –

because we're not talking about cruising, we're talking about Michael on the limit – the degradation of the tyre, and other external things that may affect your performance … Well, for me, his consistency is something that is not human.' Clearly, though, Michael Schumacher is a warm human being. This is why he has friends and has created such loyalty and support around him within his team.

In this high-technology age, some have suggested that it is easier for the drivers, that they are not much more than mere chauffeurs at the wheel of a vehicle controlled by machines. But this demeans all drivers, past and present. In Domenicali's view, despite all of the devices available, Schumacher has proved himself. 'You could say that Senna's death pushed Michael to glory, but Michael could have beaten him,' he insists. 'That was the old era, and Michael is the most technological of all the drivers. He knows how to use what's around him to go faster and faster and faster. Formula One is full of telemetry data, and he is interested in it because it's part of what he needs. He learns so well too. He would make a good fighter pilot.'

Learning is what it was all about in his early years with Ferrari, and not just in terms of settling in with the team and creating an effective working environment. For a sporting hero, Schumacher has not always had an easy ride with the media, and after the European Grand Prix at Jerez in 1997 in particular, he suffered a serious image problem. Critics with longer memories added other incidents to that one with Villeneuve, including his 1994 title-clinching race at Adelaide in the Australian Grand Prix where a controversial collision with Damon Hill was decisive. Their conclusion was that, at times, Schumacher was a cynical and over-aggressive driver. 'If we go back, he had a couple of occasions during a long career, and I think that he has learnt from them,' says Domenicali, defending his man. 'But once again we are talking about a proportion that is so small in terms of what he did overall. I think that every aspect of his career, including the negative bits, has an explanation. For sure it starts with the fact that when he's racing he wants to win. Sometimes he's unable to control the stress that surrounds himself, and sometimes he will make a mistake, as he did in Jerez. He was so close to the achievement, so close to giving Ferrari success after they had waited so long to win a title, that he felt frustrated, especially as the tyre was not performing well. Then you get desperate. That was the situation he was in, but he has learnt from it.

'I think that when he was with Benetton, it was a different part of his career,' Domenicali muses. 'He was in a period where he wanted to show he had that kind of grit a brave driver has. Not in a negative way, but you want to show something because a driver sees his business as a bit special. When you pull down your visor, as a driver you are selfish, even if it's with your brother or son. By nature, every driver wants to win awards to show the others that he's the number one. You can be number one not only because you have the talent, but also because you can show the others that you are more offensive, or you can keep the throttle on a little bit longer than the others. It's something that's a part of all drivers.'

Schumacher's capacity for all kinds of work, as we have seen, is phenomenal, and at Ferrari he did indeed work hard to recover from these setbacks and regain the kind of popular image he once enjoyed in his earliest days in Formula One. Domenicali agrees, somewhat surprisingly, that Schumacher has shown himself to be a bad loser, but does not believe that it is a part of his character, only a by-product of frustration in specific, highly stressed circumstances. 'I would say that maybe he was a bad loser many, many years ago, and now he doesn't

CHAPTER TWELVE

ON THE BENCH

*We had to prove to him that Ferrari could
provide success, so I have to say all the team
was working for Michael.*

Ferrari race engineer Luca Baldisserri

Like any man involved in a team sport as an outstanding individual, Schumacher is only as strong as the weakest link in his side. Since he first burst on to the Formula One scene at Spa-Francorchamps in 1991, he has improved his performances every season and built up Team Schumacher around him. He has had personal media managers, fitness experts, advisers, lawyers and accountants, like everyone else, but he has also made the most of his relationships with key personnel in all the teams he has worked for. He has developed certain ways of working with the media too, keeping closer to trusted reporters and steering clear of others. After fourteen years in the paddock, he knows his way around and he knows how to stay out of trouble.

Among the many people who have been a part of his exceptional success story, from Benetton all the way through the glorious years at Ferrari, there are some who played valued and important roles for a period and then moved on. They came in and out of the team, acting, as it were, like substitutes. They are the squad members rather then the first team. Harry Hawelka and Balbir Singh, for example, his personal physiotherapists and fitness men. Each has made a contribution to the Schumacher era, as have his personal media managers, Heiner Buchinger and then Sabine Kehm. Team drivers, too. Other people, at different times, have carried out other duties. All have played a part.

Pat Symonds was Schumacher's race engineer during his championship years with the Benetton team when Ross Brawn and Rory Byrne were there, and he has followed Schumacher's career closely. His views offer an insight into how Schumacher developed from his first days in the sport. 'I had a very high opinion of Michael very quickly,' he says. 'He actually arrived at Benetton when I was on a sabbatical at

Reynard. I came back to the team at the end of 1992 and started working with him at winter testing, and it was obvious he knew what he was doing. He was still developing a lot then as a driver, but I have a very high regard for those guys who went through the Mercedes-Benz training programme in sportscar racing, and Michael typified that. He thought a lot about what he was doing and looked at every aspect of his job – which might sound an obvious thing to do, but surprisingly few drivers actually do that. So I think that what struck me initially was his attention to detail. I found it pleasurable to work with him. It was almost like working with an engineer – the same sort of mindset.'

It wasn't long before Symonds was won over by Schumacher's warmth too. He saw the German as an outgoing young man and refutes claims from some quarters that he has drunk from the poisoned chalice of success. Many believe – the media for one – that Schumacher is cold and insular, keeps himself away from the limelight and steers away from any intrusions. He does, to a certain extent, but that does not mean he is not an affable character in the right environment. 'I think he is still the outgoing guy I first met back then,' Symonds says. 'He is a professional and he is able to separate work from play. When he was at a test or in a race or in the car he was very focused, but outside that I think he is genuinely a very nice guy. In those days we used to mix with the drivers a lot more than we do these days, and Michael used to come along to parties and things. He was fun. The British press paint quite a dark picture of him, and I think that is largely down to 1994 and 1995 when he was racing against the great British hopeful [Damon Hill]. But in my mind it is not a justified image. I can't believe being at Ferrari for ten years has done anything to change that. When I see him these days he is as friendly as ever. Maybe he brackets people – there are some he likes to deal with and some he doesn't – but we are all a bit like that.'

Symonds was disappointed to lose his working relationship with Schumacher at the end of the 1995 season, when the German was wooed away by Ferrari. He transferred his race engineering skills to the car of veteran Gerhard Berger. Then, midway during the following year, a combination of the prospect of hooking up with Schumacher and a series of personal clashes with team boss Flavio Briatore over the management structure of the organisation led Ross Brawn to quit the team and join Ferrari after a period of 'gardening leave'. In many ways Symonds should have been the cornerstone of Team Schumacher. He was offered a chance to move to Maranello, but he chose to stay put at Enstone after Brawn recommended him as the ideal man to take on the vacant technical director's role. He has never regretted the decision. 'The reason I didn't go was I wanted to take on a new challenge,' says Symonds. 'I couldn't see any point in just doing the same thing again with a red shirt on rather than a blue shirt. I was attracted to going to Italy, and to the name of Ferrari, but before Ross left he recommended I take over as technical director and I thought that was a much more interesting challenge. I thought there were better things to do in life, and I am very pleased that I took that decision.'

Symonds makes it clear that Schumacher was a huge motivational force within Benetton, but that his drive and determination to succeed, firmly displayed in his demeanour both on and off the track, belied a character that relied as much on the strengths of trusted others as it did on self-belief. 'Michael was a team player,' he says. 'He appreciated what it took to win. There are many drivers who think they can do it all themselves, that what is around them is irrelevant, but Michael knew that was not true. He did a lot to motivate everyone, the mechanics and everyone, all the way through the team, and I think he identified in the Benetton team what were the good aspects and the bad aspects. I think it was very logical for him to move to Ferrari, which was a team that was nowhere at the time. And he knew his ability alone was not enough to turn Ferrari into winners. He needed back-up, and Ross and Rory were very instrumental in turning the team around.' He has no doubts, however, that both Brawn and Byrne joined the Scuderia for their own personal challenges, not simply to team up with the driver they had helped nurture for four years at Benetton. While from the outside it appeared that Schumacher was the pied piper and his technical chiefs were the ones dancing along behind, that, insists Symonds, was far from the truth. 'If you take the case of Ross, Rory and myself, I think we are all independent thinkers,' says Symonds. 'I don't think we would follow a pied piper. Certainly in my case I didn't. Ross and Rory, for equally good reasons, decided they would go. We thought Rory was retiring, so maybe it was just a question of second thoughts in his case. I am sure Ross saw it as a challenge, and anyway, Ross didn't always see eye to eye with Flavio.'

That four-year period at Benetton was crucial in planting the acorns from which the now mighty oak of Team Schumacher has grown. Brawn and Byrne had worked together for years before the young German Formula Three champion arrived from Jordan, and the trio had already established a good working relationship before Symonds returned from his spell with Reynard. Schumacher was clearly the catalyst that transformed the group from one that won races into one that challenged for greatness, but he did not have an overriding influence, and each of the men within the group had his own ambitions. 'Michael and the Benetton team grew up together,' Symonds says. 'They had been around a while before Michael paid more than you if you don't believe they are as good as you? It's all about self-esteem. If you are prepared to do something for less than the next guy and you are doing a better job, then I would say that is a character flaw. I can well believe Michael was motivated to be the best and have the rewards that recognise him as the best, but in terms of whether there is an extra million in the bank this year, I cannot believe that is particularly important. I mean, when he left us at the end of the 1995 season, we had negotiated with him for 1996 and beyond, and he wanted what was in those days a hell of a lot of money to carry on driving. Actually it wasn't really a discussion point for us because what he demanded and what we could afford just did not meet. But it wasn't acrimonious at all. Never did we think he was being greedy. We just felt, "Yeah, the guy is the best, he is worth it," but we simply could not generate that sort of money. Or, to put it another way, if we had paid him what he asked we couldn't have run the team properly. So it just didn't happen.'

Since Schumacher's departure from Benetton the team has been swallowed up by the Renault organisation, under whose name it now races. Symonds still heads up the technical side of the team and has seen many drivers pass through over the past ten years. The increase in technology over that time makes it hard to compare the aptitude of those drivers, but the same basic principles of understanding technical details apply no matter what level or era you are in, and the first point of talking technicalities is to make sure that communication between driver and engineer is on an appropriate level. Symonds remembers well the qualities of Schumacher that made it easy to talk to him on these and other matters. 'I think Michael is pretty exceptional in those human aspects,' he says. 'His attention to detail, his team player attitude, his personality – they were very strong. Michael saw the value of the team at a very early age, I would say, and over the many years and the many drivers I have worked with there are not many drivers who see it like that.'

Schumacher's relentless approach to testing is perhaps one of the strongest indicators of just what it takes to achieve the unprecedented success he has achieved. Even back in the early days, Symonds can recall wet trips to backyard British venues such as Snetterton in Norfolk and Pembrey in Wales, where Schumacher's unending desire, his almost robotic need for information on how the car reacted with new tyres, new suspension settings or new brakes, drove the team on to push themselves further than before. The five o'clock morning calls to attend a hastily arranged shakedown test two hours later did nothing to dampen his enthusiasm, and Symonds reckons the results Schumacher's work ethic achieved both for himself and the team sent a clear message to the next generation of Grand Prix drivers. Follow my lead, or be blown away. 'One of the great things about Michael that makes him different from most drivers is he thoroughly enjoys working,' says Symonds. 'I said before that he has this incredible attention to detail, and holds this view that you have to work in every area to succeed, and he regarded testing as a vital part of that. Many drivers see it as a necessary evil, but Michael wasn't like that at all. He could go testing on a bloody miserable day in the middle of nowhere, and from lap one in the morning he was quick, blisteringly quick. He was just on it all the time, all the way through to when he left. Maybe there were some like that in the past, like Jody Scheckter, but in this era he was the first driver to appreciate that fitness was so important. He worked very hard at his fitness, and one of the benefits of that was that he could test all day, on the pace, with no problems at all. He also appreciated that testing is not about finding better solutions all the time, it is also about proving something doesn't work. He the German's side at Adelaide in 1994 when his controversial collision with Damon Hill handed the title to the Benetton driver, does not think it is the case at all. 'People do seize on it and say that's his weakness,' he says, 'but Michael is under pressure so many times, and there have been many, many times when he didn't make mistakes, so I don't accept that argument. In fact, my view is almost the contrary. Certainly when he was driving for us, and I have seen it since he went to Ferrari, he actually made mistakes when he wasn't concentrating, when he wasn't under pressure. When he first started driving for us, we still had a manual gearbox and no over-rev protection and things like that. Michael used to over-rev engines on his in-lap, never on his fast lap – he was always very precise with that. But on the in-lap he would be thinking about the run he had just done, and he would go and stick it in the wrong gear. If anything, he makes mistakes when he is *not* being pushed 100 per cent.

'If he makes a mistake or has a bad race, he just wants to work out why it happened. I am exactly the same. If things are going badly I am very quiet and pissed off, and so is he. That is a good characteristic. It's a characteristic of someone who cares deeply. I think all successful people are like that, to be honest.'

Throughout any racing career, a driver's biggest rival is always his team-mate. He is the only man who has equal machinery and an equal level of opportunity to get the job done. Some of the most hard-fought rivalries in the history of the sport have been between team-mates, whether it was the gentlemen's rivalry between Juan Manuel Fangio and Stirling Moss at Mercedes-Benz in the 1950s or the bitter hatred between Alain Prost and Ayrton Senna at McLaren in the late 1980s. The relationship with your team-mate can be one of pleasure or pain, depending on whether you stand out or suffer.

Schumacher has comprehensively trounced every one of his team-mates since the very beginning of his Formula One career. That is down almost entirely to his work with Team Schumacher, his ability to galvanize those around him into working with him. Also, he is a great driver, no doubt, and with Formula One drivers being such fiercely competitive creatures, who in their right mind would want to be paired with the most successful driver of all time in a team that was, although they regularly denied it, firmly focused on him? That simple fact was evident early in the 2005 season when Ferrari were linked with a move for McLaren star Kimi Raikkonen for 2006. 'I don't think Kimi would fancy Ferrari,' said McLaren boss Ron Dennis, laughing off the rumours that the star driver at his team would want to line up alongside the already well-established star driver of their scarlet rivals. 'Even if he was guaranteed to lead the team when Michael retired, there's not a chance in hell he'd sign to be his number two for a year or two first.'

Dennis's comments hint that Formula One's dominant team of the decade was resorting to employing second-rate drivers, but how much of this was down to drivers not wanting to play second fiddle, and how much was down to Team Schumacher itself? It is well known that Ferrari is built around Team Schumacher, at whose centre is Michael Schumacher. To guarantee his number one status within the team, it is likely that Schumacher has been influential in hand-picking his team-mates since first joining the Scuderia. Indeed, in recent years it has even been openly suggested by people inside the paddock that Schumacher may have a performance clause in his contract, not from the team demanding his full commitment – that is a given – but requesting a superiority over any driver who lines up alongside him. Who could have predicted Eddie Irvine being picked for the role alongside Schumacher when David Coulthard and Gerhard Berger were available? The official reasons for not signing either man centred around them wanting joint number one status, something that Schumacher allegedly blocked as a condition of his own deal. Even earlier at Benetton he was known to make it difficult for his team-mates, with claims that he would use his pace as a justifiable reason for using his team-mates' data but rarely sharing his own.

First Schumacher had to earn his wings, though. He had to prove he had the speed to be there in the first place. First came Andrea de Cesaris, a veteran Italian driver with a penchant for crashing cars on a regular basis. By the end of qualifying for Spa in 1991, Schumacher was seventh and de Cesaris eleventh. Beginner's luck? Hardly. After jumping ship to Benetton for the next race in Italy, he outqualified his Brazilian team-mate Nelson Piquet, a three-time world champion, in his first four races. Schumacher only failed to complete the clean sweep on Piquet at Adelaide, a track he had never even seen before.

For 1992, he was paired with British driver Martin Brundle. Since his retirement from driving in 1996, Brundle has become one of the most respected TV commentators in the Formula One paddock, and has been able to furnish his viewers with insights on the subject of Michael Schumacher as few others within the media can. As a broadcaster with a wealth of experience, he observes that it is much more than Michael's driving that makes him the dominant champion he has become. 'He psyches people out just by the way he carries himself around the paddock,' says Brundle. 'He glistens with health, and his totally relaxed demeanour and look of total confidence just kills the opposition. He's already done the job before he gets in the car. He's able to think long and hard. I've always said a great driver uses 70 per cent of his ability to drive and 30 per cent to think about things, while a good driver uses 80 and 20.'

Having seen Schumacher as a driver in his formative stages at Benetton, Brundle knows a different, more sensitive side to him, a side many outsiders have only recently begun to believe exists at all. He cites 'Austria-gate' in 2002 as a prime example of Schumacher being naive enough to think that he would get no negative reaction from the crowd after Jean Todt instructed team-mate Rubens Barrichello to move over for him virtually on the finish line of the Austrian Grand Prix after the Brazilian had led the whole race. The boos on the podium seemed genuinely to shock the world champion. Brundle points to a childhood lost to a life of relentless go-karting as a reason for that. 'He's less streetwise than some, but I don't think it's relative to education,' he says. 'His intellect is equal to any of the greats. I just wonder whether he would understand some of the reactions better if he were a bit more streetwise. But then again, if he were Joe Regular he wouldn't be winning world titles and earning £20 million a year, would he?'

Brundle also sees a flaw in Michael's attitude towards racecraft. It is as if he is cocooned in his own little world where anything goes. Seeing other great drivers from history push themselves and their rivals to the very limits of what is acceptable on-track has inspired him to win, no matter what the cost, he says. 'Schuey's just like Senna and Prost. He has a natural gift and the incredible self-belief that goes with it. These guys are winners who will push the limits beyond everyone else. They have the most intense, almost dangerous desire and need to win at all costs, and somehow they convince themselves they are not wrong. He tried to convince himself that what he did at Jerez in 1997 [when he collided with Jacques Villeneuve in a bid to secure the title] was right. I can understand that. He's seen

Stowe corner, Schumacher snatched a front brake and careered off the track into the tyre barriers. The resulting leg break kept him out for six races and pushed Irvine into the number-one role in the team. Suddenly, the impetus was with Irvine, and he nearly made it too. With Brawn, the tactical master, now concentrating on the other side of the great divide, Irvine won the Austrian, German and (with the returning Schumacher's help) Malaysian races, but ultimately lost the championship to Mika Hakkinen. Baldisserri is convinced that had Schumacher been in the car, a first drivers' title since 1979 would have come Ferrari's way, and he lays the blame for that not happening firmly on Irvine's shoulders. 'I don't think Eddie was able to work as first driver,' he says. 'He had these things in his mind that he was always under Michael, and psychologically it was completely different when he had to do the job. When you have to work at the top, you need a completely different mentality to drive yourself and the team, and I don't think Eddie was ready for that. Ultimately our weakness in 1999 was Eddie himself.'

Drivers come and drivers go, and for this reason it is impossible to consider any one of Michael's team-mates as an integral part of Team Schumacher. The man who has come closest is Rubens Barrichello, who joined Ferrari in time for the 2000 season. Eyebrows were raised when the signing was announced, because although nobody doubted the Brazilian's speed, there were question marks over his mental ability to deal with a team-mate like Schumacher. As the number two driver in all but classified status, the talent Barrichello possessed, which many believed could be world champion material, would be suppressed. Barrichello had previously been Irvine's team-mate, the very man he was replacing in the scarlet machine, during their time together at Jordan between 1993 and 1995, where the brash Ulsterman did little to improve the mindset of the Brazilian. Neither did the death of his idol, friend and countryman Ayrton Senna, whose accident in 1994 left Brazil crying out for a new hero. The pressure of expectation on Barrichello was too much to bear, forcing him into a deep depression from which it took him fully half a season to recover.

Still, Barrichello's inauguration into the team went well: he was second on the grid in Australia, alongside his team-mate and less than a tenth down. He followed it up with a second place in the race, and Brawn was quick to praise him. When questioned after the Spanish Grand Prix that year, he pointedly remarked, 'I think Rubens has done more for us in four races than Eddie did in three years.' By the end of the season, Barrichello left nobody in any doubt as to his mentality. The once shy, introspective youngster who had burst on to the scene with a memorable, if unrewarded, drive for Jordan at the 1993 European Grand Prix at Donington Park was making jokes in press conferences and had his chin up all around the paddock. Clearly his first race win at the German Grand Prix had helped, and it seemed that Barrichello was gearing up for a challenge in 2001, after spending a year observing the traits of the (by that time) triple world champion. 'Of course Michael is quick,' he said at the time. 'But, like Eddie, I am using him as a target. We can all improve as drivers, and in F1 you never stop learning. Next year I am going to be better still, I promise. Just watch!'

We did, but he wasn't. The 2002 season went the same way, the Austrian Grand Prix putting Barrichello firmly in his place, and in 2003 Ferrari's struggles were such that the team had to concentrate on Schumacher to be assured of retaining both titles. By the early spring months of 2004, Barrichello reckoned on having the measure, at least in part, of Michael, and was ready to take him on at his own game. He declared publicly, perhaps naively, that there was no contractual obligation to defer to

CHAPTER THIRTEEN

SURVIVAL INSTINCTS

*None of us are new to this and we accept that
our competitors are doing a better job than we are
right now. But we've survived more difficult
moments in time in the last couple of years,
and we'll survive this as well.*

Michael Schumacher, 2005

One of the films in the original *Star Wars* series was called *The Empire Strikes Back*. The concept may have to be revisited, in motor racing terms, in 2006. For in 2005, after five years of unbroken supremacy, the Ferrari success factory was put under siege by the Formula One aliens known to the normal world as Renault and McLaren. Michael Schumacher found himself in the unaccustomed position of playing second fiddle to not one, but two other drivers, one from Spain and one from Finland.

A new generation was scrapping for the glory of winning the champions' crown, and the 'dream team' were left fighting for their dignity as the season progressed. The Scuderia, and their tyre suppliers Bridgestone, an organisation that recognised and praised the considerable input from the seven-time champion, were overshadowed. Bridgestone's French rivals, Michelin, were winning at ease. The only 'victory' Ferrari claimed before the championship was decided and their titles were taken from them came in June during an extraordinary fiasco of a race at Indianapolis, where Michelin were unable to vouch for the safety of their tyres. As a result, all of their teams withdrew, only six cars started – the Ferraris, the Jordans and the Minardis – and the race was no more than a miserable contrivance for television. The sad state of affairs for Team Schumacher was emphasised further by the manner in which Michael claimed his victory. After a pit-stop, he came perilously close to colliding with team-mate Rubens Barrichello. The sombre faces on the podium and the embarrassing wording of the Ferrari news bulletin released afterwards spoke volumes. Optimism for the future was subdued. The team knew their cars were not the quickest, that their driver would soon no longer be champion, and that their once supreme dominance could be over.

It was entirely predictable that over the following months –

as Weber faced charges in Stuttgart that were unproven, and as the 'dream team' struggled to overcome the problems created by an uncompetitive car-and-tyres combination that resulted, notably, in their first pointless return on home soil at Monza for a decade – speculation about the future would intensify. Stories suggesting that the rising young Finnish star Kimi Raikkonen was unhappy at McLaren Mercedes-Benz began to circulate; then that he was set to move to Ferrari in 2006 or 2007, as a replacement for a disillusioned Schumacher. Soon after that it was suggested that Schumacher would move the other way and return to the roots of his career with the Stuttgart-based manufacturer. At Monza, in September, an Italian magazine even ran a picture of Raikkonen in Ferrari overalls on their front cover. The allusion to changes required was easy to understand, but it had little or no effect. By then, the Spanish champion-elect Fernando Alonso had also been drawn into the debate about the future, and about his own ambitions. He made it clear he would prefer to stay with Renault rather than move to Maranello and take a risk in Schumacher's footsteps. He believed, he said, that his chances for the future would be better served by remaining where he knew he could succeed.

The speculation was a reminder that time marches on; it waits for no man. Even Team Schumacher was vulnerable, though no one could say when the end would come. At Monza, where both the drivers' and constructors' titles were moved beyond academic reach, where Maranello for the first time in years could no longer call itself the home of the defending champions, Michael conceded that he had been prepared for such a sad moment for months. But, in fighting talk, he refused to discuss giving up the battle to regain competitive speed and win again in the future.

One word was not uttered in the post-race post-mortems: Bridgestone. It was as if the cars' rubber was a sacred and unmentionable part of the package. For the first time in years it seemed the team's 'one for all, all for one' philosophy must come under strain, but there was no evidence of a fracture. The team stuck together, even when the long-serving Barrichello decided that after six seasons as the supporting player to Michael he was leaving to join BAR-Honda. No one could have failed to notice that Barrichello had been more, much more, than a supportive player in the unbroken success story enjoyed by Team Schumacher. His years at Ferrari had coincided with the triumphant domination, even if he was not one of the inner sanctum members regarded as the 'dream team'. His departure, too, was a signal of the changing times, a first crack in the bulletproof skin of the team. His move gave Ferrari a chance to bring another Brazilian, Felipe Massa, to Maranello to race alongside the old master, but the changes meant questions were asked. Was the team in serious decline? Did Rory Byrne's retirement spell the end? Was the motivation and desire that had fuelled the creation and sustained success of this exceptional group of people now on the wane?

Chinks in the Team Schumacher armour had appeared from the start of the 2005 season. For years, the rule-makers had faced pressure from critics, and Ferrari's rivals, to try to create an environment in which the other teams, and other drivers, had a better chance to win. In 2005, there was a change in tyre design, due to a new regulation demanding that race tyres must last a full distance. The introduction of this, if not declared openly, was clearly an attempt to slow the Scuderia down. New engine rules, too, that demanded the power-units last for two races rather than one, were introduced; and so, too, were revised qualifying regulations, introduced after the sixth race of the season, which saw the running order for the grid-deciding session formed by the finishing order of the previous race. This further encouraged continued success while making it difficult for struggling teams to come back.

The heat was on the team, and for the first time they struggled to respond to the new pressures. It was not voiced of course, but one critical component, Bridgestone's tyres, seemed to be underperforming. Ferrari's challenge was made more difficult by having an exclusive relationship with the tyre supplier. 'We are the only top team with Bridgestone,' Jean Todt explained after the Turkish Grand Prix in August. 'If we would be with the same tyres, with another very top team, it would be easier to find out what the problem is and to answer it, but at the moment we don't know . . . We are alone fighting with Bridgestone tyres. As I have said, Bridgestone is a great partner – great, yes, because we've won more than anybody else with them. But if we have the slightest problem, which is the case at the moment, we end up with eight cars in front of us. But do I complain? No. I want to finish in the best position in the table as possible. I've lost the dream to win both championships, but now at least we have to secure third position if possible.'

Third position. *Third*. Not at all what the team had grown used to achieving.

But the problem was about more than just tyres. Ross Brawn, at around the same time, conceded that for the first time in six years it may have been that his design team had proved fallible. Or human. 'It is unrealistic to expect Bridgestone to turn a magic switch and solve the problem,' he admitted. 'With the change of rules, we didn't interpret that direction as quickly as other teams clearly have done. We ended last season in a competitive position and we started this season in a less competitive position, so over the winter other teams made more progress than we did. We've got to find solutions for the car as well. For sure, if we have more power and more downforce the car handles better and it uses the tyres better. But we've got to improve the handling, we've got to have more power, we've got to have more downforce – all the things that make a good racing car. The more we can go in that direction, the better. And, also, the drivers can then manage the situation, because they have some, let's say, spare capacity to handle the situation. That's what we need to create. But we know it won't be an overnight change. It'll be step by step, and it'll be a hard slog.' It was, of course, a hard slog to get to the top in the first place: Ferrari's first constructors' title was six years in the making, their first drivers' prize seven years.

But the situation presented by the 2005 rule changes was not entirely new: the team had coped with a similar set of pressures in 2003, when significant changes, including a dramatic rescaling of the points-scoring system, pushed them into the clutches of their closest rivals at the time, McLaren. Then they performed a near-miraculous escape from the jaws of defeat, and with a magnificent effort retained both their world championship titles, Schumacher holding on to his crown by just two points despite winning five more races than closest rival Raikkonen. His eighth-place finish in Japan was enough finally to confirm him as champion again. His spectacular, if controversial, alcohol-fuelled celebrations included throwing a television through a window at the Suzuka race circuit – the kind of high jinks once thought the private property of rock stars. It showed just how much emotion and pressure had built up over the previous few months. In 2005, the same emotions were not there for him because he was never able to defend his championship. He had not been able to build any momentum. 'This year it is not possible,' he admitted in Istanbul in August.

'So, for us, it is natural that there is only one target now: to go for the next championship.'

Such is the fighting spirit embodied in Michael Schumacher and his team. It has been there all through his motor racing career. If they win one race, they look to win the next. No further than that, no title aspirations, just the next race. If they lose, they do not dwell on the past, they look to how they can improve. When Renault won the opening three races of the 2005 season, the writing was already on the wall for the team, but that setback did not stop Michael from buckling down to the hard work required for the next race, the San Marino Grand Prix at the end of April. 'What pleased me was how much fight Michael had in him,' observed Brawn after witnessing Schumacher come back from that near-disastrous start to the campaign and chase championship leader Fernando Alonso all the way to the chequered flag at Imola. 'He is so competitive, and what you always see is that he's still got the ability. At his age he's got this huge passion and huge hunger to do well, and he's still got that raw ability. I think he's got lots of mileage left in him. He relishes the competition. I think Fernando is going to be a very tough guy to beat this year, but even if we get beaten this year, I suspect Michael is going to want to redress the balance next year.

'We often joke with him that it wasn't bad today for an old man, and he takes it all in good humour. With any driver you are waiting for that point where they start to go down the other side, and he's just not doing that. He's still fantastically fit, hungry and passionate, and you can see it all in his performances. He was so angry. To come out and put in the performance he did at Imola just shows how exceptional he really is.' He had shown that fighting spirit at the season-opener in Australia too, where he was eighteenth on the grid because of a heavy downpour in qualifying. He fought his way through the field, but became beached in a gravel trap after colliding with Nick Heidfeld's Williams-BMW as he tried to hold on to the final points-scoring position in eighth place. Even then he was determined his season-opening race would not end that way, as Brawn recalled. 'Michael was keen to get back on track, but his car was too damaged. He had just got into a points-scoring position and he was determined to get back into it.'

For a time during the 2005 season it seemed that the loss of performance was likely only to be temporary, but in truth, the Scuderia had lost their way. 'This is probably as tough a challenge as Michael has faced,' Brawn admitted. 'Fernando is driving extremely well, much better than we've seen before.' The real problem for Ferrari and Schumacher was that they were rendered unable to reach the competitive level they had taken for granted for years. The team knew they were slow – they were forced to admit that – but the greatest concern to all involved was the fact that they did not know why. Throwing blame at the Bridgestone tyres would not have solved the problem; it was the overall package that failed. As they had always said, they win and lose together. It was all about the package. Unfortunately, it was a package in 2005 that was not good enough to be victorious.

'Today the situation is very different to the past, and all we can aim for is to make progress,' mused the long-suffering Jean Todt. 'We are aware that there are no miracle cures, and at the moment, staying united is the most important thing . . . I know racing so well after so many years. I know that things are never easy, and that when there are cycles, those cycles can end at one moment or another. I hope the cycle that came to an end at the start of this season is simply a temporary feature, and that's what we hope to prove very quickly. The atmosphere is very strong in the team – to work harder if necessary. Of course we prefer success, but as I have said before, we had so much success so we must be prepared for this kind of situation. That's maybe why we never enjoyed our success as much as we might have done, because we knew we would have some tough times. So we are prepared to have a tough time, but we are prepared to have better times as well. The situation already seems very dark, very bad, but I think there's not a lot missing. I am convinced we will overcome this difficult period.'

Schumacher spoke openly too. He showed his frustration at times, and talked of the team going backwards. There were inconsistencies in the performances that, save for the 2003 lull, had not been there in the past. The team made developments, Bridgestone made developments; sometimes they went the right way, sometimes they went the wrong way. They were experimenting, trying to dig themselves out of a hole – a big and, it seemed, ever-expanding hole. Todt, the alchemist, was facing his biggest challenge since the 1990s, and knew he had a major task to perform. Not only did it appear that Bridgestone were struggling to perform, so too was the design department.

Years of sustained success had taken their toll, and in many respects it was inevitable. Sooner or later all great sports teams break up or slide into decline. The key to real greatness in management lies in anticipation of that and making preparations to ensure that the strength of the whole is not diminished by alterations to the component parts. It is Todt's job to ensure that the Scuderia does not crumble, his responsibility to stay on and assemble another 'dream team' beyond Team Schumacher to provide an inheritance for Maranello. Brazil, the greatest soccer-playing nation on earth, earned their right to that title by winning the World Cup not once, or even twice, but five times over several decades of development and progress. Sir Matt Busby, the great manager who inspired and led

Manchester United to their first European Cup triumph in 1968, was later to be remembered as much for the disarray in which he left the club when he retired as he was for the moment of joy he gifted to millions of supporters.

Michael Schumacher is a seven-time world champion. He took his last five titles at the ages of 31, 32, 33, 34 and 35. But he is not yet too old to perform. Despite the stress and all the wear and tear, he is still among the fittest in the paddock, and he still has time on his side. The great Juan Manuel Fangio took his last title at the age of 46; Australian Jack Brabham took his third and last title at 40. Graham Hill and his son Damon were both older than 35 as world champions; so, too, were Mario Andretti, Nigel Mansell and Alain Prost. But the demise of Ferrari in 2005 signalled that Team Schumacher needed something special if they were to climb back to the top. And at the age of 36, with more money invested and saved than many of the world's small nations, many asked the obvious question: why should Michael Schumacher feel a need to continue, especially after the departure of Rubens Barrichello?

For the German's perennial number two, the man whose ambition five years earlier had been to become Ferrari's number 1B, had had enough. Barrichello, off his own bat and with a clear sign of patience running out, had decided that playing second fiddle to the man at the epicentre of the Ferrari system was too much for someone of his talent to endure. He asked Todt if he could leave, and Todt reluctantly accepted. He was off to BAR-Honda, with hopes of a world championship in his own right burning bright. The secrecy of the Scuderia means the reasons for Barrichello's sudden change of heart, just one and a half years after matching Schumacher, Todt and Brawn in committing to the team until 2006, will remain a mystery. But it appeared to be rooted in a disagreement Schumacher and

Barrichello had in Monaco. On the final lap of that race, Schumacher was ninth behind Barrichello. Then, stunningly, he slid past him at the chicane in what Barrichello described afterwards as a dangerous move, one he would never have attempted. To the team, it was brave and worthy of praise, and they softly hinted that Barrichello might not have been aggressive enough in defence. An internal row, no doubt expanded to its limits by the German and Italian media in particular, commenced. And with the noise, the doubts about Barrichello's position began to surface.

A month later in the United States the Brazilian came close to snatching the lead through the pit-stops when the Ferrari pair were racing each other for victory with all but the back-marker teams ruled out of the race through tyre problems. Schumacher pushed him wide on to the grass. Again, it was an aggressive move from Schumacher – exciting racing, a display of commitment. Had Rubens done the same, however, the views of the team might have been a little different. The situation made something clear to Barrichello. 'I saw it was going to be very difficult for me actually to try to win the championship with Ferrari,' he said. 'Michael has been there longer, and I saw my chances as much higher with a team that has not yet won a race, but has all the desire and the good ingredients to do it. Every change brings a new motivation, but it is the resources, the people, everything, that was more the fact that took me there [to BAR]. I still dream of being world champion, and it is thanks to Jean Todt that I was able to make the move. I was talking to BAR for a long time, but it was just this year at some point that everything started to happen a little bit. Then I went to Jean and said, "If I want to leave, will you be happy to let me go?" And he said, "You have one week to decide that because I am counting on you for next year." But then I came back with the news.'

Ferrari were both surprised and disappointed. Why on earth would anyone want to leave the team? For Barrichello, it was simple. He had spent season after season being second best to Schumacher, and now, with Schumacher virtually committed to Ferrari for his racing future, he had the opportunity to go to a team that was actually performing better than his current outfit. It still seemed, too, that he felt he was not respected. 'People ask me what is the worst time I had at Ferrari, and they might think it was Austria 2002,' said Barrichello, who in that race was controversially forced to pull over and hand Schumacher the win. 'But I think that was the best time. It was great because that was really good to change things around. It was really good in terms of respect, because they knew I could win races without the help of anyone. It was probably the turning point of my racing career there.' But not, it appeared, a U-turn from back-up man to equal challenger.

Brawn defended Ferrari and the team against the implications of Barrichello's claims that he was never respected, but admitted that simply in being Schumacher's team-mate the Brazilian was always going to be on a losing wicket. 'We've had a very good period with Rubens and I've said many times he has the toughest job in Formula One because he's trying to beat Michael Schumacher in the same equipment, and nobody's ever managed to do that. I took him as a serious racer all the time, so there was no change from our side at any point. He would have been world champion if Michael Schumacher hadn't been there – at least once, maybe twice. That, to me, is the standing of Rubens. It can be a very frustrating experience racing against Michael, but he's always tried hard, worked hard, and done a very good job. I was disappointed with what happened, but I can understand why it happened.'

Nigel Stepney, too, respected Barrichello's efforts. The

Brazilian may not have been a key player inside the group we refer to as Team Schumacher – he was merely one of those 'on the bench' – but at least he had had a good crack at his task. 'He's competitive and he wants to win, so it is very hard for him,' said Stepney. 'He has the same equipment. People make out that it's different and it's only Rubens who has the problems, but we know the equipment is the same. We build the cars the same, using the same bits. We do it because we want Ferrari to win. It hurts us if we make one car slower than the other. We put more effort into making sure the things that happen don't happen again. The cars have been bulletproof, and that's down to how we build them, run them, strategies, all kinds of things. We try to be bulletproof to cover every possible thing that could go wrong. Sometimes things go wrong for Rubens, but we work for Ferrari, not Michael Schumacher.' Speaking before the Barrichello decision was revealed, and quite probably before it was made, Stepney's opinions were honestly put, and almost clairvoyant. 'Rubens could always go somewhere else if the money is all he cared about, but it's not,' Stepney added. 'He wants to win races, and that's why he stays here. It's his motivation. He could get offered the same money to be a leading driver at BAR. You go there, you know nobody, you build a team from scratch. Do you sacrifice what you have at Ferrari for that? I wouldn't.' But Barrichello did in the end. What was the point, after all, in not choosing to sacrifice what he had at Ferrari when all he had was an apparent number two status and a team that was showing signs of falling off a precipice? Stepney insists, however, that if Barrichello felt he had a number two status, it was all his own doing. 'You get out what you put in,' he said. 'And I don't honestly believe Rubens puts in as much effort as Michael. If he did, he would challenge him more.'

And so the team will move on into 2006 with a new man 'on the bench'; a man Schumacher has already worked with; a man who, many observers believe, is being groomed to take over from the master. Massa, another Brazilian, has already played a bit part in the story as one of the team's test drivers, during 2003. He is young, energetic and enthusiastic. He shows it in his driving, sometimes a little too much, but if Todt can impart his calming influence and team-building skills on the new charger then, as Stepney said, it is possible to imagine the impact a younger and possibly faster, if less experienced, man might have on the team. With Barrichello gone, Stepney felt that the Scuderia needed something else, not just raw aggression. 'Not more competitive, but able to give more of himself,' he suggested. 'I don't think he'll have to push us more. I remember the Andretti–Peterson days. If a driver wants to learn how to be the complete Formula One driver, he just has to follow Michael, just as Peterson used to sit behind Andretti. That's what Rubens should have been doing, and he was not doing it. You need to be right in behind that number one driver.'

It seems that Barrichello's decision to leave came because he felt that through good or bad times the team would always stick behind Schumacher and not him. Massa will have to command respect very quickly if he wants to continue the Ferrari success story, but he could be offered a helping hand if Schumacher decides he is the right man to groom as a replacement. It is unlikely that Massa will become the creative fulcrum of anything close to a group, a 'dream team', like that created by Schumacher because the seven-time champion has had an exceptional and unique career and is a man of equally unique talents. A heavy weight, therefore, may rest on Massa's young shoulders in 2006. He will be required not only to help Schumacher and his team resurrect the glory days, but also to persuade Ferrari that there is a long-term future beyond the Schumacher era.

Massa arrives at a time when the team's success has ended but key members of the special group remain. Each one of those vital players, however, remains tied to the team only for a limited time, and each is looking, no doubt, at a private version of the future after a decade of hard work chasing the same goals. Even Jean Todt, when asked what his biggest priority in life is, revealed that he had things on his mind other than motor racing. 'At the moment, it is my son,' he said. 'I don't think there is just one thing because your life is cluttered. So, on one side, I have one son and I love him. Then there are my friends. And then what takes up most of my time at the moment, my work. Every single thing is important, but I don't think you can say only one thing because you have to share your life with other things.'

Stepney, a key cog in the smoothly oiled Team Schumacher gearbox, also turned his thoughts to his private life. For him, however, glory with the 'dream team' came at a cost. He now felt his home and family life might be due some attention. 'Home is where you relax,' he said. 'You come back from a long day, or a race, and just collapse on the sofa and don't even think about Formula One for the rest of the day. I've never needed someone who would be really happy and active when I got home. All I wanted to do was relax. So, I have to say, I've got through a few relationships. I've been married three times! The job is tough on my private life, and I know a few people who've been through the same thing as me. But then, look at Ross. He has his family right behind him. It depends on who you are and how stable and how volatile you are. My private life has changed over the last eight months. I know I still want to win Formula One world championships, but after destroying so many relationships, now it's time for a little bit of stability. At 46,

I'm happy with how my private life is going. My partner, Ashama, is half-Asian and half-Portuguese . . . I think it's time I settled down a bit.'

No team in motorsport has had sustained success quite like Team Schumacher. The great Fangio had a very full trophy cabinet, but that silverware was won with different teams. In recent years Williams, Benetton and McLaren have had mini-eras, but none has managed to stay at the top, brushing aside rule changes and resurgent opposition, to retain both titles for such a time. It is inevitable that it will end, but when? Rory Byrne wants to return to Thailand; Todt is to re-marry; Brawn has eased beyond his 50th birthday and may well be satisfied after six championships with Ferrari. Yet, vibrant and dramatic as ever, the Schumacher driving force has continued, and if anyone can convince the 'dream team' to stick together, it is Michael. 'Michael works as a leader, tugging everyone,' observed Bridgestone's Hirohide Hamashima. 'He demands many things from everyone. He gets everything and he shows good results, so that makes them stronger and more keen to work together.'

But perhaps only a handful of members of Team Schumacher remaining hungry for the task ahead is not enough. Ferrari prides itself on being a team, but it can only be as strong as its weakest link. 'Michael and myself, we wouldn't have achieved anything [on our own],' reflected Todt. 'For me, what we have achieved is a result of a combination of a lot of people. Of course, we have an order, so some people are more important than others, but what is unique is the achievement of all those people put together. It's not only Michael, and it's not only Ross and Rory. It's all of us working together. I always take the example of the sailing boat. If you are going against the wind, even the most sophisticated sailing boat will not work. However, if you have just a normal boat, but with a strong wind blowing in the right direction, then that boat will go very quickly. It's the same for working with our partners.

'Michael loves what he does, and he loves trying to raise the standards of excellence. But in motor racing it is not just a question of the driver. You need to have the car, the engine, the team – you need to have a lot of things. In life, you must always understand why you fail and why you have success. We are humble in this respect. We talk a lot about stability in this business, but stability can be a disaster. If you have stability with bad people, all you have is a stable disaster. Only if you have very good people in a stable situation can you do a good job.'

INDEX

and 2000 world championships 186, 187
and 2005 season 285-286
birth and early life 135-136
and Bridgestone 282
and death of Michael's mother 218
father 135, 136
and Ferrari leaving Formula One (2004/5) 190-191
joins Ferrari 130, 132-133, 138-140, 188-189, 194, 202, 248
and Michael 133-134, 147-148, 153
organisation and leadership 14
as Peugeot team manager 132, 137-138
priorities in life 291, 293
as rally co-driver 135-136
regulations and limits stretched and broken 82-83
and 'team orders' 75, 272
Todt, Nicolas (son) 134
Toleman, Ted 163, 164
Toleman Group Motorsport 158, 163-164 *see also* Benetton F1 team
Toleman TG181: 158, 179
Toleman TG280: 163-164
Tottenham Hotspur FC 236
Tour de France Rally 136
Touring Car Championship, European 192
Toyota F1 team 136
Trella, Jorg 116
tsunami, Boxing Day, 2004: 28, 153
TWR (Tom Walkinshaw Racing) 53 *see also* Jaguar sportscars

U
United States GP – 2002: 78-79, 174; 2003: 200; 2005: 200, 279, 288
universities 64-65, 66-67
Unser, Robby 137
USF&G investment company 52

V
van der Grindt, Kees 231-233, 234-235
Vatanen, Ari 137-138
Verstappen, Jos 273
Villa d'Este Hotel, Lake Como 107,

108, 113
Villeneuve, Gilles 210, 272-273
Villeneuve, Jacques 20, 24-25, 44, 49, 139, 140, 256, 268, 272
Vodafone 151, 227
Von Trips, Wolfgang 210
Vufflens-le-Château, Switzerland 220-221

W
Wagenhauser, Udo 119-120
Walkinshaw, Tom 52-53, 109, 111
Warmbold, Achim 136
Warr, Peter 196
Warwick, Derek 52
Warwickshire county football team 191
Weber, Heidemarie 105
Weber, Willi 25, 26-27, 70, 91, 92, 95, 103-106, 109, 120, 121, 122-125, 206, 227
birth and early life 114-116, 118-119
bribery charges 103, 104-105, 280
discovers Michael 116-118
father 118
and Michael joining Benetton 110-111, 112, 113, 114
and Michael joining Ferrari 126, 152, 265
and Michael's scuba-diving incident 218-220
Sports Illustrated article 106-107
West 125-126
wigs, celebratory 49, 185, 187
Wilkinson, Jonny 43
Williams, Frank (now Sir Frank) 52, 56, 61, 203
Williams Grand Prix Engineering F1 team 24, 44, 52, 54, 56, 58, 61-62, 81, 141, 142, 144, 151, 171, 228, 230, 293
Wimbledon tennis titles 43
Winkelhock, Joachim 116
Witwatersrand University 161
Wolf, Walter 61
World Cups, football and rugby union 43
World Health Organisation 28-29
World Rally Championship 137